The Japanese Consumer

M000087591

By the late twentieth century, Japanese people were renowned as the world's most avid and knowledgeable consumers of fashion, luxury and quality, while the goods that embodied their tastes and lifestyle were becoming a part of global culture. Penelope Francks' book offers an alternative account of Japan's modern economic history from the perspective of the consumer. Reaching back into pre-industrial times and tracing Japan's economy from the eighteenth century to the present, she shows how history has conditioned what Japanese people consume today and compares their experiences with those of their European and North American counterparts. In so doing the author presents a lucid and informed account of everyday life in Japan, exploring what people eat, how they dress, the household goods they acquire and their preferred shopping and leisure activities. This beautifully illustrated book succeeds in making economic history palatable and entertaining. It will be a treat for students and all those interested in Japanese society and culture.

PENELOPE FRANCKS is an Honorary Lecturer in Japanese Studies in the Department of East Asian Studies at the University of Leeds. Her recent publications include *Rural Economic Development in Japan* (2006).

The Japanese Consumer

*An alternative economic history
of modern Japan*

Penelope Francks

CAMBRIDGE
UNIVERSITY PRESS

CAMBRIDGE UNIVERSITY PRESS
Cambridge, New York, Melbourne, Madrid, Cape Town, Singapore,
São Paulo, Delhi

Cambridge University Press
The Edinburgh Building, Cambridge CB2 8RU, UK

Published in the United States of America by Cambridge University Press,
New York

www.cambridge.org
Information on this title: www.cambridge.org/9780521699327

First published 2009

Printed in the United Kingdom at the University Press, Cambridge

A catalogue record for this publication is available from the British Library

Library of Congress Cataloguing in Publication data
Francks, Penelope, 1949–
  The Japanese consumer : an alternative economic
  history of modern Japan / Penelope Francks.
     p. cm.
  ISBN 978-0-521-87596-7
  1. Consumption (Economics)–Japan–History.   2. Consumers–Japan–
  History. I. Title.
  HC465.C6F73 2009
  339.4′70952–dc22   2009026027

ISBN 978-0-521-87596-7 hardback
ISBN 978-0-521-69932-7 paperback

Contents

List of illustrations   *page* vii
List of tables   ix
Acknowledgements   x
Notes on the text   xi
Map   xii

1   Japan and the history of consumption   1

2   Shopping in the city: urban life and the emergence
    of the consumer in Tokugawa Japan   11
    The great cities as centres of consumption   12
    Consumption and everyday life in the cities   27
    Goods, the state and society   40

3   Country gentlemen, ordinary consumption and the
    development of the rural economy   47
    The rural elite and consumption   48
    Everyday consumption in the countryside   54
    Consumption and 'rural-centred' economic growth   66

4   Civilising goods': consumption in the
    industrialising world   74
    Newspapers, trains and electricity: the birth of the
    modern infrastructure of consumption   76
    'Civilising grain': food and drink in the emerging urban
    industrial world   87
    Clothes and household goods: fashion, novelty and
    changing tradition   97
    Consumer goods and the path of economic development   102

5   Living with modernity: the emerging consumer of the
    inter-war years   108
    Cities, suburbs and shopping   109
    Everyday life in the modern world   123
    Attitudes to modern consumption   136

6 The electrical household: consumption and the
   economic miracle   145
   From war and occupation to economic miracle: state, society
   and mass consumption   146
   Consuming the bright life   163
   Consuming and saving: the individual and society   176

7 New tribes and nostalgia: consumption in the late
   twentieth century and beyond   183
   Shopping in the city, late twentieth-century style   184
   Consumption in practice in the post-miracle years   193
   The ambivalent consumer   207

8 The Japanese consumer past and present   218

   Statistical appendix   223
   List of references   231
   Index   242

Illustrations

2.1 The Mitsui textiles store in Edo   *page* 18
2.2 A traditional comb shop   20
2.3 An Edo-period cosmetics salesman   21
2.4 An Edo-period food and drink stall   23
2.5 Working men relaxing at a bar   24
2.6 A large-scale *kamado* cooking stove   37
2.7 An Edo-period kitchen   38
2.8 A guide to restaurants in Edo   44
3.1 A rural kitchen   64
3.2 A rural family gathered around an *irori* hearth   65
3.3 A vegetable peddler   68
4.1 A bazaar in Tokyo   84
4.2 Traditional small shops   85
4.3 Advertisement for Sapporo Beer   86
4.4 A sake bar   96
5.1 Interior of the Mitsukoshi department store   114
5.2 The Lion Beer Hall   116
5.3 Schoolboys queuing at a provincial cinema   119
5.4 Cover of a dressmaking magazine   122
5.5 Curry-rice and cutlets   126
5.6 Fashions in *meisen* kimono   130
5.7 A housewife in an advertisement   132
5.8 A family meal at a table   135
6.1 An electrical-parts stall in Akihabara, Tokyo   150
6.2 A street of shops and stalls in Ameyokochō, Tokyo   151
6.3 Kitchen and living room of a 1950s apartment   155
6.4 A noodle restaurant   167
6.5 Electrical goods advertised as gifts   174
6.6 Advertisement for televisions   181
7.1 A contemporary shopping street   189
7.2 A Tokyo hardware shop   190

7.3 A shop selling imported tea in Motomachi,
    Yokohama   192
7.4 Billboards advertising attractions in Asakusa, Tokyo   192
7.5 Rice of different varieties on sale in Kyoto market   196
7.6 Mushrooms on sale in a market   197
7.7 Accommodating car, washing and garden in
    contemporary Tokyo   203
7.8 A contemporary version of an *irori* hearth   204

Tables

1 Share of consumption in gross national expenditure, 1885–1995   *page* 224
2 Consumption in the overall growth of the economy over long-swing phases, 1887–1969   225
3 Growth and structure of private consumption expenditure, 1874–1940   226
4 Growth and structure of private consumption expenditure, 1955–1995   227
5 Per capita consumption of selected goods, 1875–1940   228
6 Average annual quantities purchased by households, selected consumer items, 1965–1995   229
7 Percentages of households possessing selected consumer durables, 1964–1995   230

Acknowledgements

The idea for this book arose in the course of discussion with Marigold Acland of Cambridge University Press one day over a cup of coffee in Leeds, and her continued enthusiasm and support for the book throughout its gestation have been much appreciated. Others to thank for helpful suggestions at various stages include Ellis Tinios, Andrew Gerstle, Richard Smethurst, Saitō Osamu, Tanimoto Masayuki and Kiyokawa Yukihiko, as well as participants in seminars on the project at the Nissan Institute in Oxford, the Japan Research Centre at the School of Oriental and African Studies, University of London, the Department of Economic History at the University of Tokyo and the Department of East Asian Studies at the University of Leeds.

I am also most grateful to the British Academy and the Daiwa Anglo-Japanese Foundation for funding my visit to Japan in 2007 to collect material for the book. The Great Britain Sasakawa Foundation provided additional funding in support of the illustrations, and its director, Stephen McEnally, supplied cheerful encouragement beyond the call of duty just when it was needed.

Every effort has been made to locate the copyright holders of material used in illustrations, and I am grateful to staff at a number of Japanese publishers and museums, as acknowledged in the text, for help with this. The publisher would be happy to receive any information in relation to cases where the copyright holder could not be located and to make acknowledgement in any future edition of the book.

Richard Francks took all the contemporary photographs included in the book. He also organised everything and achieved an unrivalled mastery of the Tokyo transport system in the search for obscure museums. As always, without him the book would not have been written.

Notes on the text

Japanese personal names are given in the Japanese order, with family name first, except in the cases of Japanese authors writing in English.

Macrons are used to indicate long vowel sounds in Japanese, except in the cases of the most familiar place names.

TŌHOKU

KANTŌ

Tokyo (Edo)

KANSAI   Yokohama

Kōbe   Kyoto

Nagoya

Osaka

Fukuoka

KYŪSHŪ

Map of Japan

1 Japan and the history of consumption

Visitors to 21st-century Tokyo experience above all a world of goods. Standing at the crossroads of wherever is the currently fashionable shopping district, they will be awed by the constant flow of dedicated consumers and the extraordinary array of goods to be enjoyed in department stores, boutiques and specialist shops. Young people, hurrying about their business or stepping out with their friends, display their individual takes on current fashion, while their elders discreetly show off their designer labels. All around, shop windows, billboards and flashing TV screens give out images of products of every kind. Meanwhile, whole sections of the city are devoted to the practice and enjoyment of consumption in a range of facilities that reaches from the unbelievably expensive bar or exclusive restaurant to the tiniest noodle shop or the sleaziest massage parlour.

Eighteenth-century visitors standing at similar spots in the city then called Edo experienced the same awe. They saw shops – indeed the ancestors of present-day Tokyo's department stores – selling all kinds of clothes, food and household goods. They admired the outfits of the rich and fashionable or mingled with the crowds of ordinary shoppers; they enjoyed the entertainment offered at the theatre or the geisha house, and they refreshed themselves at eating and drinking establishments that ranged from elegant riverside restaurants and fashionable tea-houses to cheap eateries and open-air bars. Advertisers targeted them with fliers and product placement in prints of celebrities and, like their present-day counterparts, they needed shopping and restaurant guides to help them to decide where to shop and what to eat among all the choices on offer.

From the eighteenth century to the present day, the consumer has existed as an integral part of Japan's economic life, acquiring, utilising and enjoying the ever expanding quantity and range of goods that Japanese producers have created. Once, many of these goods – kimono, sushi, futon and much more – were peculiar to Japan, but by the nineteenth century the range was expanding to include Japanese versions of the goods with which the world of American and European consumers was increasingly populated. Eventually Japanese goods themselves – the products both of 'Japanese tradition' and of Japanese high technology – were to become a part of global consumer culture: the electrical goods by means of which Japanese people re-created their everyday lives in the post-Second World War decades were finding their places in Western homes by the 1970s, while in due course Japanese food, fashion and popular culture – noodles and sake, karaoke, manga and anime – translated more or less directly from their Japanese originals, were to spread around the world.

These developments have been intimately tied up with the story of Japanese economic growth over the past two centuries, as well as with the social, political and cultural change that has accompanied the country's emergence as a major global power. The changing world of goods and their consumers embodies Japan's economic history – from the first appearance of the thriving commercial economy that had established itself by the early nineteenth century, through industrialisation and the post-Second World War 'economic miracle', to emergence as an economic superpower within the global economy of the late twentieth century – as it worked itself out in everyday lives. This world of ordinary things and activities – of food, clothes and household goods; of shopping, cooking, travelling and being entertained; of trying to look nice and live comfortably – may seem far removed from the account of technical change, business management, government institutions and macro-economic policy that is normally taken to represent Japanese economic history. But, as Adam Smith's famous dictum puts it, 'consumption is the sole end and purpose of all production',[1] and consumption history can reveal to us what the rise of the Japanese economy has ultimately been about. The aim of this book, in telling the story of the Japanese consumer, is also to illuminate, from the angle of ordinary people and everyday life, the developments that have produced the superpower economy whose goods we all nowadays use and enjoy.

This 'demand-side', 'bottom-up' approach is not the one to be found underlying the usual account of Japan's economic history. There, Japanese people typically appear as savers and workers, as managers, entrepreneurs and government bureaucrats, but seldom as those who have eaten, worn and used most of the goods that the Japanese economy has succeeded in producing in ever-greater quantities. Anthropologists and sociologists have lately discovered the contemporary

---

[1] *The Wealth of Nations* (1776), Book IV, Chapter VIII.

Japanese consumer, recognising that the study of consumption behaviour represents a remarkably productive route into an understanding of how Japanese society works. But the consumers they study appear timelessly modern, or post-modern, divorced from any of the historical economic, social or political processes that might have made them what they are today.

This is despite the fact that historians of pre-modern Japan nowadays delight in describing what was undoubtedly a world of consumption to be enjoyed in the great cities that had come into existence by the eighteenth century. The literature of the period tells of the food, clothes, entertainment and luxury goods that were consumed – not just by the elite – in a milieu of rising incomes and shifting status that long pre-dated Japan's first exposure – from the middle of the nineteenth century – to the modern, industrial, consumerist West. Thereafter, however, the Japanese consumer disappears into a history of saving and investment, technological change and management practice, on the assumption that, through the subsequent years of economic growth and change up to the Second World War, most ordinary people, in the cities and in the villages and small towns of the countryside, were simply engaged in the process of acquiring 'daily necessities'.[2] Once the post-Second World War economic miracle took off, Japanese people at last began to be able to enjoy modern consumer goods – the mass-market electrical products, cars and junk food that their Western counterparts had begun to consume in the pre-war period – but it was still typically for their saving, not their spending, that they were studied and famed.

Underlying this account of Japanese people, throughout their history, as workers and savers for whom goods were simply necessary for survival in the short or long term is the analytical framework once standardly utilised by Japanese historians studying their own country. Here Japanese workers and farmers are seen as necessarily exploited, first by a feudal ruling class, then by a land-owning elite and ultimately by a capitalist bourgeoisie, leaving them with little scope for the purchase, much less enjoyment, of anything other than the necessities of survival. The persistence of very small-scale, peasant-style farm households, many of them renting land from landlords, was seen as evidence of the 'excess' population on the land and 'surplus' labour, which brought about low wage levels in town and country and restricted the growth of purchasing

[2] See, for example, Shimbo and Hasegawa's standard modern account of the growth of the commercial economy of pre-industrial Japan (Shimbo and Hasegawa 2004: e.g. 164, 177).

power. Japanese businesses, unable to develop markets for their products at home, sought them overseas in Japan's pre-war empire and later in the export markets of Europe and the United States. The concept of the 'narrowness' of the Japanese domestic market was in this way an important element in the analysis of the links between the economy and the emergence of Japanese imperialism and militarism in the pre-war years, later re-born in the structural relationship between Japan's high rate of saving (hence low growth in consumption) and the trade surplus that was plaguing its international economic and political relations by the 1980s.

In recent years, a wide range of studies has come to challenge this picture. It is now clear that, for a long period from the late eighteenth century through to the late nineteenth, steady economic growth was taking place in Japan, albeit involving the production, much of it in rural areas, of 'traditional' goods using 'pre-industrial' technology. As a result, given the low rate of population growth and the inability of the ruling elite to capture all of the benefits of economic growth, living standards were rising, especially in the countryside, as rural households began to acquire the food and drink products, textiles and household goods once available only in the cities.[3] The modern urban industrial growth that took off from the 1890s certainly caused conflict and new inequalities, but it also fostered the gradual diffusion of new consumer goods, alongside continuing growth and change in the consumption of the 'traditional products' that still accounted for the bulk of ordinary consumption in urban as in rural households. The rapid growth in incomes produced by the economic miracle of the late 1950s and 1960s, following on from the hardship of the war-time years, encouraged Japanese people to acquire in quick succession the symbols of modern life, from the washing machine and black-and-white television to the family saloon and fancy stereo, while at the same time re-building and increasing their savings. Nonetheless, although the expanding production and distribution of an ever widening range of consumer goods are implicit in any account of Japan's modern history, the consumption of those goods – and the people who consumed them – rarely merits more than a passing mention.[4]

By the 1980s, Japanese people were at last beginning to be recognised not only as the world's greatest savers, but also, especially

---

[3] For a wide range of evidence for rising living standards and quality of life in this period, see Hanley 1997.
[4] A notable exception to this is Simon Partner's work on electrical goods in the post-Second World War period (Partner 1999).

as they took advantage of the high-value yen (resulting from the trade surplus) in the luxury stores of London, Paris and Milan, as its most discerning yet voracious consumers. Anthropologists and sociologists began to see in the Japanese consumer the apotheosis of the post-modern consumerist world of signs, dissecting in detail a best-selling novel composed almost entirely in brand names.[5] But the Japanese ladies who queued to stock up at Gucci or Prada, the businessmen who spent unimaginable sums on nights out or golf, and the teenage girls perfectly and universally attuned to the latest craze all seemed to spring from nowhere. Economic historians, brought up on the idea of the 'narrowness' of the Japanese market, had nothing to contribute, as Japanese consumers frenziedly spent their way through the rise and collapse of the 1980s 'bubble economy'.

This book narrates the history of those consumers, demonstrating how its discovery opens up the neglected world of everyday life – of eating and drinking, dressing, furnishing homes and socialising; of women and children as well as their more visible menfolk; of ordinary goods produced elsewhere than in the gleaming, or Satanic, factories and offices of the 'modern sector'. It was within this world that the material expressions of Western consumerism – from the pocket watches and beef stews that symbolised modernity in the late nineteenth century to the mobile phones and Starbucks lattes of the present day – had to find their place. As subsequent chapters show, Japanese people have been honing their skills and developing their particular tastes and characteristics as consumers for two centuries and more, and their history remains embedded, if we but look for it, in the vibrant post-modern consumerism to be observed on Tokyo streets today.

Japanese consumers are of course not unique in having a history, and this book draws inspiration from the by now large literature on the consumption history of other parts of the world, most significantly the first industrialising nations of Europe and North America. As has been the case with Japan, the economic history of the rest of the industrial world was once largely focused on the 'supply side', analysing developments in production, technology, business organisation, trade and government policy from a largely top-down and as far as possible quantitative perspective. However, in the wake of Neil McKendrick's seminal 1982 paper postulating a 'consumer revolution' in eighteenth-century England, historians of 'the West' have (re-)discovered consumption, recognising that widespread growth in purchases of food products, clothes

---

[5] See Field 1989.

and accessories and all kinds of more or less decorative household goods represented, as McKendrick put it, a 'necessary analogue' to the industrial revolution.[6] This literature enables us to view Japan within the comparative context of the earlier industrialising countries of the West and opens up a whole range of issues in relation to the role of consumption in the history of the modern world.

For McKendrick, the driving force behind the eighteenth-century consumer revolution had been the possibilities offered – by widening trade, communications and markets, as well as rising cash incomes – for emulation of the goods that had once been the prerogative only of those of wealth or high status. The use of goods to demonstrate status had, of course, a long history, but studies of parts of the world as diverse as Renaissance Italy and Ming China were to find evidence of the growing propensity of the elite to acquire possessions as a means of showing off their wealth and taste and indeed as an enjoyable activity.[7] However, by the eighteenth century, in England and in other parts of Europe, more and more people were finding themselves wanting, and being able to acquire, 'populuxe' copies of the fashion accessories – fans, gloves, buckles – and household goods – clocks, mirrors, china – with which the rich were surrounding themselves. In London and Paris alike, shopping was becoming a central part of the urban experience, while superior tourists complained that it was getting impossible to tell from appearances who was servant and who was master or mistress.[8]

However, others argued that emulation alone was not enough to explain the profusion of goods that the evidence suggested was accumulating in the homes of the 'middling sort' and indeed others below them on the income scale. Nor could it explain the changing forms in which everyday goods – food and drink, clothes and household goods – were consumed, as social and working lives changed with the growth of cities and of industrial employment. The purchasers of tea services, decorative metal-ware and dining tables and chairs, as of the tea, coffee and sugar to go with them, were carving out for themselves both the material surroundings for new forms of social and family life and the signs of their own identity and respectability in the modern world that was emerging by the nineteenth century.[9]

---

[6] McKendrick 1982; for a survey of this literature, see Glennie 1995.

[7] Jardine 1996; Welch 2005; Brook 1998.

[8] On shopping in eighteenth-century England, see Walsh 2006; on populuxe goods in Paris, see Fairchilds 1994.

[9] For this argument, see Fine and Leopold 1990; for evidence of the growing importance of possessions in England, see Weatherill 1996 and Shammas 1990. For a more recent analysis, see Berg 2005.

The techniques of mass production that were eventually born out of the industrial revolution accelerated the diffusion of goods, often in new forms, to more and more consumers, giving rise to the mass market and the techniques of distribution and advertising that went with it. As a result, despite the continuing efforts of historians to unearth the long history of the Western consumer, the consumerism with which we are now all familiar has largely come to be viewed as a phenomenon of the modern industrialised world, in which fashion drives the never ending development of new products and people define themselves by means of the goods they consume. The emergence of the consumer has there-fore come to be seen as bound up with the availability of the 'modern' goods, produced and marketed in 'modern' ways, that resulted from the industrial revolution in the West.

For the world beyond the original sites of the industrial revolution, therefore, consumerism, as it is now understood, is something that arrives as part and parcel of the imported industrialisation that brings modern goods to domestic markets. Although it is of course recog-nised that consumer markets are not the same the world over and are conditioned by 'cultural' factors, and while historians of Europe and North America continue to discover earlier and earlier evidence of the existence of the 'pre-industrial consumer', the Japanese, and nowadays Chinese and Indian, consumer is still largely defined in terms of his or her purchases of Western fashions, electronic goods, Coca-Cola and McDonald's.[10] The 'non-Western consumer' springs fully formed and without a history into the market for modern consumer goods, and the many areas of consumption activity (and the production that supplies them) apparently unrelated to the 'Western impact' are largely ignored by all but intrepid anthropologists.

Consumerism in contemporary Japan clearly embodies many of the features that define its Western counterpart, from the primacy of fash-ion and advertising in determining consumer choice to the use of goods to signify status and individuality. However, it cannot be assumed that it was only as a result of the impact of the West that Japanese people came to ascribe meaning to goods in these ways, nor that the place of goods within their society is necessarily the same as that elsewhere. Much of their consumption expenditure is still devoted to goods and services which are not to be found, except as exotic imports, in other parts of the world; Japanese and other East Asian consumers are often thought to display an 'ambivalence' towards consumption, hence a pro-pensity to save, that is almost incomprehensible in the American or

[10] For a critique of this approach, see Trentmann 2004.

British context; the social ramifications of consumption are argued to weigh more heavily on Japanese consumers than on their individualistic, pleasure-seeking, Western counterparts.[11] All this would suggest that history does indeed condition the pattern of consumption growth and the emergence of the consumer as an aspect of modernity, and that Japan, as the first non-Western nation to achieve industrialisation and modernisation, represents a crucial case study within the comparative context of consumption history.

In presenting such a case study, this book uses a broadly chronological structure within which to describe the evolving world of the Japanese consumer. It begins in what is usually known as the Tokugawa (sometimes Edo) period, the two-and-a-half centuries (from 1600 to 1868) of relative peace, stability and 'seclusion' from the Western world when overall government lay in the hands of shoguns from the Tokugawa family. During this time, cities grew up, the market economy developed and growing numbers of people began to work in, and enjoy the products of, the manufacturing and service industries that emerged alongside an increasingly productive agriculture. Most historians now conclude that this 'traditional', 'pre-industrial' economic expansion continued beyond the overthrow of Tokugawa rule in the 1860s, providing the basis for the growth of the economy until at least the 1890s.

Nonetheless, the breakdown of the Tokugawa seclusion policy, caused by the arrival of Western warships and traders in the 1850s, did result in the first steps towards the introduction into Japan of not just the technology and business structures but also the products and lifestyles that the industrial revolution had generated in the West. It was not until after the turn of the century that these were to have any widespread impact on the everyday lives of most Japanese people, but the late nineteenth century saw the beginnings of the process of accommodating the methods and products of the industrial West into the pre-existing structures of consumption in Japan.

From the 1890s, however, the modern industrialisation and urbanisation initiated by the opening to the West, together with the subsequent establishment, under the Meiji Restoration of 1868, of a new system of government, began to produce significant changes in the ways in which Japanese people led their lives. As more and more of them moved from the traditional family environment of the countryside to work and eventually set up their own households in the towns and cities, so new

---

[11] These issues are raised in an East Asian context in Garon and Macachlan 2006.

goods were acquired, new kinds of household structure established and new forms of social activity devised. By the time that Japan, by now an imperial power, became embroiled in war in China and the wider Asia Pacific in the late 1930s, half of the population lived in urban areas, relying on the market for all that they consumed and developing urban lifestyles and patterns of consumption, while those who remained in the countryside were becoming less and less immune from the influence of the 'modern life' of the cities. Nonetheless, the vast majority of the goods that Japanese people ate and drank, dressed in and furnished their houses with were 'traditional' products, though now consumed within the new context of modern urban life.

By 1945, the war effort itself, combined eventually with the effects of bombing and the loss of imperial and international trade, had reduced much of the Japanese population to struggling for subsistence amidst the debris of the economy. Recovery was relatively swift, however, and by the 1950s Japanese people, by now overwhelmingly urban or suburban, were on the road towards the modern consumer lifestyle, under the influence of factors such as the post-war, predominantly American, occupation of their country and the re-opening to trade and communications with the increasingly consumerist Western world. Nonetheless, in the homes that they crammed with electrical goods, Japanese families maintained and adapted many elements of the consumption patterns that had emerged before the war. So they sat down at their new Western-style dining tables, dressed in jeans and T-shirts, to eat rice and side dishes which, though now bought pre-packed from a supermarket and advertised ad nauseam on television, their parents and grandparents would have recognised. By the time that the economic miracle culminated in the bubble economy of the second half of the 1980s, the Japanese consumer was able to spend with abandon, not just on designer handbags and the most expensive golf equipment, but also on connoisseurs' sake, obscure species of gourmet fish, and rice from the most prized fields in the most prized regions of the country. The long history of consumption in Japan was eventually to reach its apotheosis in the complex consumer life of the contemporary Japanese family.

Within the book's overall chronological structure, individual chapters will look at the various factors that conditioned the development of consumption in Japan and, through them, at the changing lives within which that consumption took place. Consumption by the trend-setting elite, whether the urban merchant classes of the great Tokugawa-period cities, the 'modern boys' and 'modern girls' who enjoyed all things Western in the 1920s, or the 'parasite singles' with money to burn in the 1980s, will take up part of the story, but it is ordinary lives in town and country that provide the main focus of attention. Throughout the book, changing consumption patterns in food and drink, clothing and household goods will provide the way into the everyday lives of households and families experiencing pre-industrial growth, modern industrialisation, economic miracle and post-industrialisation. The goods with which such families increasingly surrounded themselves reflect their responses to these changes, as much as they do the supply-side investment and technical change that produced them and the culture of marketing and advertising by means of which they were sold.

For each period, therefore, we will consider how and why goods were acquired and used, within the patterns of everyday life. In order to find evidence of consumption practices, we need to enter areas well beyond those conventionally mined by economic historians. What people bought and used was determined not simply by their absolute and relative incomes, but also by the changing infrastructure within which they lived, worked and shopped; the family patterns and gender roles that structured their day-to-day lives; the popular culture, advertising and media environment that surrounded them; and the prevailing thoughts and ideas conditioning the meanings that material goods, in general and in particular, held for them. However, the existing body of work on Europe and North America demonstrates how the wide range of social, political and cultural factors that came together in the growth of consumption cannot be ignored if we are to understand how economic development and industrialisation have taken place in Japan as in the Western developed world. Some aspects of the growth of consumption as a central element in the emerging modern economy can be understood on the basis of quantitative data (assembled in the statistical appendix), but many can be glimpsed only through the kinds of qualitative evidence produced by anthropologists and ethnographers, literary and cultural scholars and non-economic historians of many kinds.

Of course, the supply side that produced the growing abundance of goods and services available to Japanese consumers matters for any understanding of Japan's development process and its wider significance as the first non-Western example of industrialisation. However, the demand side offers a different angle on that process, one in which the everyday activities of ordinary people play a significant role. It is this that is the subject of what follows.

2 Shopping in the city: urban life and the emergence of the consumer in Tokugawa Japan

> Ancient simplicity is gone. With the growth of pretence the people of today are satisfied with nothing but finery, with nothing but what is beyond their station or purse.[1]

> She does the hair
> even of the maidservant
> just for her own sake.[2]

Throughout the history of consumption, from the Renaissance to the present day, cities have been the sites of the conspicuous spending, emulation and fashion-creation that have represented the first expressions of the consumer revolution. London was already a lure for shoppers and fashionistas by the late seventeenth century, and the emergence of the 'season', which brought much of the social elite, along with their retinues of servants and hangers-on, up to town for part of each year, consolidated the city's role.[3] Pre-revolutionary Paris was the stage for the fashionable spending not only of the aristocratic elite, but also of consumers of populuxe clothes, accessories and household goods much further down the income and status hierarchy.[4] As communications between town and country improved, the great cities developed both as the chief shopping sites for consumer goods across the range and as centres from which fashion and the knowledge of it were transmitted throughout the country.

In the seventeenth and eighteenth centuries, Japan was one of the most highly urbanised countries in the world. Edo (present-day Tokyo), with a million inhabitants, was probably the largest city in the

---

[1] From Ihara Saikaku's collection of stories, *The Japanese Family Storehouse* (Nippon eitai-gura), first published in 1688, as translated by G.W. Sargent (Ihara 1688/1959: 26).

[2] Poem in *senryū* form, from a collection published in 1765; translated by R. H. Blyth and quoted in Leupp 1992: 56.

[3] On the attractions of shopping in eighteenth-century London, see Berg 2005: 261–4; on the impact of the season, see McKendrick 1982.

[4] Fairchilds 1994.

eighteenth-century world, while Osaka and Kyoto had populations approaching those of London and Paris, the largest cities in the West at the time.[5] Initially established as bases for government, administration and trade, these great cities emerged as centres of consumption, with population and work-force structures, infrastructure and institutions, and even arts and ethos reflecting a consumer culture that was eventually to be transmitted out to the rest of the country. It was here, in the urban context, that Japanese people first began to engage in, and enjoy, market-based consumption and the practices and choices that went with it, so that in Japan, as elsewhere in the world, it was the city that gave birth to the consumer.

The great cities as centres of consumption

Japan's urban boom took off in the early seventeenth century and was in many ways a consequence of the political arrangements that accompanied the establishment, after 1600, of a national government system headed by shoguns from the Tokugawa family. Given their primary role as centres of government and administration, towns and cities produced few of the goods they needed within their own boundaries and, as their populations mushroomed over the first half of the century, they came to constitute large-scale markets drawing in products from throughout the country. City dwellers, from the great lords and merchants to the lowliest servants, of necessity relied on the market for much of what they consumed, and the resulting development of facilities for shopping and leisure spending opened up new opportunities for the acquisition and enjoyment of goods that underlay the flourishing urban culture of Tokugawa Japan.

The urban population and the market

In the years around 1600, the leading general Tokugawa Ieyasu, employing a mixture of military conquest and political negotiation, established control over the two hundred or so feudal lords, known as *daimyō*, who had governed and fought over the territory of Japan during the preceding decades of conflict and instability. Ieyasu established a new castle and base for himself and his successors as shogun, or military leader, in what was initially the tiny fishing village of Edo on the Kantō plain, some three hundred miles north-east of the old imperial capital of

---

[5] Nakai and McClain 1991: 519. In 1700, there were five cities in Japan with populations over 100,000, compared with fourteen in the whole of Europe.

Kyoto where the emperor remained. As shogun, Ieyasu left the *daimyō* in charge of their individual domains, which they were expected to tax and govern from the castle-towns that acted as their capitals, but retained substantial territory in the hands of the Tokugawa house to provide income for the administration by means of which he exercised overall control of national government. In order to ensure this control, trade and other contact with the outside world were restricted and the lords were required to spend half their time in Edo, demonstrating their allegiance to the Tokugawa shogun and dissipating any funds they might otherwise have built up to finance opposition to the national government. As a result, they found themselves obliged to travel back and forth regularly between their domains and their Edo residences, accompanied by suitable retinues of retainers and servants, in a ritual that became known as *sankin kōtai* or alternate attendance.

The establishment of the Tokugawa system generated rapid growth in urban populations and a large-scale urban construction boom. Most domains required the samurai military retainers of the lord, redundant as fighters now that national peace had been established, to move into their castle-towns where they would work in the administration of taxation and government. There they lived, as an exclusive hereditary class, on stipends provided by the lord from his tax revenue, within a hierarchical structure of status and office. As housing and other facilities were constructed for them, the craftsmen, merchants and labourers who could supply the goods and services they needed were also drawn in. The castle-towns of the greatest lords grew to be major cities, while smaller versions became established in domains everywhere.

Meanwhile, on a much larger scale, Edo expanded rapidly into a great city, as the shogun set up his military and administrative headquarters there, *daimyō* built and staffed their mansions and traders and workers flooded in to meet the resulting demands. Given the remoteness of Edo from the most developed areas of agriculture and manufacturing in the Kansai region around Kyoto, Osaka, as that region's port, came to act as the assembly and distribution point for goods and people making their way to Edo and beyond. With Kyoto still supporting the imperial court and the aristocracy that surrounded it, seventeenth-century Japan found itself the site of three great metropolises, as well as a network of towns and cities throughout the country.

The structure of the urban population, and the housing and living arrangements that it produced, reflected the raison d'être of the cities as centres of administration and commerce. In Edo and, to some extent, other castle-towns, it was the establishment of the bases for *daimyō* administration and residence that initiated urban growth. The samurai bureaucrats who ran the shogun's own administration probably numbered, along with their families and servants, about 250,000. A roughly similar number manned the *daimyō* residences in Edo, looking after the lord's family – required to remain in the city as hostages to his good behaviour – and carrying on the domain's business there on a day-to-day basis.[6] This permanent population was substantially augmented from time to time by the influx of samurai retainers and servants high and low who accompanied the lord on his *sankin kōtai* trips to Edo.[7] The supplies necessary to support all those permanently or temporarily part of the *daimyō*'s Edo establishment could to some extent be brought in kind from the domain, where the lord's taxes were typically received for the most part in rice or other agricultural produce, but much had to be purchased in the city. Samurai who lived on the stipends received, often in kind, from the shogunate or their own *daimyō* had no choice but to convert their incomes into cash (or credit) to support themselves while on their lord's business in Edo.

The political elite of lords and samurai, together with all their dependants and servants, therefore came to rely on a non-samurai commercial population that probably equalled that of the samurai in number by the early eighteenth century.[8] Its members ranged from those who ran great trading houses dealing in rice, textiles, sake and an ever growing variety of more specialised goods, through financiers and money-lenders, craftsmen in many different more or less skilled trades, purveyors and shopkeepers, to porters, palanquin-bearers and construction labourers. While samurai stipends remained by and large fixed – and a massive drain on the tax income that domains were able to squeeze from their farmers and other inhabitants – and their ethos forbade samurai from engaging in any kind of commercial activity, those from the merchant and artisan classes who were successful in the business of trade and finance grew richer and themselves began to constitute a market for the goods and services available in the cities.

Meanwhile, the construction boom and the subsequent growth in urban population and income provided opportunities for a whole army of servants and labourers, permanently or temporarily supporting themselves in the cities. Probably at least 10 per cent of the

---

[6] McClain and Merriman 1994: 13–14. A large domain such as Tosa maintained a permanent staff of 700–1,000 at its Edo residence, as well as 100 or 200 in its smaller establishments in Osaka and Kyoto (Vaporis 1997: 30).

[7] Gilbert Rozman estimates that typically 20–30 per cent of the city's population were on *sankin kōtai* business, while a further 20,000 seasonal migrants regularly spent the winter there (Rozman 1974: 100–1).

[8] McClain and Merriman 1994: 14.

population of the cities were domestic servants of one kind or another, with the proportion rising to 20 or 30 per cent in the most prosperous wards, and a relatively large number of households employed one or more servants.[9] Many servants and apprentices lived in their masters' households, although often receiving cash wages in one form or another on top of their board and lodging, while day-labourers and temporary workers stayed in boarding houses and hostels, or in the tenements of 'row-houses' thrown up by speculative builders. The nature of urban employment meant that single men tended to preponderate in the labour force and, although girls and women did go to the cities to work as servants, waitresses, entertainers and prostitutes, relatively few married and settled there. As a result, the 'mass market' of the towns and cities was dominated by the demands of single men for food, drink and entertainment.

In addition to the fluctuating population of *sankin kōtai* travellers and seasonal workers, great cities such as Edo, Osaka and Kyoto also drew in growing numbers of tourists and visitors.[10] Business brought provincial traders up to town but the cities also offered many more enjoyable attractions to those able to journey to them: temples and shrines were the objects of pilgrimages, as well as the source of the material souvenirs sold at festivals and in arcades of permanent stalls; the famous sites and personalities of the cities were advertised in widely available prints; and of course the best shops and local food specialities were not to be missed.

By the end of the seventeenth century, the great construction boom was over, and urban growth slowed down as the focus of economic activity shifted out to the countryside. However, by then the cities had established themselves as large-scale markets with populations – high or low, long-term resident, temporary migrant or tourist – dependent on commercial supplies for almost everything they consumed. This necessitated the development of the distribution and retail facilities that turned the cities into the centres of fashion and enjoyable consumption pictured and described in the flowering urban culture of the time.

The birth of shopping

With their large-scale concentrations of consumers largely reliant on the market for everything from everyday food and clothes to the kimono, swords and calligraphic scrolls produced by the greatest craftsmen

[9] Leupp 1992: 29–41.
[10] On the attractions of cities for tourists and travellers, see Jansen 1989: 65.

and artists of the day, Tokugawa-period cities drew in goods from throughout the country by means of increasingly specialised networks of production and distribution. Market gardeners in the agricultural areas around the cities supplied fruit and vegetables, while local fishermen provided fish and shellfish; craft producers in Kyoto continued to serve the upper-class market for textiles, furnishings, pottery and all sorts of clothing accessories; particular regions developed the food-processing expertise necessary to supply the large urban markets with sake and soy sauce; in domains throughout the country, rural producers came to specialise in differentiated forms of textiles, ceramics, paper, lacquer-ware and all manner of household goods. The distribution and retailing system that made these goods available to urban consumers was central to the creation of the urban culture of consumption that characterised the period.

Given its location in relation to key agricultural and manufacturing regions and its port and road connections, Osaka emerged in the early seventeenth century as the central hub within the distribution network that served Edo and other cities. Numerous wholesalers, dealers and agents were already establishing themselves, some specialising in particular products, such as the cotton grown in the surrounding region which was manufactured into cloth for sale to consumers in the north of the country, others in the products of particular regions, such as the agents from Satsuma domain who traded in the sugar, camphor and *shiitake* mushrooms of southern Kyūshū.[11] By the early eighteenth century, an enormous range of processed and manufactured goods was being shipped from Osaka to Edo and beyond, ranging from basic commodities such as vegetable oil and cotton cloth, through processed food (large quantities of sake and soy sauce, for example), household goods (ceramics, kitchenware, wooden furniture) and clothing accessories (sandals, *tabi* socks, fans, umbrellas), to cosmetics, medicines and even books and manuscripts. A group of 124 pharmaceutical shops in Osaka held a monopoly on sales of all imported medicines, which they assessed, packaged and sold on to retailers throughout the country. Osaka's substantial outcaste (*eta*) community produced and shipped out large quantities of leather goods, ranging from samurai armour to sandals and leather-soled *tabi*.[12] The 'thousand and one' everyday goods sold by Osaka producers included 'engraved signature seals, lacquer-ware, gold leaf, umbrellas, *shamisen* strings, carved whalebone, pictorial votive offerings, folding screens, storage chests, sliding doors, raincoats, carpenters' tools, mirrors, lanterns' and much more.[13]

---

[11] McClain 1999: 59–60, 67.   [12] McClain 1999: Table 3.2, 65, 71.
[13] McClain 1999: 72.

Such goods found their way into complex and varied retail systems in the cities. For fresh food, there were markets specialising in vegetables and fish, and door-to-door sellers of fish and other fresh produce were readily available. The wholesale and retail fish market at Nihonbashi in Edo/Tokyo existed from the early Tokugawa period until the Great Earthquake of 1923, after which it was moved to its present location in Tsukiji.[14] Osaka's Three Great Markets, all established in the first half of the seventeenth century, specialised in fruit and vegetables, fish and rice respectively.[15] Processed food could be bought from specialist shops such as confectioners, rice merchants and noodle-sellers, while ordinary grocery shops were to be found in every residential quarter. Records in Edo list peddlers selling vegetables, sweets, incense sticks, straw sandals, flowering plants, bean curd and soy sauce.[16] In the area around the bridge at Edobashi, dealers in seasonal fruit and vegetables, as well as the pine branches used as New Year decorations, fetched up year after year, alongside permanent tea-houses, fortune-tellers and shops selling a huge range of cosmetics, hair and clothing accessories, love potions and 'sexual gadgetry'.[17]

At the same time, large-scale stores and city-centre shopping districts drew in resident and visiting shoppers from far and wide. The Mitsui family, originally based in Kyoto, opened their textile shop (Echigoya) in Edo in 1683 and by the 1730s were employing over 200 people there (Fig. 2.1).[18] Their building had a long shop-front and large sales area, as well as a range of facilities including a customer toilet and garden. Another Kyoto-based retail organisation, Shirokiya, opened a store in Nihonbashi in Edo in 1662, selling high-class textiles and accessories, which was successful enough to be employing 150 staff by 1749 and supporting three other branches in Edo.[19] The two great Osaka dry-goods stores (Echigoya/Mitsui and Masuya) spread out along the city's central streets.[20] Alongside such large-scale stores were assembled specialist shops that included pharmacies, tobacconists, sellers of every kind of clothing accessory, book and antique shops and second-hand stores of many kinds.[21]

Of course, in many respects, the retail experience of Tokugawa-period consumers was not the same as that of their modern counterparts.

[14] Bestor 2004: 98.
[15] McClain 1999: 56–8, which shows contemporary prints of the busy scenes at all three markets.
[16] Leupp 1992: 139.   [17] McClain 1994: 113–14.
[18] Nakae 2007: 58; Dunn 1969: 118.
[19] Hayashi 1994: 215.   [20] McClain 1999: 73.
[21] For a visiting samurai's assessment of competing second-hand shops, and for more on shopping in Edo, see Vaporis 1997.

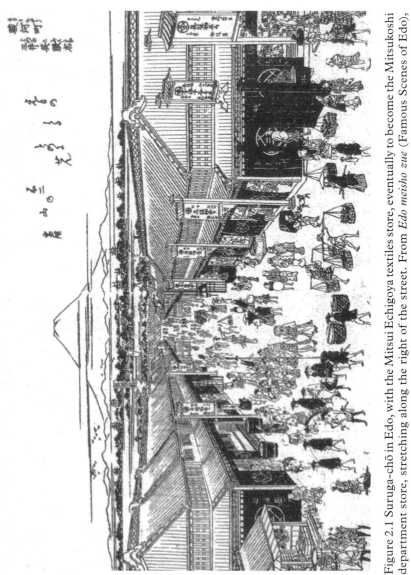

Figure 2.1 Suruga-chō in Edo, with the Mitsui Echigoya textiles store, eventually to become the Mitsukoshi department store, stretching along the right of the street. From *Edo meisho zue* (Famous Scenes of Edo), published in 1834–6. Nakae 2007: 59, courtesy of the National Diet Library.

The big dry-goods stores tended to cater to particular clienteles within urban society. They did not as a rule display fixed-price goods for window-shopping, but instead employed sales assistants (usually men) to demonstrate goods to customers, at their homes or in-store. Sales were typically made on account, with settlements twice a year at the time of the mid-summer Obon and New Year festivals, although Echigoya was unusual in selling at fixed prices in cash. More ordinary shops were essentially the opened-up front rooms of the houses where shopkeepers and their families lived, and row-house tenements were often constructed to include shop units that opened out on to the street (Fig. 2.2). Here fishmongers, greengrocers, confectioners and sellers of ceramics, household utensils, cosmetics and second-hand clothes operated alongside craftsmen who manufactured and sold from their homes. Palanquin-bearers stored their vehicles in such units and waited to be called out on a job, as the Edo equivalent of a taxi service.[22] Meanwhile, much shopping could be done at home, as travelling salespeople came to call (Fig. 2.3).

In such an environment of personalised and local shopping, fashion trends tended to be spread by word of mouth and by example, but retailers also came to engage in significant amounts of advertising and promotional activity. Product placement within the popular wood-block prints of *kabuki* actors and famous geisha was common;[23] stores had already discovered the potential of the umbrella as a space for displaying logos;[24] handbills, fliers and striking shop signs were widely used to attract customers. Textile shops produced beautiful catalogues of prints displaying their current patterns and designs.[25]

There seems little doubt therefore that, as the Tokugawa period progressed, shopping in the city was becoming an enjoyable activity that went well beyond the requirements of purchasing the necessities of survival. For the rich and fashion-conscious, the smartest shops offered wide ranges of goods from which to choose in pleasant surroundings; for those with scholarly tastes, visiting antique, curio and book shops in search of a prize item for the collection was a major attraction of the urban experience. For all and sundry, meanwhile, fairs and festivals at temples and shrines offered opportunities to buy all kinds of

[22] Nakae 2007: 60–1.

[23] Mundane products such as soap, toothpaste, face powder and sake were involved, as well as high-fashion clothes and accessories. See examples displayed in the Advertising Museum in Shinbashi, Tokyo.

[24] Moeran 1998: 150; Vaporis 1997: 49.

[25] A number of well-known *ukiyoe* artists began their careers or supplemented their incomes producing prints for such catalogues (Noma 1974: 128–9).

Figure 2.2 Shop making and selling wooden combs in the manner of its Tokugawa-period forebears, still operating in the Ueno district of Tokyo in 2007.

Figure 2.3 A travelling salesman demonstrating cosmetics and hair ornaments. Adapted from an Edo-period text in Takenaka 2003: 46.

goods from stalls, while eating, drinking and being entertained. Buying things – whether treats or bargains from the fishmonger or grocer, gifts or souvenirs to take home from a *sankin kōtai* visit, the most beautiful kimono fabric or the smallest trinket from a peddler – was becoming an essential part of the art and enjoyment of being in the city.

Eating, drinking and being merry

Meanwhile, Tokugawa-period cities also experienced an explosion in the provision of facilities for another form of pleasurable consumption: eating and drinking out. Prior to this, social eating and drinking outside the household had typically taken the form of the large-scale formal banquets put on by those seeking to impress invited guests with their power to command resources. The emphasis had consequently been placed on the quantity and appearance, rather than the taste, of the food. At a more humble level, communal festivities, when local groups would get together to brew sake and provide accompanying food, continued to take place. In the context of the social and economic development of Tokugawa-period cities, however, new forms of social eating were to emerge, so that, by the nineteenth century, in the commercial world of urban Japan, eating away from home had become an element in private or small-scale social life, a focus of fashion and style for those who could afford it and of enjoyment for many more.[26]

Tea-houses and inns, serving refreshments to travellers and visitors to shrines, temples and other attractions, began to appear throughout the country, as travel and tourism expanded during the early Tokugawa period.[27] By the first half of the eighteenth century, city tea-houses were beginning to serve a wider range of food in differentiated styles, and by the early nineteenth century, the restaurant sector in Edo and the other great cities was booming.[28] At the top end of the scale were large, fashionable establishments, offering private rooms and elaborate cuisine, many located in the riverside pleasure quarters of Edo. Here, and in their equivalents in other cities,[29] the rich and fashionable, mainly from the merchant classes who could afford it, dined on seasonal specialities in the company of actors and geisha, while intellectuals met for discussion over drinks and superior snacks. In establishments such as these, food, and the experience of dining on it, became a matter of fashion and taste. Restaurants competed fiercely with each other through the introduction of new foods and forms of preparation; their chefs became celebrities and their waitresses had to be pretty (and possibly available). Most served some form of multi-course (*kaiseki*) menu and the presentation of food on the necessarily distinctive and large range of plates and bowls was also an important part of a restaurant's image.

Meanwhile, those lower down the income scale were also being offered a widening range of opportunities to eat or drink out, whether out of necessity, when unable to prepare food for themselves at home,

[26] Ishige 2001: 107, 113, 120–1. It has been suggested (e.g. Takenaka 2003) that the restaurants set up in Edo after the Meireki fire of 1657 were the first in the world, pre-dating any in France or England by at least a century. This may depend what is meant by a restaurant; there were apparently establishments that could be called restaurants in China as early as the tenth century (Ishige 2001: 117), but certainly dining out for pleasure at a commercial establishment seems to have been an accepted practice in Japanese cities well before it was in Europe.
[27] For the history of restaurants in Japan, see Ishige 2001: 117–24.
[28] A survey of 1804 recorded over 6,000 eating places in Edo (not counting those in the theatre and pleasure quarters), or 1 per 170 inhabitants (Ishige 2001: 122).
[29] For example, the Sumiya restaurant in Kyoto, which is still open to visitors.

Figure 2.4 Stall selling food and sake. An illustration from an 1851 version of the puppet-theatre play *Keisei Awa no Naruto* (Courtesan at Naruto in Awa), written and illustrated by Rakutei Saiba and Utagawa Yoshitora; courtesy of Waseda University Library.

or for pleasure and social interaction. Eating and drinking places ran the gamut from the high-class restaurants through simpler and cheaper establishments for drinks and snacks, fast food or noodles, to street stalls selling boiled fish and vegetables (*nimono*), cheap stews (*oden*) and sake (Fig. 2.4). Informal bars/restaurants known as *izakaya* emerged as places in which to drink and snack on simple food, while sitting at benches in a noisy and raucous atmosphere; mobile *yatai* stalls provided outside eating and drinking facilities, as they still do (Fig. 2.5). Street vendors carried braziers on poles over which they warmed boiled vegetables, tofu and rice as they did the rounds of the *daimyō* mansions where

Figure 2.5 Working men relaxing at an open-air bar in Ameyokochō, Tokyo, much as their Tokugawa predecessors might have done.

visiting *sankin kōtai* samurai lodged.[30] Sushi of many different types was sold in sushi restaurants or by street vendors who dressed in distinctive outfits to distinguish their wares.[31] By the nineteenth century, shops selling bowls of *soba* or *udon* noodles and soup, much as appear on the menus of small restaurants today, were apparently to be found on almost every block in Edo. The large proportion of single men – live-in servants, migrant labourers and so on – in the populations of cities such as Edo, paid wages or pocket money in cash and free to spend on eating and drinking as they liked, presented a ready market for prepared food.[32]

It also, of course, created a considerable demand for alcoholic drink. In volume terms at least, per capita consumption of sake in Edo at peak times was possibly as high as present-day per capita consumption of alcohol of all kinds, and refined sake brewed in the specialist brewing areas of the Kansai region around Osaka was shipped into the city in large amounts, in its distinctive barrels, using dedicated shippers.[33] Urban drinkers, reliant on commercial supplies, almost universally drank the refined product produced by larger-scale breweries, rather

[30] Nakae 2007: 70–1.   [31] Nishiyama 1997: 171.
[32] Nishiyama 1997: 174; Ishige 2001: 122–4.   [33] Kanzaki 2000: 149.

8 The great cities as centres of consumption 25

than the unrefined, home-brewed or village-made product of the countryside, and differentiation by quality, brewer or region of origin began to be accepted.[34] The male populations of the great cities, uprooted from rural practices of communal, festive drinking, increasingly appear to have been consuming sake, often alongside snacks and fast food, as a private social activity with friends or fellow workers. Similarly, the middle and upper classes came to drink sake more and more as a pleasurable accompaniment to private meals rather than as a part of rituals, ceremonies and formal banquets. Sake-drinking practices that are now accepted as 'traditional', such as serving the drink warmed, became firmly established. By the middle of the Tokugawa period, the use of purpose-made sake cups and flasks both at home and in bars and restaurants was widespread, creating significant backward linkages to the ceramics industry.[35]

Tokugawa cities also offered many other occasions and venues for social and leisure activities and the consumption associated with them. Tea-houses, grand or simple, continued to provide facilities and refreshments for social gatherings and tea-drinking as relaxation became an established practice.[36] Tobacco smoking, first introduced to Japan by foreign visitors in the late sixteenth century, spread widely over the course of the Tokugawa period, and many catering establishments provided smoking equipment for their customers, male and female. The style of smoking that developed in Japan involved the use of very finely shredded tobacco (grown in Japan) in long, thin pipes (kiseru), and tobacconist's shops, as well as sellers of a wide range of smoking paraphernalia, from the basic to the highly artistic, were common in the cities.[37] Public bath-houses (sentō) offered the opportunity to relax and chat as you soaked, while men at least were able to repair to their upper floors to play shōgi (Japanese chess) and go and to enjoy tea and cakes.[38]

Meanwhile, the cities came to offer a growing range of leisure and amusement facilities. The kabuki theatres were by no means exclusive establishments, and armies of fans bought prints of their favourite actors, as well as bentō picnic boxes to eat in the intervals. Edo was

[34] Watanabe 1964: 255. Sake was brewed in the Edo region but the products of the big Kansai brewers were regarded as much superior, as well as being improved by spending time in barrels during the sea voyage to Edo. An annual Beaujolais Nouveau-style race took place to bring in the first of each year's new brew (Nakae 2007: 66–7).
[35] Kanzaki 2000: 147–8.   [36] Takenaka 2003: 56–7.
[37] See Takenaka 2003: 90 and exhibits at the Tobacco and Salt Museum, Shibuya, Tokyo.
[38] Nakae 2007: 86–7.

famous for its fireworks displays, drawing thousands to the riverside viewing spots on hot summer nights. Outings to view spring blossom and other seasonal sights presented excellent opportunities for showing off fashionable clothes and elegant picnic equipment. Amusement quarters (*sakariba*) began to emerge, offering many kinds of entertainment as well as facilities for shopping and refreshments. Here tiny theatres, charging little more than the price of a bowl of noodles for admission, provided venues for practitioners of the art of dramatic story-telling (*rakugo*).[39] Temples and shrines were the sites of festivals and fairs at which peddlers plied their wares, fortunes were told and well-organised beggars engaged in a wide range of busking. Sumo wrestling became an established spectator sport in the seventeenth century, and the top professionals were celebrities, portrayed in wood-block prints alongside actors and geisha. Gambling in many forms was a common pastime, and facilities for prostitution, from the most basic brothel to the most glamorous geisha house, were widespread. No day off in Edo was apparently complete without 'nomu, utsu, kau' (drinking, gambling, buying).[40]

Residents of the great cities of Tokugawa Japan did not therefore lack the facilities they needed to choose and acquire marketed goods and to consume them in new ways that fitted their changing private and social lives. Markets, shops and door-to-door sellers provided them with the fresh and processed food items required by urban eating styles; shops, large and small, offered textiles and accessories, from the most ordinary to the most exquisite and fashionable; household goods of every kind could be bought from craft producers, shops, stalls and travelling salesmen; restaurants offered everything from gourmet delights to street snacks. Although some might still bring produce from the country or continue to make miso (fermented bean paste) or pickles at home, most relied on the commercial facilities that the cities offered to meet most of their needs and desires. These facilities were themselves embedded in wider networks of supply and commerce, in the surrounding regions and further afield, through the commercial hub of Osaka or, in due course, along other supply routes linking directly with producing areas. The Tokugawa period thus saw the establishment of the infrastructure of consumption that enabled many in the great cities to begin to practise and enjoy the life of the consumer.

[39] McClain 1994: 123.
[40] Kanzaki 2000: 150. The 'buying' was probably of sex, it has to be said.

Consumption and everyday life in the cities

The developing infrastructure of consumption in the cities presented urban people with new ways to acquire a growing range of goods. What they actually bought reflected the lives they were coming to lead there and the expanding and changing role of goods within them. Through the food they cooked and ate, the clothes they wore and the household goods with which they surrounded themselves, they adapted to the changing economic and social world around them and created patterns of everyday consumption that have continued to shape and condition Japanese day-to-day life ever since.

Food and drink

In the 1560s, Oda Nobunaga, one of the founders of the Tokugawa shogunate, reportedly failed to appreciate the fancy but tasteless dishes prepared for him by the captured chef of an aristocratic household, preferring the ordinary rustic food he had been brought up on.[41] Before long, however, his successors were presiding over a society within which food, drink and cuisine were becoming ever more matters of interest and significance to urban people. Different schools of cookery emerged, and cooking began to be regarded as an art, with secret traditions and special 'ways'.[42] The gourmand and food snob became recognised characters, and a well-known saying had it that while Kyoto people ruined themselves through extravagance on clothes, Osaka people did the same on food. Cookery books and restaurant guides were published in growing numbers, increasingly not just for the food snob: the runaway success of *Tōfu hyakuchin* (A Hundred Tofu Curiosities) of 1782 inspired not just a 'hundred more things to do with tofu' but 'hundred recipe' books on a whole range of foods.[43]

Different types of cooking and eating had come to be recognised even before the establishment of the Tokugawa regime and ranged from monastic vegetarian diets to the massive, sake-fuelled banquets of the feudal upper classes. However, as the cities grew through the seventeenth century and the infrastructure of markets, shops and food-processing facilities became established, a widening choice of food possibilities opened up for urban consumers. As a result, the differentiated

---

[41] Nishiyama 1997: 144–5.
[42] Roberts describes a samurai officer in the domain of Tosa copying out books, including 'a cookbook of favorite household recipes created by the samurai of his domain' (L. Roberts 2002: 27).
[43] Ishige 2001: 126–7.

forms of eating and drinking that the commercial economy made possible could be enjoyed and utilised as indicators of status, style and fashion. Across urban society, food became more varied, more fun and more distinct from the basic food of the countryside, in ways that were closely associated with the forms of economic and social life emerging in the cities.

What was to develop out of this process was what we now think of as 'traditional' Japanese cuisine. The basic meal structure that became established during the Tokugawa period is often referred to as the *kaiseki* style and is generally thought to be a sort of happy medium between the slap-up medieval banquet and the austere forms of eating and drinking that had developed earlier as part of the tea ceremony, with a new emphasis on quality – producing food that looked and tasted good – rather than quantity. *Kaiseki*-style meals centred around rice, cooked and eaten on its own but served alongside as many varied side dishes and accompaniments as appropriate to the situation and the purse. Miso soup in one form or another was a fixture in a *kaiseki* menu, as was green tea, and sake accompanied it when alcohol was appropriate. What else was included depended on what was available and on the culinary resources of the cook. Side dishes involved vegetables, fish and pulses, sometimes fresh, sometimes salted or dried, depending on the season. These might be boiled or grilled and were often seasoned or pickled, using soy sauce, miso paste, vinegar, sake lees and so on. Meals were usually served on individual trays, placed before each participant and set with separate bowls or plates suitable to the elements of the course. Elaborate *kaiseki* meals involved many courses, hence many trays; simple versions consisted of no more than rice, miso and one or two side dishes of fish, vegetables or pickles, in forms that still constitute the basic elements of Japanese home or restaurant cooking.

Meals of this structure appear to have become standard across the urban social spectrum during the Tokugawa period, but offered enormous scope for differentiation in the quantity and quality of ingredients and side dishes: in the establishments of the *daimyō*, lord and servant followed the same pattern, but with the best dishes of course going to the lord; ordinary samurai households, struggling to keep up appearances, prided themselves on pure and simple, home-made side dishes to go with their rice; *nouveau riche* merchants flashed their wealth as they bought up the most fashionable, new-season items to include in their *kaiseki* spreads; single workers bought bowls of rice, tea and pickles from stalls and street sellers.

The establishment of this kind of eating – distinguished from the one-pot stews and variety of grains typically consumed in the countryside (see ch. 3) – as standard in the cities had many implications. First, it placed polished white rice, boiled or steamed on its own, at the centre of 'civilised' eating. Much of the demand thus created was met from the rice collected as taxes in kind by the feudal lords. The lords would use this rice for their own household consumption and to pay the stipends of their samurai, but whatever remained after this could be shipped to market – much of it to Osaka, where the domains maintained ware-houses for it – and sold to raise cash revenue. Farm households also marketed rice when and where they had it to sell. Merchants, artisans and other urban residents without sources of income in kind bought rice from retail rice merchants, of whom there were about 2,000 in eight-eenth-century Edo.[44] When eaten in *kaiseki* style, rice was meant to be pure white and unadulterated, and rice-polishing therefore employed a significant number of the unskilled male workers in Tokugawa cities.[45] Polishing results in the loss of key nutrients from rice, and those who came to consume the heavily rice-centred urban diet, from the imperial family down to the servants in the lords' households, contracted beri-beri as a result of the thiamine deficiency that it produced. None-theless, the association of pure white rice with a civilised Japanese way of life was established and set to become the single most important factor conditioning food consumption patterns and agricultural policy ever since.[46]

The adoption of the 'rice plus side dishes' meal pattern also led to a growing reliance on the commercial infrastructure of the city for many of the other ingredients that had begun to play a part in a 'civi-lised' diet and way of eating. Fresh fish and vegetables clearly had to be acquired from markets or door-to-door sellers, but *kaiseki*-style menus also required processed-food elements for which home-made substitutes proved increasingly inadequate. Miso is relatively easy to make at home, and it was generally not considered proper to rely on 'shop-bought' miso, so that many households, urban as well as rural, continued to produce their own well into the twentieth century.[47] Proper soy sauce, as opposed to its precursor, *tamari*, which is a by-product of miso-making, is much more complex to manufacture and was a com-mercially supplied product from the beginning, in eastern Japan at least. The explosion in demand for soy sauce in Kyoto from the middle of the eighteenth century led to rapid rises in its price and the emergence of

---

[44] Hayashi 1994: 224–6 provides a detailed description of the distribution system that supplied rice to the Edo market.

[45] Leupp 1992: 137.   [46] For this argument in full, see Francks 2007.

[47] However, it was often necessary to buy the ingredients: soya beans, salt and the grain-based starter (*kōji*) that produces the necessary fermentation (Hayashi 1994: 220).

new producers from outside the city, who could undercut local brewers and force an end to their officially sanctioned monopoly.[48] Meanwhile, specialist soy-sauce brewers became firmly established in the Noda and Chōshi regions to supply the Edo market, the most successful of them eventually to metamorphose into the multi-national Kikkoman enterprise.[49] Dishes seasoned with soy sauce, from the most expensive sashimi to ordinary stews and noodles, were essential accompaniments to sake-drinking, especially in Edo, where the food was notoriously 'karai' (salty) as a result.

Meanwhile, although the basic 'rice plus side dishes' pattern became the model for urban eating, whether elaborate or simple, home-cooked or restaurant-prepared, urban life also offered alternatives or supplements, particularly in the form of processed or ready-prepared takeaway food, available from shops, stalls and street vendors. Noodles in various forms could be bought everywhere, while fashions in sushi spread through Edo and beyond: the first restaurant to sell Edo-style sushi in Osaka was opened in the early 1820s and soon had competitors there.[50] Perhaps the most highly developed field of prepared or processed food, however, was that of Japanese-style confectionery. As in Europe, white sugar, from imported sources, had been used by elite consumers as a medicine or spice from early on and continued to be imported via Nagasaki through the Tokugawa period. By the late eighteenth century, however, domestically produced brown sugar was becoming available, much of it used in confectionery, alongside ingredients such as *mochi* (pounded rice) and bean paste. Confectionery-making became something of a boom industry, as producers competed to create distinctive types of sweet or cake, particular shops developed their own shapes and tastes, and shrines and temples moved into the souvenir market with their own specialities. *Manjū* (buns filled with sweet bean-paste) from a particular shop in Osaka were known nationwide; *mochi* wrapped in special kinds of leaves sold in large numbers as souvenirs from Edo temples; the Portuguese-inspired sponge cake known as *kasutera* was widely available, as were versions of Chinese 'moon cakes'. Different kinds of confectionery were produced for particular uses – for ceremonies, religious offerings, gifts, banquets and so on – but merchants and samurai also took to eating something sweet with their morning cup of tea on an everyday basis.[51]

---

[48] Shimbo and Hasegawa 2004: 187–8.
[49] See Fruin 1983.
[50] Nishiyama 1997: 171.
[51] Watanabe 1964: 252–3, 250. There are clear parallels here with the early growth of sugar consumption in pre-industrial Europe; see Mintz 1985.

By the nineteenth century, therefore, for those with access to the facilities of the cities, a variety of food was available, even for the servants at the bottom of the table in the great households or the day-labourers subsisting on cheap takeaways and leftovers. For those who could afford it across quite wide strata of urban society, food had come to represent a source of enjoyment and an expression of status and refinement. Obtaining and cooking it required a rising level of knowledge and skill, with large households employing specialist chefs and a range of kitchen staff. In less exalted households, wives had to learn how to manage food preparation, whether by themselves or by servants. Particular kinds of processed-food product had come to be widely used as gifts and souvenirs and, despite regulatory attempts to stop it, acquiring the first-in-season of particular fish, fruit or vegetables, even if at an exorbitant price, was already the competitive business it still is today. Regional varieties of food products were clearly differentiated and appreciated by connoisseurs. Much of the practice that surrounds food consumption in Japan to this day – from the rice-based structure of menus, through regional product differentiation, to competitive connoisseurship – was thus being formed within the commercial economy and shifting status structures of Tokugawa-period cities.

Clothing

A formal kimono or informal *yukata*, as displayed in the areas of department stores still devoted to the Japanese-style clothes that Japanese people today wear, at one extreme, on the most formal of public occasions (weddings, funerals, New Year shrine visits) and, at the other, to relax in at home, do not on the surface look very different from those worn by the beautiful men and women and cheerful servants portrayed in Edo-period prints. However, despite the constancy, and indeed simplicity, in its basic conception, traditional Japanese-style clothing offers enormous scope for differentiation, display and the operation of fashion. This was reflected in the use of particular kinds of clothing to represent status from early on, and by the Tokugawa period detailed sumptuary legislation was attempting to restrict the spread of 'inappropriate' clothing styles among the lower classes, most notably by banning anyone of non-samurai status from wearing silk. For the merchant classes of Tokugawa cities, such rules represented a challenge they were able to overcome with ingenuity, as they launched the process of fashion-creation that would eventually turn growing swathes of the population into clothing consumers.

The basic garment that we label a kimono is made from a standard length of cloth cut into eight pieces which are then sewn together again along straight seams to create the full-length body, the sleeves, and the lapels and collar that form the neckline. There is no shaping to fit the individual, nor any fastenings, and the outfit is held together by a sash formed from another straight strip of cloth and called, in its more elaborate forms, an *obi*. The effect of the outfit is created by the colour and design of the material, which can range from plain stripes and all-over patterns to elaborate painted or embroidered flowers or scenes, in combination with the decorative elements, in particular the *obi*. The materials used have ranged historically from the linen and cotton worn by ordinary people and for everyday use to high-quality silks woven and dyed in many different ways. By the early Tokugawa period, both men and women were wearing kimono-style outfits, although distinctions between male and female costumes emerged over the course of the period, and distinctive male garments, in particular long pleated trousers (*hakama*) and short loose jackets (*haori*, versions of which women also wore), did develop.

Despite its simplicity, however, there has always been more to a kimono outfit, even an everyday one, than meets the untrained eye. What we think of as the kimono is in fact an outer garment (*kosode*) which can itself be lined or padded, depending on the season. On all but the most relaxed occasions (sleeping, for example), it is necessary to wear at least one undergarment below the *kosode* and the combination of colour and design among the inner and outer layers is a key element in determining the fashion and style of an outfit. Formal *obi* are composed of layers too, creating elaborate bows at the back, and the whole ensemble can be topped with a short jacket or shawl. When stepping out in Tokugawa-period cities, various accessories, such as fans, combs and umbrellas/parasols (or swords in the case of samurai men), would be tucked into *obi* or carried in sleeves or purses. Hair was always worn up, sometimes in elaborate shapes decorated with pins and flowers, and neither men, with their topknots, nor women typically wore hats.[52] Sandals, and their accompanying split-toed *tabi* socks, completed the outfit and ranged from the highest platform-soled *geta* to the most basic straw flip-flops. While a complete high-fashion kimono outfit was a work of art and highly restricting and inconvenient to wear, ordinary women donned aprons over their simple *kosode*

[52] Various kinds of headscarf were worn, however, and the wide straw hats used to protect ordinary people from the sun and rain are a common feature of Edo-period prints.

and men tucked up the bottoms of their kimono in their underwear and got on with their work.

Japanese-style clothing therefore offered considerable scope for differentiation, hence the expression of status, taste and fashion. This scope was further widened by clear distinctions that emerged between the types of kimono appropriate not just to different seasons but also to different levels of formality and different class status. Summer and winter styles differed not just in the thickness of materials but also in the patterns and designs deemed suitable to match the season. Meanwhile, as in all clothing systems, different styles went with different kinds of activity. Tamura Hitoshi simplifies this by distinguishing four categories of clothing: (1) that for highly formal occasions such as weddings and funerals; (2) 'Sunday best' clothes for high days and holidays (*hare* in Japanese); (3) clothes to wear when going out on more relaxed and informal occasions; and (4) everyday and work clothes.[53] Samurai men and women continued to choose *haute couture* materials and designs, while the merchant classes experimented, and what was relatively informal for a samurai might be formal for a merchant. For those who could afford it, therefore, a full wardrobe would include a choice of summer and winter outfits suitable to his/her class for each level of formality, with *kosode* and *obi* in appropriate materials and patterns and a complete set of undergarments and accessories. The trousseau of the daughter of a rich Edo merchant family, marrying in 1866, contained 213 items, including 30 *obi*, 61 *kosode* (some lined, some unlined), and the accompanying full range of undergarments, accessories, footwear and night-clothes.[54]

Such an investment in clothing was clearly intended to be a long-term one. Materials were made to last and, since any given kimono will fit anyone, there is no possibility of growing out of it and it can be handed on from mother to daughter, or indeed pawned or sold into the second-hand market.[55] This might be expected to inhibit the development of fashion in clothing, but there is no doubt that, amongst the well-off urban merchant classes of the second half of the Tokugawa period, fashions mattered and changed. By the late seventeenth century, the development and spread of complex weaving and dyeing techniques, in response to demand for new and different colours and designs, was making possible more elaborate and faster-changing fashions in textiles.[56]

[53] Tamura 2004: 16.   [54] Tamura 2004: 263–6.
[55] On the second-hand clothes trade and the use of clothing as a saleable or pawnable asset, see Saitō and Ozeki 2004: 177–8.
[56] Shively 1964: 127–8.

The leading geisha of the big-city pleasure quarters saw themselves as fashion setters and the prints made of them served as fashion plates. By the middle of the eighteenth century, merchants' wives were competing to display the most sumptuous and ornate outfits, but by the later part fashions had shifted towards more subtle and sophisticated colours and styles. Designs of narrow stripes in high-quality cotton or cotton/silk mixes succeeded one another as the top-fashion materials of the late Tokugawa period, in cycles reckoned by the fashion experts to last about ten years.[57] Rising incomes and expenditure among the urban merchant class thus meant that, despite the substantial long-term investment that a high-class kimono involved, there was a growing market for the latest fashion.

At the same time, the nature of a kimono outfit meant that it was not always necessary to invest in an expensive new *kosode* in order to keep up with fashion trends. Kimono had to be regularly taken apart for washing and could be revamped with, for example, new collars and cuffs in fashionable materials. New linings or undergarments could change the look of an ensemble: even before the opening of Japanese ports to full-scale foreign trade in the 1850s, imported woollen material, with its soft texture and bright colours, was being snapped up by the fashion-conscious, who used it to add a touch of stylish colour – scarlet or purple – in collars, linings and undergarments.[58] Part of the success of the Mitsui store in Edo was put down to its willingness to sell cloth in small pieces (as opposed to the standard kimono length), which could be used to revamp existing outfits.[59] Accessories, from hair ornaments through fans and bags right down to the textile straps on sandals, represented relatively inexpensive ways of demonstrating style.

As a result, the consumption of fashion in clothing was not necessarily restricted to the rich merchant elite. Through small-scale purchases of accessories or populuxe copies, the wives and daughters of artisans and craftsmen could follow fashion trends, and continuing developments in the design and production of cotton fabrics meant that fashions were embodied in the cheaper items intended for more informal wear, as well as in expensive silk. The large servant population of the big cities was also significantly exposed to changing fashions in clothing. Decorative servants, elegantly attired and ideally with not much to do except look good, were widely accepted status symbols, so that masters and mistresses were obliged to provide their maids and menservants with smart outfits and beauty tips. Commentators widely complained that it was

[57] Tamura 2004: 309.   [58] Tamura 2004: ch. 1.   [59] J. Roberts 1973: 19.

becoming impossible to judge status from dress, and in some cases it was the maid who had the real eye for fashion and instructed her *nouveau riche* mistress.[60]

By the first half of the nineteenth century, therefore, for the inhabitants of Japan's great cities, clothing had long since ceased to be a straightforward reflection of political status and class. The sumptuary regulations that attempted to codify the relation between dress and status were being flouted, in one way or another, by high and low alike, as money and taste increasingly became the determinants of what merchant-class men and women, and their servants, wore. Rising incomes and responsive producers enabled consumers, ranging from the super-rich in the market for high-fashion items to the servants picking up fans and hair ornaments at temple fairs, to increase and change their stock of clothing and hence to use clothes in new ways as vehicles of fashion and style.

Household goods

The design of 'traditional' Japanese housing does not perhaps offer the same scope for the use of furniture and household fittings as did, for example, the seventeenth- and eighteenth-century English houses that became increasingly cluttered with the tables and chairs, beds and curtains, clocks and ornaments that went with new forms of social and family life. In the context of Tokugawa-period, and to a large extent later-era, Japan, home improvements took standard forms, such as the construction of verandas and corridors connecting more rooms, the laying of *tatami* matting in guest rooms and dining and sleeping areas, the building of impressive walls and gates and the installation of *tokonoma* alcoves for the display of family relics and heirlooms. The tenement-like row-houses built to house the influx of urban craftsmen and workers typically provided apartments too small to accommodate much in the way of possessions. Furniture was for the most part, for rich or poor, either built in, as in the case of the cupboard space used to store futon, or small-scale and movable – cushions, tray-tables, braziers, the dowry chests used to store kimono.

Nonetheless, as in Europe, the commercialising economy of the cities and in particular the changing patterns of food consumption and associated social life encouraged the acquisition of a growing quantity and range of some kinds of household good and necessitated the provision of new facilities and equipment, especially for preparing and serving food and drink. *Kaiseki*-style dining depended on the ability to cook more

---

[60] Leupp 1992: 54–5, 121–2. See also Shively 1991.

than one dish, including rice cooked on its own, at the same time. This was difficult to do with the standard form of cooking device used in the countryside – a brazier or fire-pit over which a pot was hung.[61] More elaborate cooking required the construction of a stove, or *kamado*, of brick, stone or earth, in which a fire could be lit and, as such a device could not be accommodated in the living area of the house, a separate dirt-floored kitchen area away from the rooms in which meals were eaten. Large urban households were equipping themselves with *kamado* from early on in the Tokugawa period, and the grandest houses had *kamado* ranges and large kitchen areas in which servants worked, typically sitting or kneeling to perform their tasks (see Figs. 2.6 and 2.7). By the eighteenth century, merchant townhouses too were being constructed with kitchen areas separate from the living quarters.[62] With a *kamado*, it was possible to cook polished white rice in the desired form, using specially designed cooking pots, while simultaneously preparing side dishes. The spread of the charcoal brazier (*hibachi*) also made more careful and controlled cooking possible, and expenditure on charcoal, for cooking and heating, became a major element in the budgets of urban households.[63] Those without access to a *kamado* could make do with the small, charcoal-fuelled, portable version known as a *shichirin*, which was widely available by the middle of the Tokugawa period.[64]

More complex forms of cooking also involved a range of increasingly specialised utensils. Kitchen knives made by the top craftsmen were already being endowed with something of the mystique accorded to swords – the maker's name was engraved into the blade, as with a sword – and serious chefs needed a dedicated set of knives for different tasks.[65] More mundane pieces of equipment, such as chopping boards and pestle-and-mortar sets (*suribachi*), were also becoming standard kitchen items.[66] Serving vessels, in particular rice tubs and purpose-made sake flasks, lined the kitchen shelves in large households (as in Fig. 2.7).

Above all, however, *kaiseki*-style meals, depending on their complexity, required a relatively large number of individual wooden, if possible lacquered, and ceramic bowls, plates and trays. Developments in design

---

[61] See Figs. 3.2 and 7.8.   [62] Kosuge 1991: 22–6.
[63] Mochida 1990: 19; Hanley 1997: 62–3.
[64] Nakae 2007: 84–5.   [65] Ishige 2001: 206–12.
[66] Koizumi Kazuko's compilation of data from the inventories of goods belonging to lower-income households (typically those of executed prisoners or exiles) in early nineteenth-century Edo reveals them all owning similar sets of cooking equipment, including portable stoves, knives, chopping boards, pestle-and-mortar sets and various earthenware and iron cooking pots (Koizumi 1994: 351–2).

Figure 2.6 The large-scale *kamado* stove at the Edo-period Sumiya Restaurant in Kyoto. Courtesy of the Sumiya Hozon Kai.

and production techniques in the ceramics industry, partly inspired by the influx of Korean potters following Japanese military campaigns in Korea in the late sixteenth century, made it possible to meet the demand for differentiated shapes and styles of ceramic-ware.[67] Concentrations of potters emerged in particular areas, creating distinctive products both at the top end of the market, where artistic pieces were collected and displayed by connoisseurs, and in ordinary day-to-day items such as bowls, big and small, deep or shallow, sake flasks and tea bowls.[68] Lacquer-ware, in particular trays, soup bowls, chopsticks and a range of storage boxes and stands for specific purposes, was produced in growing quantities, and lacquer-ware production, like that of ceramics, grew to be a major industry in a number of parts of the country.[69] Better-off households came to possess large stocks of specialised types of bowls, trays, boxes, flasks, cups and so forth especially for use when receiving guests and entertaining at banquets, picnics and so on, while those lower down the scale, though not in a position to entertain guests,

[67] Ishige 2001: 100–1.   [68] Watanabe 1964: 259.
[69] See e.g. Wigen 1995: 79–81.

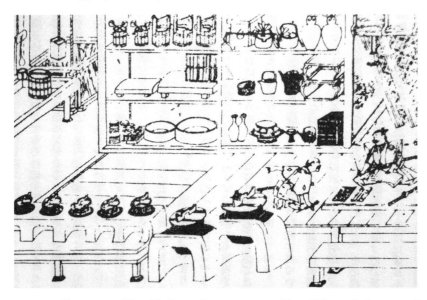

Figure 2.7 The kitchen of an upper-ranking Edo-period samurai household. The *kamado* and additional rice-cooking stoves are shown in the bottom left of the picture, while dining equipment – somewhat larger than life – is arrayed on the shelves at the back. Adapted from a contemporary text in Kosuge 1991: 22.

continued to accumulate more basic bowls and serving equipment for their own use.[70]

Meanwhile, urban households were also buying and using a growing quantity of other kinds of household goods. Over the course of the Tokugawa period, houses tended to become larger and better constructed and to offer more scope for the use and display of the furniture and ornaments which fitted into Japanese-style housing and which once only the grandest households had possessed.[71] The use of bedding, for example, ceased to be the preserve of the rich and important, and houses eventually came to be fitted with the built-in cupboards still used for futon storage during the day. Portable heaters (*kotatsu*) came to be widely used, and even relatively ordinary homes began to be equipped with clothes racks and small chests and screens.[72] Buddhist altars for the home, though expensive, were also increasingly common purchases.[73] Items such as vases and scrolls to display in *tokonoma* alcoves, mirrors and make-up boxes, portable writing desks and sewing boxes were clearly being quite widely acquired.

[70] See Koizumi 1994.   [71] Hanley 1997: ch. 2.
[72] Takenaka 2003: 112–13.   [73] Koizumi 1994: 350.

This accumulation of household objects was reflected in the proliferation of specialised storage containers. Households with the space and resources to construct detached storehouses were able to accumulate freely and if possible protect their belongings from fire. Others managed with chests, specially designed to hold clothes or particular classes of object, such as medicines, tea-ceremony items or writing materials. During the Meireki fire of 1657, huge wheeled chests blocked the streets as the inhabitants of Edo tried to flee with their possessions.[74] The practice of putting together sets of clothes and furnishings, together with the chests to keep them in, for brides to take away with them spread down from the upper classes during the period, so that 'these furnishings ceased to be the showpieces of upper-class weddings, but now met the everyday needs of a lifetime'.[75]

Furniture and household goods by no means exhaust the range of items with which the urban population was coming to surround itself as the Tokugawa period progressed. Like elites in China and other parts of Asia, the scholarly better-off enjoyed scouring book-stores and antique and curio shops for scroll paintings, calligraphy, books, ceramics and tea-ceremony equipment. For those lower down the social scale, there were the prints of actors, beautiful women and scenery to collect and display. Just as the rich and fashionable in eighteenth-century London were transported in the most elegant carriages, so their Edo equivalents moved around in luxury palanquins, borne by livery-clad servants. Ordinary people were technically forbidden from using palanquins but the availability of much less classy ones suggests that they did so nonetheless.[76] Toys and games – kites, tops, battledores – were everyday items, persisting into the era of the video game as 'traditional crafts'. A 'flourishing trade' was done in dolls at the time of the doll festival in the spring and, 'by encouraging periodical changes in design, the traders concerned sought to increase demand for them'.[77] Tokugawa-period manufacturers appear to have been far ahead of their Western counterparts in inducting children into the consumer culture of the cities.

As the cities established themselves and developed over the course of the Tokugawa period, therefore, consumers put together new and changing arrays of the food, clothes and household goods now available to them through the facilities provided by the urban environment. These arrays reflected the changing social and economic situations in which they lived – the shifting social hierarchy and income distribution, as well as the patterns of work and family life – but were also clearly being

[74] Hanley 1997: 44.   [75] Koizumi Kazuko, quoted in Hanley 1997: 48.
[76] Leupp 1992: 12–19.   [77] Dunn 1969: 167–8.

used to construct identities and to locate individuals within a world in which fashion and taste were increasingly significant determinants of the acquisition and use of goods. Such shifts in the relation of people to goods did not go unobserved, either by the state, in its efforts to control and regulate the economy and society, or by the artists and intellectuals who participated in and sought to make sense of the emerging urban world of consumption, and it is to these responses that we now turn.

Goods, the state and society

The inhabitants of Tokugawa-period cities were clearly able to experience a growing abundance of goods, as producers throughout the country expanded their output to meet the demand for more highly differentiated and faster-changing items of food, clothing and household goods. This experience was linked to, and facilitated by, developments in the ways in which people used and related to material goods. Equally, such developments were themselves interlinked with the social and political, as well as economic, changes taking place during the period. Goods which, at the beginning of the period, had been used to demonstrate the power and status of a feudal elite were, by the nineteenth century, embedded in a world of fashion and enjoyable consumption dominated by those whose social and economic positions depended on commercial and manufacturing success, rather than military and political prowess. Thinkers and writers wrestled with the moral and cultural implications of these changes, while the political authorities struggled, ultimately in vain, to control the expanding world of goods and those who prospered and enjoyed themselves within it. Meanwhile, those consumers themselves were busy devising the structures of emulation, fashion and refinement by means of which goods could be used to demonstrate their identity as individuals or members of society.

As in medieval Europe, the powerful in Japan had come to engage in the conspicuous display of goods – castles, elaborate clothes, symbolic accessories and so on – to demonstrate their status and to awe their subjects. The feudal lords, having used the periods of civil warfare of the sixteenth century to consolidate their local power, displayed their status by means of armour, horses and their accoutrements, weapons, the provision of large quantities of food and drink and the ultimate status symbol of an impenetrable castle. With the establishment of peace under a system in which the local feudal lords managed the internal affairs of their domains while offering allegiance to the greatest of their number – the shogun of the Tokugawa family – as national overlord, this symbolic use of goods was codified. Possessions thereby came to act as clear indicators of social and political status within the rigid class hierarchy by means of which the shogunate sought to exercise overall regulation and control of the country. What you wore, how big your house was, what and how you ate were all determined by your class status and hierarchical position. Even the shogun himself was subject to a strict (and apparently unappetising) dietary code that guaranteed his pure and superior status.[78]

Nonetheless, this system designed to control and limit the use of goods held within itself contradictions which were to undermine it by stimulating the very growth in consumption activities that it was meant to restrict. In particular, the establishment of the *sankin kōtai* system, which required feudal lords to travel around the country in suitable state and to maintain appropriately impressive residences and lifestyles both in their domains and in Edo, was in part intended to encourage them to spend and not accumulate funds that they might use for other, perhaps political, purposes. This very spending, however, put pressure on the budgets of the lords, obliged to lay out large amounts of their revenue on conspicuous spending outside their territories, and encouraged them to find ways to promote and profit from the growing production of differentiated consumer goods for 'export' from their domains to the rest of the country.[79] Meanwhile, the expansion of the urban population, which had resulted from the establishment of the Tokugawa system – intensified as it was by the periodic influx of lords and their retinues – necessitated the development of manufacturing and commerce. This growth increased the economic power of the merchant class, which was supposedly outside – and superfluous to – the hierarchy of political power and social status.

Hence, amidst the economic development that the Tokugawa system in practice facilitated, the ruling class – burdened by their relatively fixed incomes and the restrictions that their status placed on the ways in which they could spend what they had – found themselves obliged to stand by and watch as their social and political inferiors expanded their consumption expenditure and became the leaders of fashion and style. It was successful merchants who patronised the restaurants and theatres of the pleasure quarters and their wives and daughters, together with their 'kept' geisha, who sported the latest fashions; even craftsmen and artisans had the money to enjoy eating and drinking in *izakaya* and acquiring populuxe versions of the latest fashion accessories. Lords and their samurai, meanwhile, made a virtue of necessity by extolling the morality of a pure and frugal way of life, appropriate

[78] Mochida 1990: 20.   [79] See L. Roberts 1998 for a case study of this process.

to one's station, but clearly found it difficult to resist the temptations of urban consumption to which their limited incomes often really did not run.[80] Their growing indebtedness and the intensifying conviction, among sections of them at least, that all was not well with a world in which goods no longer reflected proper political and moral status would eventually prove significant factors in mobilising the movement that overthrew the Tokugawa system in the 1860s.

Meanwhile, the increasing use and enjoyment of goods among wider and shifting strata of society was reflected in the more and more frantic efforts of the political elite to hold back the tide of inappropriate consumption by means of sumptuary laws. From the late seventeenth century through to the nineteenth, regulations were continuously being issued detailing the forms of expenditure appropriate to all the various ranks within the complex hierarchy of Tokugawa society, proscribing ever more precise lists of goods that were not to be consumed by particular classes, forbidding manufacturers to produce excessively sumptuous items and setting maximum prices. Clothes and accessories, as the most visible forms of conspicuous consumption, were a particular focus of attention but food and drink, household goods, furnishings, buildings and even leisure pursuits came within the scope of regulations, which reveal much about the nature of consumption spending among the urban better-off. Attempts to ban the selling of particular seasonal food items before certain dates in the year reflect the ways in which fashion competition had entered the world of urban dining; the link between changing patterns of eating and drinking and expenditure on related household goods and equipment is demonstrated by proscriptions concerning sake-cup stands and cake boxes and on the number and quality of dishes and trays to be used at banquets; ladies-in-waiting at Edo Castle were told they should not 'frequently replace [their] garments with fine ones'.[81] The need to re-issue regulations on a repeated basis indicates that, as with sumptuary legislation almost everywhere,

---

[80] In Saikaku's 1688 *Japanese Family Storehouse*, a rich man lists the things from which one must abstain if one is to become a millionaire. They include: 'expensive clothes, expensive women, silken suits for day-to-day wear; private palanquins for wives; private lessons in music or poem-cards for eligible daughters; ... kickball, miniature archery, perfume appreciation, and poetry gatherings; a craze for the tea ceremony, and for remodelling the best rooms on tea principles; flower-viewing, boating excursions, baths in the middle of the day; evenings out with friends, gambling parties, playing Go or backgammon; ... sake with supper, excessive pipe-smoking, unnecessary journeys to Kyoto; ... collecting fancy sword accessories; familiarity with Kabuki actors, and with brothel quarters' and a good many more such temptations (Ihara 1688/1959: 59–60).
[81] Shively 1964: 135, 148, 145.

the attempt to maintain the link between goods and political status was doomed, in the face of the desire of those profiting from the growth of the commercial economy to demonstrate and enjoy the fruits of their rising incomes.

Meanwhile, writers and thinkers were also exercised over the implications of the spread of 'luxury' outside the ruling political elite. Saikaku, as the best-known recorder of the urban culture and society of the first half of the Tokugawa period, lovingly describes the clothes and accessories of the merchant classes, while at the same time warning against the dangers of overspending and bemoaning the breakdown in the relation between goods and status which had led to the inappropriate flaunting of goods once the preserve of the samurai. Extravagant women who 'forget their proper place', should, he declaimed, 'be in fear of divine punishment'.[82] For the philosopher and moralist Ishida Baigan, it was not only socially correct but also morally virtuous to dress appropriately to one's station.[83] Just as in eighteenth-century London and Paris, the sight of fashionably dressed servants and ordinary people wearing copies of the smart accessories of the rich provoked outrage.

Clearly, however, neither the force of law nor the strictures of moralists could do much to curb the desires of the merchant classes not just for the status symbols – silk clothes, white rice, elegant furnishings – that had once marked out the samurai class, but also for the fashionable goods that identified them as members, ideally leaders, of smart and sophisticated urban society. Edo was 'a closed world... in which vogues, led by the theatre and the pleasure quarters, spread like contagions. People knew their stores, and stores knew their people.'[84] Finding one's way around the world of consumption choices – getting fashions right, not making a fool of yourself, knowing whether items were within your budget – was no simple matter, but before long guides were available to help. Restaurant guides were published in growing numbers, some in a portable broadsheet form modelled on the well-known league tables of sumo wrestlers (Fig. 2.8).[85] An 1848 guide to eating in Edo listed 595 establishments: alongside the high-class restaurants, about a third of the entries were middle-range, *kaiseki*-style restaurants and another third sushi or *soba* restaurants catering to ordinary working people.[86]

---

[82] Quoted in Shively 1991: 764. The association of women with 'mindless materialism' runs through the history of Western thought about consumption too. See Styles and Vickery 2006: 2–3.

[83] Shively 1991: 755–6.   [84] Seidensticker 1983: 109.

[85] As Naomichi Ishige (2001: 127) points out, these began to appear at the end of the eighteenth century, a hundred years before the first *Guide Michelin*.

[86] Watanabe 1964: 217–19.

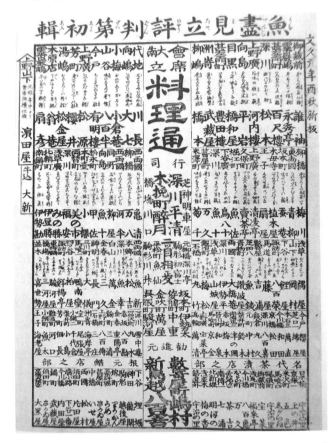

Figure 2.8 Early nineteenth-century guide to restaurants in Edo in the style of a *banzuke*, the traditional league table of sumo wrestlers. Takenaka 2003: 62; courtesy of the Tokyo Metropolitan Library.

There were specialised shopping guides to book and antique shops and even, as is well known, rating systems for geisha. Prints of actors and geisha served as guides to clothing fashion. The existence of such publications confirms that the choice of goods and services to buy was recognised as involving both individual tastes and social identity, as well, of course, as price and availability.

Behind these developments lay evolving approaches to life in the material world which were based on an aesthetic appreciation of particular modes of behaviour and forms of beauty and emotion, but one which could be expressed through clothes and other aspects of personal appearance and through styles of eating and drinking and engaging in leisure pursuits. By the later eighteenth century, the competitive wearing of ever more elaborate and sumptuous clothing had become commonplace among the urban rich, and the truly cool reacted by developing the concept of *iki*, often translated as 'chic', as the guiding principle in their dress and demeanour in the 'floating world' (*ukiyo*) of immediate but transient pleasures in which they saw themselves as living. *Iki* was 'an aesthetic that relies on painstakingly artless use of color, pattern and visual contrast to frame flashes of devil-may-care bravado, physical derring-do and fiscal improvidence';[87] in *iki* style, 'designs with stripes were favored over elaborate floral patterns; colours tended towards smoky light-browns', but flashes of fashionable colour were to be glimpsed beneath sophisticatedly plain exteriors.[88]

Being in fashion had thus become not just a matter of spending enough money but also of being in the know. The *tsū* – the connoisseur or man-about-town – was the man (usually) who knew the rules that distinguished the truly stylish from the boor and the phoney. By the early nineteenth century, the word *tsū* was appearing in the titles of a range of books designed to guide consumers through the world of taste and fashion, as in, for example, *Ryōri-tsū* (Guide to Cookery) or *Fūzoku-tsū* (Guide to Manners).[89] In the world of food there emerged the *shoku-tsū* or *kuidōraku* (epicure, gourmand) who claimed, for instance, to be able to tell the quality of a chef's knife from one cut of sashimi.[90] In such a world, status and worth had long since ceased to depend on hereditary political and military class and were now attached to the ability to appreciate and deploy the material goods which economic and commercial development had made available to significant sections of the urban population. Political authorities and moral thinkers might lament, but the consumption genie could not be returned to the bottle.

By the first half of the nineteenth century, for the inhabitants of the cities, goods had thus come to take on meanings that went well beyond the satisfaction of basic wants or the expression of hereditary status. For well-off merchants and their wives and children, choices of food, clothing and household goods enabled them not just to emulate the socially and politically superior samurai class but also to engage in the creation of fashion and style. For those lower down the income scale too, the availability of goods and services opened up the possibility of

---

[87] Bestor 2004: 92.   [88] Nishiyama 1997: 54.
[89] Nishiyama 1997: 58–9.   [90] Watanabe 1964: 243.

expressing individual tastes and of interacting with others in new social settings. Of course, for many, even in the cities, choices remained limited: large numbers of servants and apprentices lived in their employers' homes and had only limited cash income for discretionary spending; although the productive capacity of agriculture and manufacturing continued to rise over the long term, supplies of key agricultural goods such as rice could still be affected by natural events, driving up prices and reducing everyone's spending power; fortunes could rise and fall for the greatest merchant or the poorest labourer. Nonetheless, by the end of the period, for rich and poor alike in the cities, material goods not only surrounded them in far greater abundance and variety, but also increasingly offered the means to express identity, to define social status and grouping and indeed to enjoy life in ways that had not existed in 1600. As in Europe, the environment of the city had given birth to the culture of consumption.

The great cities of Tokugawa Japan were in many ways worlds of their own, each with their distinct atmospheres and patterns of consumption. Edo, as the political and administrative capital, Osaka, as the commercial hub, and Kyoto, as the continuing base of traditional aristocratic life, each had its own style of food and dress and its own ethos and culture.[91] Nonetheless, they were far from being isolated enclaves and the network of commerce and communications, initially promoted by the *sankin kōtai* system but eventually developing of its own momentum, facilitated the continual movement of goods and people into and out of the cities. It was the expansion of production in rural towns and villages throughout the country that made possible the growth of consumption in the cities, but the resulting interaction between city and countryside meant that the culture surrounding urban consumption could not but be transmitted, in due course, out to those gradually being made better off as a result of urban demand. As we shall now see, the Japanese consumer to whom the cities had given birth was soon to make an appearance out in the country too.

[91] For example, according to guides from the middle of the nineteenth century, for those going on an outing, anything other than a home-prepared *bentō* picnic was considered vulgar in Kyoto; in Edo, only the poor used *bentō* and the better-off expected to eat out; in Osaka, a *bentō* was *de rigueur* but should only contain food bought from a restaurant (Ishige 2001: 124).

3 Country gentlemen, ordinary consumption and the development of the rural economy

> Heaven says nothing, and the whole earth grows rich beneath its silent rule. Men, too, are touched by heaven's virtue; yet in their greater part they are creatures of deceit. They are born, it seems, with an emptiness of soul, and must take their qualities wholly from things without. To be born thus empty into this modern age, this mixture of good and ill, and yet to steer through life on an honest course to the splendors of success – this is a feat reserved for paragons of our kind, a task beyond the nature of normal man.[1]

The explosive growth of Japan's great urban centres was largely a phenomenon of the first half of the Tokugawa period. By the middle of the eighteenth century, the populations of the great metropolises and domain capitals had ceased to expand and, although Edo and Osaka remained the political and commercial hubs of the country, as well as active centres of culture and consumption, it was increasingly out in the countryside – in the market towns, manufacturing regions and agricultural villages – that the locus of economic growth was to be found. With the urban construction boom fuelled by the establishment of the Tokugawa system now over, and the feudal lords – now well set up with residences in their local castle towns and in Edo – becoming more and more concerned about the costs of their urban lifestyles, the forces that had led to the expansion of employment, incomes and spending in the cities were steadily weakening. The great lords no longer needed to recruit carpenters to build their mansions or new kitchen staff to prepare ever more impressive banquets, and their growing financial difficulties caused them to cut back on their *sankin kōtai* trips whenever they could muster plausible excuses. While the urban commercial classes continued to find plenty to do meeting the demands of their own increasingly fashionable and differentiated consumption, lords and samurai no longer provided the stimulus to new consumer spending that had driven the urban growth of the recent past.

---

[1] From Ihara Saikaku, *The Japanese Family Storehouse* (Ihara 1688/1959: 13).

Out in the countryside, on the other hand, the urban expansion of the seventeenth century had, by the middle of the eighteenth, created the conditions for the spread of new patterns of consumption outside the world of the urban commercial and political classes. The improvements in communications, by land, river and sea, brought about by the *sankin kōtai* system, the growth in demand for an ever widening variety of agricultural products and manufactured goods and the lack of both ability and, in many cases, incentive on the part of the governing elite to prevent rural producers and consumers from joining in the growing market for goods and services: all contributed to the commercialisation and rising incomes that drew rural people into the market for consumer goods. The leaders in this process were the 'rural elite' households, which typically combined farming and renting out land with commercial and manufacturing activities. In many parts of the country, however, ordinary cultivating households were also beginning to find the means to acquire and enjoy a wider range of food, clothing and household goods, as they too took their first steps into the world of the consumer.

The rural elite and consumption

Under the Tokugawa system, the government of the provinces lay in the hands of the hereditary class of lords and samurai. Although the lords and their families, together with a proportion of their samurai retainers and household servants, spent significant periods of time each year in Edo, their bases and main residences remained in the castle-towns of their domains. The lords had their castles, varying in size and grandeur with the scale of their domains, as measured by their respective taxable values in rice. Although a few domains left their samurai living on the land, most required that they too reside in their local castle-town, where their houses and lifestyles reflected the status of their household within the hierarchy of the domain bureaucracy and the corresponding stipend that they received from their lord. In terms of political power and status, the samurai, constituting, together with their wives and families, about 6 per cent of the total population, certainly represented an elite, and their contact with the wider world, especially in Edo, provided them with experience of urban life beyond that of most of their provincial compatriots. However, their economic and social position meant that it was not, for the most part, they who led rural society into the world of consumption.

This was the result of constraints imposed partly by income and partly by the nature of the philosophy that underpinned the role and status of the samurai as a governing elite. Domain revenues were limited, theoretically and in large part practically, to whatever share it was possible to collect from the rice crop produced by those farming the agricultural land of the domain. Although most domains began to find ways to convert taxes into cash and to supplement their incomes by means of loans, monopoly trading in local manufactured goods, devices to tax non-rice agricultural production and so on, most failed to expand their revenue in line with their expenditure and fell increasingly into debt to traders and financiers from the merchant class. Samurai stipends, as the largest element in most domain budgets, often took the brunt of economy measures and certainly did not rise sufficiently to enable the mass of samurai households to afford the consumer lifestyle that some in the – formally inferior – commercial classes now enjoyed.[2]

At the same time, the position of the samurai as an essentially feudal elite meant that they continued to some extent to live in a world where goods acted as markers of status and symbols of social relations, rather than as expressions of fashion and identity or sources of enjoyment. The clothes they wore, the food they ate, the size of their houses and the accoutrements they accumulated were all in theory governed by their position in the hierarchy of the lord's retainers and were typically locked into traditional forms, from swords and scholarly scrolls or texts to the paper hair-ties with which they decorated their top-knots. Many possessions were handed down through the generations and took the traditional durable forms of kimono, bridal chests, antique books and scrolls, ceramics and such like, leaving little scope for the purchase of transiently fashionable or enjoyable items. Income received in kind, usually as grain, provided the basis of the household's diet and although some rice often had to be sold to meet cash needs, it clearly made sense to store as much as possible for use through the year. Many samurai households were also granted plots of land on which they grew their own fruit and vegetables. Gifts in kind, typically traditional food items, passed up and down their hierarchies, cementing the social relationships between households, while traditional entertaining in the correct seasonal forms marked the passage of the years and the major events in the life of the household.[3]

Nonetheless, it was members of samurai households who, very often, were best placed within the society of the rural towns and villages to

[2] On the problems of running domain budgets, in the light of the growth of manufacturing and consumer activity, see Ravina 1999: ch. 2.
[3] For a description of the day-to-day life of a samurai household in the late Tokugawa period, see Yamakawa 2001.

learn about the new forms of consumption developing in the cities, partly through their higher level of education and wider contacts and partly as a result of *sankin kōtai*. The *daimyō* of important domains were taking around 2,000 men with them on their processions to Edo by the late seventeenth century, those of smaller ones 100 or 200. Given rotations amongst those who went each time, this would mean that a significant proportion of the upper-level samurai of a domain, together with their retainers and servants, would have had the opportunity to travel to Edo at some point.[4] The diets and other areas of consumption of the lords themselves were governed by strict codes that limited their ability to enjoy anything new. On their travels, they took many of their supplies with them and stayed at specially designated guest houses where their particular needs could be met, precluding them from sampling the regional menus available in the inns and tea-houses patronised by less exalted travellers.[5] However, the lower-ranking samurai retainers, not to mention the numerous attendants and servants who accompanied them, were freer to enjoy the sights and tastes available both en route and once they got to Edo. Shopping, for oneself and for gifts and souvenirs to take home, was clearly a significant element in the *sankin kōtai* experience for many. The scholarly came home with books, scrolls and tea-ceremony equipment, the lower ranks with food, typically of particular kinds not available at home, clothing and accessories, lacquer-ware and ceramics, and the prints and temple souvenirs that proved you had been there.[6]

Once in Edo, the servants and attendants of the great lords' households enjoyed the range of food, drink and entertainment that the city offered: superior samurai visited restaurants and tea-houses, when they could afford it, for intellectual and artistic discussion; the lower ranks and the servants ate sushi and *soba* from stalls and drank in *izakaya*, and everyone went to the theatre. Servants often ate the same meals as their masters and used the bath and bedding available to the household, while it was they who did the day-to-day shopping.[7] Their exposure to city ways clearly pointed up the contrasts with life back in the domain: on their return to their provincial homes, they were supposed

---

[4] Vaporis 1997: 31. Women very rarely took part in *sankin kōtai*.

[5] For descriptions of the provision made for *daimyō* and their retinues at a post-town on one of the routes to Edo, see the early chapters of Shimazaki Tōson's novel *Before the Dawn* (*Yo-ake no mae*), originally published serially in the 1930s but based on his family's experience of the period around the Meiji Restoration (Shimazaki 1987).

[6] For long lists of the enormous variety of goods purchased, in Edo and en route, by *sankin kōtai* participants, see Vaporis 1997: 41–9.

[7] Leupp 1992: 113–14.

to dye, in appropriately dull colours, any of their city clothes deemed unsuitably bright for ordinary rural life.[8] Their consumption of the white rice-based urban diet left many suffering from beri-beri and also, presumably, from a more long-lasting desire for things only the city could offer.[9]

As the Tokugawa period progressed, therefore, the world of goods became a problematic one for samurai households torn between the new possibilities that it offered and the traditional role and limited incomes that they had inherited. This was much less the case, however, for the non-samurai elite that the economic development of the period had begun to produce by the eighteenth century. In the increasingly commercial context of the rural economy of the second half of the Tokugawa period, large land-holdings dependent on extended labour forces tended to break up. In the typical village, this process left one or two households, with land-holdings larger than most but manageable with family resources, in a position to prosper as the demand for the output of rural producers grew. Many such households combined their own farming with renting out some of their land, investing in and managing local manufacturing or commercial enterprises, and money-lending or other financial activities. They typically provided political leadership in the countryside, acting as village heads and representatives with the domain authorities. Their eldest sons inherited their fathers' roles, all being well, while their younger sons became teachers, or managed their own branch enterprises or land-holdings; their daughters married into similar elite families in other villages.[10]

Members of this rural elite were often in a much better position than their samurai political masters to begin to sample the world of goods that had emerged in the cities. Despite the mass of sumptuary legislation, rural elite families were clearly subject to fewer constraints and inhibitions as regards goods and possessions, and produced, acquired

---

[8] Shively 1964: 154.

[9] In *Before the Dawn*, two young men from the post-town visit Edo in the closing years of the Tokugawa period and eat at their inn. 'In the Kiso [their mountain home], people ate birds from the forest or the flesh of bears, deer, and wild boar; for a special treat, they might serve the larvae of ground wasps. When it came to fish, there were salted mackerel or sardines, or for the New Year's festivities, larger salted fish. Instead, Hanzō and Juheiji were now served with the rich raw meat of the tuna, accompanied by delicate garnishes of thin green seaweed known as "sea hair" and green shiso seeds on their slender stalks. There were also yellow chrysanthemums and, beside the grated white radish, a small mound of fierce, green Japanese horseradish.' 'In a place like this, we're just savages from the mountains', says Juheiji (Shimazaki 1987: 85–6).

[10] See Pratt 1999 for a detailed account of the activities of the *gōnō* or rural elite.

and used them in growing amounts. In some respects, their patterns of consumption appear to have been designed in the first instance to emulate, or at least impress, the samurai ruling class. They ignored or got round the rules forbidding non-samurai to wear silk; they pulled out all the stops in laying on banquets for visiting officials, hiring chefs if needed and sending to town for the appropriate seasonal delicacies; they added samurai-style reception rooms to their houses and installed *tokonoma* alcoves in which to display the calligraphy and paintings that demonstrated taste and family history. They too could play the game of using goods for political purposes, in the interests of their family businesses and their villages.[11]

However, although acquiring samurai status, for oneself or one's daughter and descendants, in return for adequate contributions to domain coffers was feasible and possibly sometimes useful, there is little evidence that rural elite families really sought to integrate with the samurai class or to usurp their superior political position. The social and economic world in which they moved was that of their villages and of other rural elite families; much of their consumption activity, therefore, reflected their efforts to establish an identity, and enjoy themselves, within this world, as well as to distinguish themselves, by their possessions and their cultural sophistication, from ordinary villagers.[12] Many were able to extend and improve their rural homes, constructing impressive walls and gates, verandas and corridors, and *tatami*-matted rooms in which to entertain guests in proper style. The social activity thus made possible, involving both other villagers and visitors from elsewhere, required appropriate food and drink, hence cooking facilities, ceramics and lacquer-ware, trays and furnishings. Rural elite daughters, going out as brides to similar families of suitable wealth and status, needed kimono and all their accessories, together with chests in which to transport and store them. All sorts of household items – books, mirrors, lacquered trays, display shelves, storage chests – helped to create a suitable ambience in which to live the life of a country gentleman and his household.[13]

---

[11] For examples, see Narimatsu 1989: 177 or Nishiyama 1997: 161–2. The rural elite diarist and family historian described by Platt writes in the 1860s of how his grandfather was an excellent exponent of *kemari*, a kind of football originally played by the aristocracy. As a result, 'he often fraternized with the great families and dignitaries around Matsushima [the nearby village centre], for at this time, *kemari* was in fashion with the wealthy crowd in the Ina district' (Platt 2000: 66). Rural gentry in China had begun to wrestle with the business of using fashion and style to impress well over a century earlier; see Brook 1998: 218–37.

[12] Platt 2000: 46, 51–2.

[13] The rural elite households of the later Tokugawa period whose extant records Koizumi has analysed possessed large quantities of goods, including clothes, furnishings,

At the same time, though, rural elite families clearly also used their growing wealth, as long as it lasted, to educate, improve and enjoy themselves. Their activities in practical fields, such as devising and disseminating agricultural improvements, have been well documented, but many also composed poetry or letters, painted or wrote local histories and engaged in perfecting accomplishments such as calligraphy skills.[14] Branches of Edo or Kyoto schools of the tea ceremony, painting, poetry-writing and flower-arranging were to be found in many rural areas, their participants coming from the new rural elite.[15] All this involved expenditure on goods and services: equipment such as paper, pens and ink; bowls and other tea-ceremony necessities; and the food, drink and home facilities that the social activities associated with such 'hobbies' demanded. A Kyūshū merchant puts on a banquet to show off tea-ceremony items obtained on a trip to Edo and Kyoto to his tea-ceremony group back home; a travelling salesman makes a living touring rural areas selling luxury goods and instructing buyers how to use tea-ceremony equipment.[16]

Rural elite involvement in wider commercial networks also led to more travel, for business purposes but also for sightseeing, shopping and pleasure. Complex relationships were built up between village-based households dealing in items such as textiles and the traders and wholesalers, in the cities or often now in other rural areas, who marketed them. These necessitated business trips around the country, during which new foods and entertainments could be sampled and new goods bought. By 1863 the patriarch of a rural elite household from the northeast could take his wife on a trip to Edo, staying with business acquaintances or at inns. The couple visited famous beauty spots, enjoyed the attractions of the city – trips to the *kabuki* and puppet theatres, for instance – and spent more than intended on presents and souvenirs – a dagger, ten soup bowls, a set of combs and so on. Amidst all this excitement, a boat trip round Yokohama harbour to see moored there the foreign ships that presaged the great upheavals of the opening to trade and the Meiji Restoration barely merited a mention in the diary of the trip.[17]

---

religious and artistic objects and the specialised storage containers in which to keep them. They were especially well supplied with meal-serving equipment – lacquerware, ceramics, metal goods – for use at banquets, on picnic outings and in all kinds of entertaining. Differences in income and status among rural elite households appear to have been reflected less in the kinds of things owned than in the quantity of them – the grandest households just had many more bowls, trays, sake flasks, picnic kettles, teapots, etc. See Koizumi 1994.
[14] For examples, see Platt 2000.   [15] Nishiyama 1997: 95–112.
[16] Maruyama 1999: 187; Nishiyama 1997: 105.   [17] Bernstein 2005: 9, 77–80.

murai, on their *sankin kōtai* trips, undoubtedly helped to
their provincial home-towns into the world of goods and the
culture that had been born in the cities, it was thus members
mercial rural elite, with their growing incomes and expanding freedom, who acted as the conduit by means of which new and
increased consumption spread into the countryside. The patterns of
consumption that they created were perhaps initially modelled on those
of their samurai 'betters' but evolved in ways that reflected the social
needs and individual tastes of the country gentleman and his family.
Through them, and through their followers and imitators, as well as the
retainers and servants that they, like samurai households, initiated into
new goods, elements of the consumer lifestyle of the cities permeated
into rural towns and villages. Here they were adapted to the demands of
rural life, consolidating the new patterns of ordinary consumption that
were in due course to become established as national norms.

Everyday consumption in the countryside

Despite the size and importance of cities in Tokugawa-period Japan, it
remained the case that the vast majority of the population – probably
around 80 per cent – lived and worked in small towns and villages in
the countryside. Most rural households derived at least part of their
living from agriculture and continued to grow or collect much of the
food that they ate and the raw materials that they used for fuel, building and clothing. However, as the growing demand for the products
of agriculture and rural manufacturing drew farm households, at first
in the hinterlands of the great cities but in due course more widely,
into the commercial nexus, enabling them to earn cash income from
sales or from part-time wage work, so the purchase of the commercial
products available in the market became possible. In some parts of the
country, farm households remained predominantly self-sufficient well
into the twentieth century, although long before that few could manage
without market-bought pots and pans, lamp oil and salt. But elsewhere
households benefiting from the widening opportunity to earn extra
income – starting with the rural elite but eventually also encompassing
others lower down the scale with access to the necessary land or labour
resources – began to sample the possibilities the market offered.

In some regions, opportunities for female members of rural households to undertake paid work, especially in textiles, at home or in local
workshops, were expanding fast by the later Tokugawa period, height-
ening the attraction of 'shop-bought' alternatives to food and other
items that were time-consuming for women to produce at home. But in

many cases the market-bought goods entering the consumption baskets of rural households were new or so superior to home-made alternatives as to constitute different products and some, though small and cheap, could hardly be classed as necessities in the homes of supposedly self-sufficient sons and daughters of the soil. 'For peasants to engage in trade or for villages to have hairdressers is to be disrespectful', grumbled a high-ranking official of the shogun's government in 1788, as he protested in vain against the spread of what he saw as inappropriately luxurious clothing and hairstyles into the villages.[18] Much as the authorities, both local and national, might wish to keep peasant noses to the grindstone of agricultural production, the first sightings of the 'ordinary consumer' could not be missed in the Tokugawa countryside.

Food and drink

Throughout the Tokugawa period, rural food-consumption patterns remained strongly conditioned by the requirements of self-subsistence that had determined the nature of agriculture in earlier times. Nonetheless, nutritional standards were clearly improving, in both quantity and quality terms, and diets were diversifying to include a wider range of items. With the spread of the use of oil-lamps to lengthen the day, three meals a day became the common pattern,[19] while rising agricultural productivity made possible the cultivation not just of more grain, but also of larger amounts of other food, for sale and for home consumption. The market for commercial food products, in the cities but also in the countryside, was steadily expanding, so that a contemporary 'Complete Guide to the Speciality Products of the Domains of Japan' was able to list a huge range of local food products for travellers to sample on their journeys.[20]

Rice, which was on the way to becoming the mainstay of the urban diet, was produced by farmers principally as the means to pay tax, though whatever was left over might be sold or consumed on the farm, and given what is known of increases in rice yields and output, it is clear that by no means all the crop could have been consumed in the towns and cities.[21] Rural elite households were beginning to adopt urban-style, white rice-based meal patterns, with all that went with them, and those lower down the scale must have been increasing the proportion of rice in their diets, as and when they got better off. Throughout Asia, rice has tended to be regarded as a luxury food, with consumption

---

[18] Hanley and Yamamura 1977: 89.   [19] Ishige 2001: 102–3.
[20] Watanabe 1964: 197–8.   [21] Kitō 1998: 54.

expanding as incomes rise; in the Japanese context, bearing as it did all the connotations of the sophisticated urban diet, it functioned as a symbol of civilisation much as white wheat bread had earlier done in Europe and America.[22]

Nonetheless, relatively few Tokugawa-period rural households would have consumed rice boiled or steamed and eaten on its own, following the urban pattern, on anything other than special occasions, so that, for most, other grains grown for home consumption continued to constitute the dietary staple.[23] What these were varied according to local conditions and tastes but included wheat, barley and millet, while sweet potatoes also spread from the southwest during the period. Rural households and many provincial urban ones, including those of lower-level samurai, added rice, if it was available, to these other grains or vegetables as they cooked and a variety of recognised combinations clearly existed, such as *mugi-meshi* (rice with wheat or barley) and *katemeshi* (rice with *daikon* radish). Grains were also consumed as dumplings or porridges, but noodles were time-consuming to make and something of a treat unless commercial supplies were available. Although the proportion of rice to other ingredients might rise as incomes or harvests improved, mixed whole-grain stews, eventually recognised as nutritionally superior to the white rice-based meals nowadays regarded as traditional Japanese cuisine, were still to be found on the tables of farm households into the post-Second World War period.

Home-grown grain thus continued to constitute the basis of the rural diet, and many of the seasonings and accompaniments that went with it were also typically home-produced in the country, if increasingly not in the towns. Farm households grew a widening range of fruit and vegetables, in the case of more exotic items, such as peppers and pumpkins, often for sale in the urban market, but also the radishes and greens that added flavour and nutrition to home-cooked grain stews and formed the basis of many pickles. The soya bean provided the major source of protein, and most rural households continued to make their own miso bean paste, consumed as a soup base and flavouring, and tofu. Woodlands provided the nuts, fungi, roots and berries that are often dismissed as 'famine food' and certainly did represent a fall-back when grain crops failed, but which were also important regular ingredients in country cooking. Animal products were consumed – chickens were

---

[22] On rice as a luxury good, see Latham 1999; on bread as a civilising good, see Sarti 2002: 171 and Bauer 2001: 87–90.

[23] For discussion of ordinary dietary patterns in the Tokugawa period, see Ishige 2001: ch. 5; Watanabe 1964: ch. 11.

kept, mainly for their eggs, and hunting for game remained possible in some areas – but not in large quantities, unless fish, from rivers or the sea, was available. A samurai from Tosa domain records in his diary that he had invited other samurai to dine at his house, as he had some beef, a rare treat.[24]

Despite this essentially home-grown basis, however, commercially acquired food was beginning, at first in the most developed areas and among the better off but gradually more widely, to enter the diets of rural as well as urban households. Fish, sometimes fresh but typically in dried or salted form, became more widely available in inland areas, bought from shops and markets in rural towns and from travelling fish-merchants. By the end of the eighteenth century, even in the remote mountain villages of Morioka, people were buying fresh fish, as well as such things as sugar-based confectionery.[25] Government officials consistently complained that, even in the country, consumers were beginning to rely on shops and travelling salesmen for items such as tofu and miso that they would once have made for themselves; they were shocked to find the kinds of fancy confectionery that urban shoppers consumed in large amounts being purchased in rural towns.[26] Tea, which had once been available only in luxury powdered form (as used in the tea ceremony) or as a rough, home-grown and sun-dried product picked from bushes planted in the spaces between fields, was coming to be widely sold as leaves grown and dried, using improved methods, by specialist producers. Tobacco was widely grown, some for home use but mainly as a commercial crop, and smoking was apparently as common in the country as in the towns.[27] However, the most significant commercial food and drink items to enter ordinary consumption were products of the brewing process, most notably soy sauce and sake.[28]

It was the rapid growth in demand for soy sauce in the cities that had spurred the emergence of specialist brewers serving the markets of Osaka, Kyoto and Edo in the earlier part of the Tokugawa period. However, by the late eighteenth century, small-scale commercial breweries were being set up throughout the country, using locally supplied ingredients and seasonal labour, and a soy-sauce brewery was a typical enterprise established by rural elite investors. Product differentiation

---

[24] L. Roberts 2002: 30. Unfortunately, the event led to a drunken argument and a murder.

[25] Hanley and Yamamura 1977: 157.

[26] Sasama 1979: 23.   [27] Takenaka 2003: 90–1.

[28] Vinegar and sweet sake for cooking (*mirin*) were also being brewed commercially on a significant scale by the late Tokugawa period (Sasama 1979: 61–3).

and branding were common: the products of the large-scale brewers serving urban markets were regarded as superior, but regional breweries catered to local tastes – Osaka soy sauce differed from its Edo counterpart and soy sauce produced in Fukuoka was sweet and sticky as consumers in the southwest liked it.[29] Purchased soy sauce remained a luxury for those lower down the income scale in the countryside and was in any case less indispensable to those eating one-pot stews than to those needing highly flavoured side dishes to accompany large quantities of white rice on its own. Nonetheless, it was much more convenient to use as a flavouring than miso and was steadily becoming a standard shop-bought item for more than just the elite.[30]

Forms of rice wine were already well known in the countryside by the beginning of the Tokugawa period. Although spirits (*shōchū*) made from sweet potatoes or whatever else came to hand continued to provide drinkers in some more remote parts of the country with the oblivion they sought, sake's near monopoly of the provision of alcoholic drink was to be maintained until at least the middle of the twentieth century. The unrefined home-brewed version known as *doburoku* was widely produced and consumed in the Tokugawa countryside: villages brewed large quantities for mass drinking at festivals, weddings and other celebrations, but households also made their own and consumed it regularly throughout the day as a kind of food, just as rural Europeans drank weak forms of wine, beer and cider.[31] However, while the larger Kansai breweries developed to supply refined sake to the cities, by the second half of the Tokugawa period small-scale local breweries, again typically financed by rural elite capital, were springing up throughout the country to meet the growing demand for refined sake in the countryside.

Such enterprises produced locally differentiated products that reflected local tastes and changing drinking habits. The rural elite bought refined sake to serve with their banquets and drank flasks of it with meals at inns on their travels, but rural towns and many villages came to contain bars, where smaller-scale social drinking took place, and shops selling refined sake for home consumption.[32] Although rural people were still brewing their own sake, especially when times were hard, into the late nineteenth century and beyond, the refined, commercially produced alternative had already become established as the

---

[29] Ioku 1999: 241.   [30] Ishige 2001: 115–16.
[31] For more on this, see Francks 2009.
[32] For example, in 1829, a village of 144 households in the Hachiōji area north of Edo had six bars serving sake and one retail sake shop (Pratt 1999: 169–70).

superior and desirable drink which rural consumers, following their urban counterparts, drank when they could afford to on private social occasions. Mass public drinking still occurred, and farmers still drank *doburoku* to give them energy for their work,[33] but even in the rural world sake was already fitting into its role in more modern forms of drinking, well before the opening to trade added new forms of alcohol to the Japanese drinking repertoire.

Throughout the Tokugawa period and beyond, most Japanese rural households, and not a few urban ones as well, supplied a significant proportion of the food and drink they consumed for themselves, without recourse to the market. But nonetheless, as money incomes rose, commercial networks expanded, and more and more people came to experience the markets, shops and restaurants of the cities, items which we now think of as firmly part of 'traditional' Japanese cuisine emerged as consumer goods, inserting themselves into the diets of rural as well as urban households. On top of the basics, such as salt, that had always had to be purchased came relatively undifferentiated items, such as dried fish, that added taste and nutrition to home-grown grain and vegetables, and tofu and noodles which were troublesome to make at home, but also the far superior commercially produced soy sauce, sake and tea, now available in differentiated regional varieties, and the sugar-based confectionery that made up treats and gifts. Even polished white rice, once the prerogative of the urban elite and central to their eating patterns, was beginning to colonise more ordinary diets as more than just a New Year treat. The poorest may never have had the cash for such 'luxuries' and continued to subsist on what they could grow or gather and keep from the tax-man, but for increasing numbers, in the countryside as in the towns, purchased food and drink items were beginning to become indispensable elements in a 'civilised' diet.

Clothes and accessories

In the subsistence economy that still prevailed in many rural areas in the early Tokugawa period, clothes had to be made from home-grown raw materials and were commonly spun and woven from hemp, cotton or ramie. The standardised one-size form of much clothing made it easy to hand down or use second-hand and to patch and repair. Sandals were chopped from pieces of wood or woven from straw; rain-capes and hats were sewn together from rushes and grasses. However, with

---

[33] For a nice example from the Meiji period, see Shinohara 1967: 79–80.

the expansion of cotton cultivation, and of the largely rural system for processing it, to meet the demand for clothing in the cities, rural consumers too began to be introduced to the possibilities of bought clothing materials, new or second-hand. The Ishikawa household, whose members farmed in the region west of Edo and kept a diary of their agricultural activities during the eighteenth century, devoted a small plot of their land every year to growing cotton to use themselves. In the 1780s, however, as the nearby silk-weaving region of Hachiōji continued to expand its demand for raw materials, they began to concentrate on commercial silk-worm raising and silk reeling, so that, by the end of the century, they were no longer growing their own cotton at all, but rather participating in a growing rural market for cotton clothing material.[34]

The growth in the market for cotton textiles, as more and more households, like the Ishikawas, found it uneconomic to devote land and labour to producing their own clothes when more remunerative forms of employment for both were emerging, has been labelled the 'cotton revolution'.[35] However, the growth and changing structure of the clothing-textile market cannot be explained entirely in terms of a simple switch from home-made to bought. Commercially produced cotton was softer and lighter, hence nicer to wear, than home-made products, and it came in colours and patterns that the home-weaver could never produce, so that while output and sales certainly increased in quantity, they also diversified into many more differentiated and higher-quality products as the market expanded through the eighteenth and nineteenth centuries. Meanwhile, in competition with cotton for the growing clothes market, cheaper silk and silk/cotton mixes became much more widely available to the better-off outside, as well as within, the cities. As their incomes rose, their contact with the wider world broadened and their daily lives changed, growing numbers of rural people were beginning to demand not just bought clothes and more of them, but also something of the variety and fashionability that their urban counterparts were now able to enjoy.

By the second half of the Tokugawa period, therefore, rural wardrobes were undoubtedly coming to include a greater range of better-quality and more up-to-date clothes. The trousseaux of rural elite brides would by this time contain a number of silk *kosode* and *obi*, as well as silk undergarments and accessories.[36] These would not typically have been the extremely expensive brocade and embroidered products of the craft

---

[34] Shimbo and Hasegawa 1988: 254.   [35] See Tamura 2004: 17–18.
[36] See the many examples in Tamura 2004.

weavers of Kyoto, but rather the more varied and fashionable textiles that the silk industry was developing to compete with cotton in the growing market. By the middle of the nineteenth century, the daughters of village headmen were being equipped with a range of seasonal *kosode* and *obi* appropriate to more or less formal occasions, even if not quite in the numbers that a rich urban merchant's daughter could command, and their outfits and accessories were recognisably in the styles fashionable, at least not too long before, in the cities.[37] Samurai daughters up north in Mito domain coveted, like their big-city counterparts, nice, soft, imported wool fabric, as soon as it became available in their local dry-goods store, for their *obi* and kimono linings – 'once one had worn it, nothing else would do'.[38] Rural young women were clearly no longer going out in the same old kimono as their mothers had worn but rather, if their husbands or fathers could afford it, in fashionable outfits that varied with the season and the occasion.

Of course, it was only the better-off in the villages who could afford to invest in wide-ranging wardrobes like this. Those lower down on the rural income scale, though, were also beginning to demand more than just everyday clothes, and the growing availability of better-quality cotton textiles enabled them to acquire if not high-fashion outfits, at least something different for special occasions. Even for the least well-off, there were accessories that could brighten up an ordinary kimono and a large-scale trade in second-hand clothes. Travellers to the provinces increasingly complained of the spread of 'luxury' that was obliterating the distinctions in clothing that had once so clearly signified class differences: in Sendai in the 1830s 'serving girls dressed as well as did their employers', and even servants and the landless had *haori* jackets, umbrellas and *tabi* socks to wear with their *geta* clogs, so that ordinary people 'seem better dressed than their superiors'.[39] Even in relatively remote and undeveloped Morioka, by the early nineteenth century, a resident was complaining that ordinary people were 'better dressed than their betters'.[40]

In the less-developed parts of the country, such as the northeast, ordinary people were still weaving cloth for their own clothing into the twentieth century. Nonetheless, over much of the country, rural demand for new clothing was clearly beginning to grow by the early years of the nineteenth, as at first the better-off, but gradually many more ordinary consumers began to acquire both the purchasing power and the need and desire for a wider range of clothes to wear in pleasing,

---

[37] Again, see many examples in Tamura 2004.   [38] Yamakawa 2001: 47.
[39] Quoted in Jansen 1989: 67, 79.   [40] Hanley and Yamamura 1977: 157, 158.

comfortable and good-quality styles. The growth in demand was sufficient to support the continued development of networks of textile traders organising distribution and sales over ever wider areas, as well as the proliferation of textile-producing districts each with their distinctive products.[41] As we will see in the next chapter, the influx of textile imports that followed the opening of the ports in the 1850s ultimately served only to stimulate the market for clothing materials and to encourage domestic manufacturers to offer more of the kinds of product that domestic consumers were demanding, as their incomes rose and their lives changed.

Household goods

Japanese-style houses, being constructed mainly from wood, are not built to last, at least not without constant renovation, so that relatively few old houses have survived compared with their stone- or brick-built European counterparts.[42] However, they are also relatively easy to expand and improve, and there is much evidence that, over the course of the Tokugawa period, both elite and ordinary houses in general increased in size and became more solid and better constructed, on the basis of the diffusion of carpentry skills.[43] Such houses were designed to accommodate a life in which people sat, slept, even cooked at floor level without need of the beds, chairs and tables that 'pre-industrial consumers' began to acquire in sixteenth- and seventeenth-century Europe. Nonetheless, they did offer scope for the acquisition, storage and use of the household goods associated with more comfortable ways of living and new forms of cooking, eating, entertaining and amusing oneself that were spreading from town to country and from the elite to the more ordinary from the seventeenth century onwards.

Samurai households, establishing themselves in the early part of the Tokugawa period as befitted their new status as the governing class, adopted and adapted what is known as the *sukiya* or tea-house style as they rebuilt and improved their houses. This involved light and airy, single-storey, wooden buildings with sliding doors and internal wall

---

[41] Saitō and Tanimoto 2004.

[42] Some examples of buildings which have survived are now preserved, however, having been dismantled in their original sites and reconstructed in a number of *minka* (people's housing) parks and open-air museums, most notably the Edo-Tokyo Open-Air Architectural Museum in Koganei Park in Tokyo. These include relatively ordinary domestic and commercial buildings, as well as others of particular historical or architectural interest.

[43] For more detail on the development of housing, see Hanley 1997: ch. 2.

panels, often constructed with verandas opening out on to enclosed gardens. Standard features of such houses included formal guest rooms, *tokonoma* alcoves, *tatami* matting and earth-floored entry areas (*genkan*) where shoes were removed prior to stepping up into the wood- and *tatami*-floored living and guest rooms. Although sumptuary regulations often forbade the use of such features in commoner housing, the rural elite, and eventually others below them on the rural income and land-owning scale, ignored or got round such rules as they expanded and enhanced their houses.[44] By the end of the Tokugawa period, village houses typically had more rooms than at the beginning (despite falling average household size), at least some *tatami*-matted rooms distinct from earth-floored working areas and some sliding shutters and wall panels to allow in more light and air than was possible in the single-room, enclosed dwellings of earlier times.

Such improvements also required or made possible the accumulation of more in the way of household equipment and furnishings. This was particularly the case with kitchen arrangements. Rural cooking had typically involved the use of a fire pit (*irori*) in the main room of the house, over which a cooking pot could be rested or suspended and around which the household gathered to eat and keep warm. This was well suited to the kinds of one-pot stew that rural people usually ate and represented an economical use of fuel for cooking and heating. When carrying out home improvements, rural households tended to retain their *irori* as the focal point of their living rooms, continuing to suspend kettles or pots over them on elegant iron hooks and to assemble around them, but also followed their urban counterparts in constructing separate cooking and food-preparation areas, equipped if possible with a *kamado* stove and a sink (Figs. 3.1 and 3.2). The different kinds of cooking that this made possible encouraged the acquisition of cooking pots, knives, chopping boards and so on, as well as bowls, plates and trays on which to serve a wider range of dishes. By the late Tokugawa period, better-off rural households had often accumulated significant amounts of ceramic- and lacquer-ware, for entertaining as well as everyday use.[45]

Beyond the kitchen too, new items of furnishing and equipment were adding to the levels of comfort possible in the other rooms of larger houses. Purpose-made bedding began to be amassed, as the cultivation

---

[44] For a description of a rather grand rural elite house, re-built at the end of the nineteenth century to replace an earlier version and still standing in the 1970s, see Bernstein 2005: 21–5.

[45] See the data collected in Koizumi 1994.

Figure 3.1 The kitchen of a farmhouse dating back to the later Tokugawa period and belonging to a rural elite household in the Kantō
area. The kitchen is equipped with a well in its earth-floored area and
a *kamado* stove, together with all sorts of fittings and utensils, in its
raised area. Kosuge 1991: 38.

of cotton was extended, at first only for use by the better-off or for guests
but gradually more widely, and built-in cupboards in which to store
bedding became features of improving rural as well as urban housing.
Shelves and chests for the storage and display of scrolls and pictures,
and of a growing range of possessions in general, were now necessary fixtures for the status-conscious. Grander houses were equipped
with bathrooms and bathtubs, although public baths (*sentō*) remained
popular social amenities where they were available. Meanwhile, many
kinds of useful or pleasurable smaller goods, ranging from mirrors and
make-up boxes, writing equipment and tea-ceremony items for the
better-off to combs, toys and trinkets for everyone, were carried by
salesmen and peddlers into the small towns and villages, the markets
and fairs, of the countryside. A bonus paid in kind to a male servant at
the end of his contract in 1826 included cash and rice but also 'bowls

Figure 3.2 A rural household still gathering around their *irori* for a meal in the 1930s. Asahi Shinbun 1933: 6.

and cups for ten persons, two sets of futon, five tea cups, a variety of agricultural implements, and kitchen utensils', giving some indication of the kinds of possession by then considered necessary to a socially acceptable standard of living.[46]

By the middle of the nineteenth century, therefore, significant numbers of rural people, following their urban counterparts, were buying purchased food items, expanding their wardrobes of clothes and accessories and accumulating useful or enjoyable household goods. This increase in consumption reflected and reinforced the growth of agricultural and manufacturing output, much of it also now taking place in the countryside. The pattern of consumption that rural people established for themselves thus played its part in what has come to be thought of as the 'rural-centred' growth and development that began in the later Tokugawa period and continued up to and even beyond the end of the nineteenth century. The next section therefore looks at the wider role of rural consumption in determining the emerging structure of Japan's economy.

[46] Hanley and Yamamura 1977: 158–9.

Consumption and 'rural-centred' economic growth

The growing demand for consumer goods in the countryside as well as the cities was intimately tied up with developments in communications and marketing networks and with the expansion of production in a wide range of industries throughout much of the country. By the second half of the Tokugawa period, the locus of output growth had largely shifted from the cities to the countryside, as entrepreneurs seeking to meet demand for textiles, ceramics, processed-food items and much more developed the means to utilise the labour of members of rural households, breaking the monopolies of the urban guilds which had controlled craft production in the earlier part of the period. These developments required the movement of goods, finance and information within and between rural areas, which in turn facilitated the establishment of the markets, shops and other distribution and retailing services by means of which rising rural incomes were transformed into rising rural demand for consumer goods. The 'traditional' industries that grew up to meet this demand dominated the not insignificant manufacturing sector of the later Tokugawa period and continued to play a major role in the Japanese economy through to recent times. The products of such industries in many ways came to define the qualities that ordinary consumers enjoyed and appreciated in the goods they acquired, conditioning the structure of industrial production and the nature of the consumer market in Japan ever since.

The development of the rural market

During the first half of the Tokugawa period, the network of transport and freight routes converged on the cities as the main markets for consumer products, with Osaka, where the facilities existed for assembling and storing items prior to shipping on to Edo or other urban markets, acting as the hub. During the latter half of the period, however, more and more goods followed routes that cut out Osaka, going directly from rural production areas to rural markets elsewhere in the country.[47] The rural businessmen who organised and financed the production and marketing of goods similarly began to travel around the country seeking out suppliers, wholesalers and retailers with whom they could deal. The result was a distribution and retail system, reaching out into the countryside, by means of which ordinary consumers could translate their increases in income into purchases of goods that their fellow rural workers had made.

[47] Shimbo and Saitō 1989: 10.

This emerging distribution system revolved around the many market towns that served rural districts throughout the country. These had originally been the sites of periodic markets, where peddlers and street traders sold goods to rural buyers, but as trade became concentrated during the first part of the Tokugawa period in the shops of the castle-towns, they came to function more significantly as links between rural producers, the local urban market and, thereby, the great cities.[48] Domain governments encouraged the development of the commercial sectors of their castle-towns, but were also keen to regulate, control and tax trade with other domains through castle-town-based facilities. Periodic markets in rural towns tended to disappear, and rural consumers relied on travelling salesmen for the everyday goods they needed to buy. The traders operating the distribution network became specialised both as wholesalers and retailers – leaving functions such as transport and finance to other specialists – and in terms of the products they handled. By the early eighteenth century, more than 5,000 *tonya*, or wholesaler/dealers, were recorded as operating in Osaka, and numbers in Edo would have been similar, dealing in increasingly differentiated lines of product – raw cotton, ginned cotton, specific kinds of cotton cloth, fresh fish, salted fish, tea, tobacco, 'West Country' soy sauce and so on – and linking producers from ever wider areas of the country into the big-city and national markets.[49]

By the latter half of the period, though, as more and more rural areas became involved in commercial production of agricultural and manufactured goods and demand for consumer goods in the countryside expanded, this network suffered growing competition from trading systems that bypassed Osaka, moving goods directly between domains and their towns and villages. These were operated by traders based in the regions, sometimes in co-operation with domain-run trading agencies holding monopolies on local products. Eventually the authorities had no option but to allow such 'outsiders' access to markets that had once been the monopoly of established urban producers and traders.[50] The opening of the ports in the 1850s, and the arrival of foreign buyers seeking to deal directly with the producers of the products they were sourcing for export, represented the final nail in the coffin of the old distribution system.

It was the emergence of these new channels of distribution and communications that made it possible for more and more of the products in which rural traders dealt to find their way into the hands of rural consumers. Initially, it was peddlers, carrying goods out from the

---

[48] Shimbo and Hasegawa 2004: 166.   [49] Miyamoto and Hirano 1996: 340–4.
[50] Shimbo and Hasegawa 2004: 189–90.

Figure 3.3 A vegetable peddler, photographed in the Meiji period. Courtesy of Nagasaki University Library.

castle-towns into the villages in baskets swaying on their shoulders, who brought this about (Fig. 3.3). In Okayama, for instance, the number of peddlers began to increase rapidly in the later seventeenth century and, judging from the unsuccessful attempts of the authorities to control and regulate them, so did the range of goods that they carried.[51] By the eighteenth century, rural towns themselves had the facilities to supply the peddlers, and growing numbers of them were based there instead of in the castle-towns. Fish merchants regularly toured villages as they did city neighbourhoods; peddlers sold vegetables, processed foods, medicines and cosmetics, pots and pans, pottery and mats; shops sent out representatives selling tea and tea-kettles.[52]

At the same time as rural demand increased, new retailing opportunities were opening up in the country towns and villages where rural

[51] Hanley and Yamamura 1977: 196.
[52] Narimatsu 1989: 178. Less reputable peddlers came to band together in gangs which controlled the allocation of stalls at fairs and demanded protection money from street sellers, thus establishing the long-standing connection between sections of the Japanese gangster (*yakuza*) world and the 'informal sector' of retailing; see Dubro and Kaplan 1987: 25–8.

people lived and spent their rising incomes. It was to shops in local towns that the elite sent for the commercial food products with which to impress visiting officials and where they found themselves able to shop for the household goods, clothes (new and second-hand), medicines, confectionery and leisure items they now sought. In 1705, the town of Hirano, with a population of 8,000–9,000 people but also serving surrounding villages, supported four silk shops, fifteen tobacco shops, fourteen confectionery shops and twenty-five hairdressers.[53] Meanwhile, more and more villages also began to support shops selling commercial food products – sake, miso, tea, noodles, soy sauce, confectionery – alongside a range of dry goods including textiles, ceramics, paper, footwear, medicines and little luxuries such as cosmetics, combs, hair ornaments, fans and mirrors.

By the middle of the nineteenth century, therefore, few rural people would have been without access to shops and other commercial facilities, even if a significant number of them still relied for the most part on their own home-grown produce for all but essentials that they could not produce for themselves and perhaps the occasional treat. For the rural elite and a growing number of the better-off below them, meanwhile, the retail facilities of nearby towns and villages now offered local access to new or higher-quality food products, cotton for clothing and bedding, ceramic- and lacquer-ware with which to eat in greater style and refined sake with which to ply guests and enjoy social gatherings. In the countryside as in the cities, the first steps towards the creation of the infrastructure of market-based consumption had thus been taken.

Consumption and 'traditional' manufacturing

There is now overwhelming evidence that by the end of the Tokugawa period the Japanese economy supported a significant non-agricultural sector, as well as an increasingly productive and diversified agricultural one. The first known survey of national output, carried out in 1874, suggested that manufactured goods constituted 30 per cent of the total. The vast majority of this manufacturing output took the form of consumer goods destined for the domestic market, with textiles and the products of the brewing industry (sake and soy sauce) dominating, but with a wide range of other processed foods and household goods also recorded.[54] While urban markets remained significant, much of the

---

[53] Hanley and Yamamura 1977: 121–2.
[54] Yamaguchi 1963: 13–14. The results of the survey are known as the *Fuken bussanhyō* (Table of Products by Prefecture). For more details in English, see Francks 2009 or Tanimoto 2006b: 7–8.

growth in output that underlay the thriving commercial agricultural and manufacturing economy reported in the survey was by then being acquired by rural consumers, drawn into the market on the basis of their expanded employment opportunities and incomes. Within the context of the overall political economy of the Tokugawa system, the patterns of this demand interacted with the development of the supply side in ways which have had repercussions for the Japanese economy ever since.

Under the conditions of the Tokugawa economy – largely cut off from technological and trading developments in the rest of the world and subdivided into its small domainal components – it was bound to be the case that virtually all of the output that found its way into the domestic market had been produced by small-scale manufacturers and farmers. The expansion of rural textile production in the second half of the period depended on the development of putting-out systems and networks of village-based workshops utilising the labour time of spinners and weavers, many of them female, still living and working in agricultural households. Cotton grown in suitable regions was supplied to rural households elsewhere for spinning and the yarn passed on to specialist dyers, weavers and finishers. Different regions competed to produce the qualities and patterns of cloth that met market demand, from the coarse and ordinary for everyday uses to the delicate cotton/silk mixes and subtle colours that the fashionable desired. A large number of locally specific designs and patterns emerged as variations on the indigo blue and white colour scheme that defines traditional Japanese textiles. An army of weavers continued to produce these for the domestic market in kimono width, even after the large-scale expansion in the production of cotton textiles, of different types, patterns and widths, for the export market in the later part of the nineteenth century.[55]

Meanwhile, many other items were coming to be manufactured by small-scale producers in local areas, often with the support of domain governments anxious to promote potential new sources of tax income and domain exports. Breweries were to be found throughout the country, using locally supplied ingredients to create their own distinctive varieties of sake and soy sauce, some sufficiently special to be picked up by connoisseurs in the city, others just for local consumption. The production of ceramic goods was also a major industry: specialist pottery-producing areas, such as that around the small towns of Arita and Imari in northern Kyūshū, developed to become the main sites of Japanese pottery production ever since, but throughout the country, local producers established themselves, making everything from expensive

---

[55] For a detailed analysis of this process, see Saitō and Tanimoto 2004.

artistic items for tea-ceremony aficionados to the ordinary tea cups, bowls and sake flasks that growing numbers of households were coming to need. Wood products and lacquer-ware, paper products, matting and straw goods and almost all of the array of household items beginning to accumulate in urban and rural houses were manufactured in homes or small-scale workshops, sometimes in the cities but more so in rural areas specialising in their own particular product, while local food processors created the confectionery, fish products and condiments that diversifying diets required. Although many of the products of such industries must have been consumed locally, the emergence of a network of communications and distribution that encompassed rural areas meant that the distinctive products of small-scale producers could also reach a national market as well.

Output growth in this form has a number of implications for the emerging scope and pattern of consumption expenditure. On the one hand, it served as a mechanism placing income in the hands of small-scale producers and their workers, many of them rural, which they spent in ways that reflected the needs and desires of their everyday lives. Rural consumers, initially elite but eventually much more ordinary, used the income they derived, much of it in cash, to buy the textiles, ceramics, metal goods, sake and soy sauce that emerged from the production networks to which they contributed their labour. Many of the employment opportunities becoming available, especially in the textile industries, were for women and girls from agricultural households, for whom commercially produced processed foods meant both a higher-quality product and less need to spend time that could profitably be employed elsewhere on the laborious household tasks of pickling, fermenting, brewing and so on. The wages earned by sons and daughters from seasonal migrant labour, in the cities or in agriculture and manufacturing in other rural regions, might be needed to pay off debts, meet rental demands and pay for next year's seed and fertiliser, but they must also have offered some scope for the purchase of new clothes, pots and pans, soy sauce and sake, and even the small-scale home improvements that were clearly going on. Meanwhile, the growing demand for primary-sector raw materials – cotton, indigo, mat-rush, vegetable oils, charcoal, the wheat and rice that went into soy sauce and sake, the fish that were dried and salted for sale throughout the country – presented rural households in many parts of the country with opportunities to earn the cash income to buy consumer goods.

At the same time, the resulting patterns of consumer demand fed back into the industrial structure and reinforced the conditions that favoured the small-scale production of locally differentiated goods.

Faced with markets, in the cities and increasingly in the countryside, made up of localised consumers who used goods within their clearly defined, domainal social hierarchies and their structured seasonal patterns of eating and drinking, dressing, furnishing and amusing themselves, the key to success in the market turned out to lie in quality, product differentiation and local specialisation.[56] Small-scale producers, and those who dealt in their products, sought out niches within the segmented market structure that they faced and, as a result, what was produced tended to reflect local skills and resources and to be highly differentiated, catering to distinctive local tastes or to particular demands at the national level.[57] *Sankin kōtai* meant that locally produced specialities found their way into the Edo market, just as Edo goods moved the other way: homesick samurai in Edo received parcels of local food products from their friends and relatives, while one of those about to return home experienced the familiar tourist nightmare of not being able to find sufficiently 'Edo-like' souvenirs to buy at the last minute; high-quality products made by local craftsmen for the *daimyō* to give as gifts to Tokugawa officials were sold off by their recipients – who could not possibly use them all – and found their way into collections in Edo and beyond.[58]

As a result, local variations of everything from textile patterns through styles of ceramics to cakes, processed fish, sake and tea found their correct niches in local and national markets. Local production areas came to specialise in particular patterns or qualities of cotton cloth, distinctive pottery designs or food products for which they could claim special characteristics or associations. The regional speciality product – the *meibutsu* that still survives in the market for gifts and souvenirs – thus became a feature of the structure of manufacturing in the 'traditional' industries of Japan. Many of these industries adapted and flourished well into the late nineteenth century and remained important through (and despite) Japan's modern industrialisation. Hence, although mass production was eventually to come to Japan, it had to adapt to a consumer market long dominated by the differentiated products of small-scale, local, often rural, producers, catering

[56] For example, for the domain of Tokushima, which specialised in the production of indigo: 'the ability ... to dominate the indigo market stemmed not from its complete monopoly on indigo production but from the consumer perception that Tokushima indigo was of distinct and superior quality. Tokushima indigo thus constituted a unique product for which standard indigo was only an imperfect substitute' (Ravina 1999: 8).

[57] For a supply-side version of this argument, see Morris-Suzuki 1994: 34–6.

[58] Vaporis 1997: 63–4, 44.

to the particular pattern of consumption that Tokugawa-period economic growth had generated.

By the middle of the nineteenth century, when Western warships first made their threatening presence felt in Japanese waters and the solid foundations of the Tokugawa system began to crumble, the world of consumption born in the cities had spread out into the countryside, so that rural people could no longer be ignored, either as producers of many of the goods available or as consumers in rural markets tied in to national ones. New goods were to come in with the encroaching foreigners, but the patterns of consumer-good production and demand were by then already well established in town and country and continued to persist, providing the framework into which the products of the industrial revolution had to fit. The foreign goods that began to become available in the second half of the nineteenth century presented themselves to potential buyers who already knew what they liked and how they might use goods to enhance their everyday lives. The Tokugawa period had seen the emergence of the ordinary consumer, in the countryside as in the cities, and the process of modernisation that the events of the 1850s and 1860s were to launch would bear the mark of this ever after.

4   'Civilising goods': consumption in the industrialising world

> The Japanese are, undoubtedly, like the Chinese, a very imitative, adaptive, and compliant people and in these characteristics may be discovered a promise of the comparatively easy introduction of foreign customs and habits, if not of the nobler principles and better life of a higher civilization.[1]

> Tokyo is a great place, full of interesting things.
> Tōfu, soybeans, nattō, coopers,
> Bamboo pipestem stores, candy stores, and stores selling sweet sake,
> Chili pepper seasonings and salted fish.
> 'Kuzuui, kuzuui!' Hear the sound of the wooden clogs being made!
> Here you can get a massage! There you can eat stew! And there they are selling Chinese dumplings!
> …
> Sushi, candy, beef, tempura![2]

In July 1853, Commodore Matthew Perry's squadron of American 'black ships' entered Edo Bay, symbolically bringing an end to Japan's two centuries and more of 'seclusion' from the Western world. In fact, Japan had been far from completely 'secluded' for much of the Tokugawa period, so that many within the governing and intellectual classes were already well aware of the political and economic challenges the industrialising and colonising Western powers would eventually present to Japan, but the debate and conflict over how to respond was nonetheless intensified by the American insistence on Japan's 'opening'. Perry's squadron included two steam-powered naval frigates, and much of the concern centred on the military and political threat that the Western powers posed. However, Perry also brought with him an assortment of goods representative of some of the ways in which industrialisation

---

[1] Report of Commodore Matthew Perry, following the signing of the Treaty of Kanagawa in 1854, quoted in Beasley 1973: 96.
[2] Tōkyō bushi (Tokyo Song), a popular song of 1919, translated and quoted in Yano 1998: 252.

was transforming the everyday lives of European and American people. These included a telegraph, various clocks and a small-scale railway, apparently a great hit with the Japanese officials dealing with the mission, who all wanted a ride on it.[3] It was clear that goods, of one kind or another, were going to play a significant part in the 'opening to the West'.

With the subsequent conclusion of treaties with various Western powers, a number of ports were opened to foreign vessels, foreigners came to settle in them and trade expanded rapidly from the low levels permitted under the seclusion policy. Foreign residents – from China and other parts of Asia as well as the West – with their exotic appearances and peculiar tastes in food, clothes and habits, were the object of stares, caricatures and indeed terrorist attacks, but most Japanese who came into contact with them recognised that it would be necessary to adapt to, and even adopt, some of their strange ways if Japan were to be accepted as part of the 'civilised' world. By the early 1860s, growing awareness of the threats and opportunities posed by the opening to the West had combined with the longer-term effects of commercialisation and economic change on the Tokugawa system to produce an alliance of domains committed to overthrowing the shogunate, with the aim of establishing a government which could ensure by some means or other – the leaders of the alliance were by no means agreed on how – Japan's national strength and independence.

The successful military campaign pursued by this alliance against the Tokugawa forces resulted in the establishment of a new government, based in a re-named Edo – now Tokyo – as capital and ruling in the name of the young Emperor Meiji. Those who came to power as a result of what is now known as the Meiji Restoration were to go on to undertake a programme of political, economic and social reform, designed to establish Japan as a military and economic power and as a modern society capable of holding its own against the threatening West. Their new military forces were eventually to succeed in defeating China (in the Sino-Japanese War of 1894–5) and Russia (in the Russo-Japanese War of 1904–5), thereby laying the basis for Japan's colonial expansion on the Asian mainland. By the time of the First World War, Japanese manufacturing industry was in a position to take advantage of the Western powers' involvement in the war to secure growing domestic and export markets. Japan had come to possess the military and

[3] Beasley 1973: 355, 452n54; see also Partner 1999: 8–9. Simon Partner describes Perry's display of goods as offering the Japanese 'a Faustian bargain': adopt our system and all these things can be yours.

industrial capacity to wage war and trade in the modern world, as well as many of the political and social institutions that characterised the 'civilised' societies of Europe and North America. The industrialisation and urbanisation that this involved, as well as the establishment of national systems of education, local government, conscription and communications, were to change the lives of the vast majority of the population in a multitude of ways.

The economic growth and internationalisation that took place over the years between the Restoration and the First World War presented Japanese people with the opportunity to acquire a range of new goods, some imported but many eventually made in Japan, and growing numbers were to discover that some of the products of Western civilisation could be useful and even fun. However, for the majority of Japanese people, the impact of the developments that began in the 1850s and 1860s on their day-to-day lives as consumers was more subtle, operating principally through the ways in which the goods they had already been coming to acquire and use were produced and marketed to them. The purchase of a watch, a Western-style umbrella or a bottle of beer did present a chance to appear interesting and fashionably modern. Nonetheless, as the steam engine and the electric motor eventually began to transform the ways in which goods were manufactured; as employment in workshops and factories, in the country but increasingly in towns and cities, became more and more significant to household incomes; and as the train, the telegraph and the modern printing press opened up and unified the national market and the national culture, it was rather through the growing and changing consumption of things such as rice, soy sauce and kimono textiles that everyday consumer lives were to be most affected by the processes of development initiated in the events of the 1850s and 1860s.

Newspapers, trains and electricity: the birth of the modern infrastructure of consumption

Although the Tokugawa economy encompassed thriving commerce at the national level, it can perhaps best be modelled as a set of domainal 'countries', trading with each other but also pursuing their own lines of development and mercantilist economic policies.[4] Consumers in the cities could indeed obtain products from all over the country, and sophisticated long-distance networks of production and distribution developed to serve them, but most ordinary consumption involved the products of

---

[4] This is the model developed by Luke Roberts (1998).

the local agricultural and manufacturing economy. Travellers brought back goods, ideas and fashions from their journeys along the highways and their stays in the cities, but it was within the structures of local economic life that such things were to be enjoyed. The development of new forms of transport and communications from the 1850s began to change this, as did the establishment of a more centralised national political economy with branches reaching out to towns and villages everywhere. Nonetheless, this was not to produce either a flooding of the country with Western-style goods and the culture embodied in them, or the imposition of a homogenised and mass-produced national lifestyle. Rather, it resulted in what might be thought of as product differentiation at the national level, as consumers picked and chose from the widening array of goods available to them, in the context of their changing ways of life.

Communications, cities and the nation

The initial impact of the opening to trade on the lives of Japanese people outside the treaty ports and the centres of government and intellectual debate took the form of a significant increase in the export demand for Japanese primary products, in particular raw silk and tea, with foreign traders seeing much more to be gained from meeting the European demand for silk than from engaging in the uphill task of selling Western manufactured goods to Japanese buyers. As a result, more and more Japanese rural households took up silkworm-raising and silk-reeling, increasing their dependence on market activities but also increasing their incomes. After 1868, the new Meiji government abolished the feudal domains, pensioning off the samurai class, and converted the taxes paid in kind (at least theoretically) to the former domain governments into a national land tax paid in money on the basis of ownership rights in cultivated land. These reforms on the one hand forced rural households further into the market, as they sold produce in order to meet tax demands in cash, and on the other removed any restrictions on free trade that remained from the mercantilist policies of the old domains. The domestic market for consumer goods, which had already begun to grow during the Tokugawa period, was further opened up, while the incomes by means of which demand for them was made effective continued, for the most part, to rise.

This growing and widening market depended on an expanding communications network, transporting goods from producer to consumer, but also bringing more and more of the population into contact with the material possessions, lifestyles and consumer culture of the

rest of the nation. Initially at least, much of this was achieved through
expansion in existing forms of freight and passenger transport. The
pack-horse routes by means of which goods had been carried through
mountainous terrain during the Tokugawa period were improved
to take wheeled wagons and rickshaws.[5] Traditional sailing ships
provided stiff competition, in coastal trade at least, to foreign, and
eventually Japanese, steamship companies.[6] River and road traffic – by
ferry or barge, horse-drawn vehicle or manpower – along traditional
routes remained the main form of inland communications well into the
twentieth century, expanding and improving through the second half
of the nineteenth century to accommodate the growing flow of goods
and people.[7]

However, the lure of the railway – the essential symbol of modern
life – was eventually to prove irresistible. The first line was completed
in 1872, and by the 1910s a network of almost 5,000 miles of track
was coming to link towns and villages throughout the country to the
wider world.[8] For freight transport, water remained more important
than rail into the inter-war period, but it was through the possibilities
opened up for passenger travel that the railways exercised their main
impact on everyday life. This was largely the result of the speed of
the train: on a major route such as the Tōkaidō (from Tokyo to Osaka
and Kōbe), while horse-drawn omnibuses and steamships had cut the
time taken down to days, compared with the fortnight or so required
to cover the distance on foot or in a palanquin, by the 1880s the train
was taking only twenty hours.[9] The relatively high initial fares meant
that most early train travellers came from the better-off classes, but
by the turn of the century prices had fallen sufficiently to mean that
ordinary families too could contemplate excursions by train. By
present-day standards, late nineteenth- and early twentieth-century
trains were not necessarily comfortable, punctual or well appointed,
but, as a result of their speed, they opened up possibilities for travel –
for business, family visits, shopping or leisure – which would simply not have been feasible with older forms of transport.[10] The rural
Tōhoku patriarch and his wife, on their trip to Edo in 1863 (see p. 53),
had walked and occasionally ridden the distance in a leisurely eight

---

[5] For an example of the development of traditional, pack-horse-based freight transport,
see Wigen 1995: ch. 2.
[6] Wray 1986.   [7] Lockwood 1968: 107–8.
[8] Ericson 1996: 9.   [9] Ericson 196: 68.
[10] For example, Anne Walthall describes three elderly ladies taking an excursion by
train in the late nineteenth century: they left Tokyo at 5 a.m. and arrived at an inn in
Nikkō at 11.15 for lunch; they hired a guide to take them round the sights, did some
shopping for souvenirs and got the 3 p.m. train back to Tokyo (Walthall 2002: 58).

days; by 1890, the train was speeding their grandson on his first visit to Tokyo and enabling him to attend middle school in a town thirty miles from his home.[11]

The significance of the railway for the life of local communities meant that they competed fiercely, by all the political and financial means open to them, to secure rail connections and to be the sites of stations. Not to have the railway could mean backwater status in social and cultural as well as economic terms. Stations, with their big clocks, newspaper stalls and food and drink stands, were important symbols of 'modern life', often becoming centres of retail and housing development, and the opening ceremonies for them represented opportunities for local initiation into new products such as beer. At the same time, train travel facilitated not just the movement of people and goods but also the transmission of information and desire: a businessman from rural Nagano in 1889, observing that a toy he had first spotted in Tokyo in March was already popular in his home-town in April, noted 'that a fashionable item should spread this quickly to the provinces is really nothing but a result of the opening of the Tōhoku line'.[12]

With the expansion of the communications infrastructure came the development of the media, diffusing information, alongside goods and people, around the country. Literacy levels in Tokugawa Japan had been relatively high, and much information was spread, amongst the rural and urban elite at least, by means of books and other documents.[13] However, developments from the 1850s onwards significantly boosted the impact of the media, as the establishment of the national education system gradually provided the mass of the population with the means to access written material. Japan's first newspapers were being produced soon after the opening of the ports, and by the 1870s, with the arrival of the modern printing press, national titles, now aiming at a wider readership, were being established, while numerous magazines each had their day.[14] Although strictly censored, the press disseminated local, national and international news to the literate in town and country, and reading newspapers aloud to those who could not read or afford them was a common practice. Meanwhile, newspapers also became the main vehicle for advertisers through to the advent of radio, so conveying direct as well as indirect news of the emerging world of goods to be experienced in Japan and beyond.

[11] Bernstein 2005: 77, 116.   [12] Quoted in Ericson 1996: 93.
[13] Regional and class differentials in literacy skills were, however, considerable; see Rubinger 2007.
[14] Altman 1986.

Town and country

Much of the information that thus came to be disseminated of course emanated from the cities, which were beginning to expand in new ways, creating new contexts for the distribution and consumption of goods as well as plenty of news. By the 1890s, urban industrial employment was starting to grow fast, generating new industrial cities alongside the growing metropolises inherited from the Tokugawa period. The population of the six largest cities – Tokyo, Yokohama, Nagoya, Osaka, Kyoto and Kōbe – grew from 2.4 million (6 per cent of the total population) in 1888 to 6.1 million (11 per cent) in 1918, with Osaka and Kōbe in particular quadrupling in population over these thirty years.[15] Still, in 1918 no more than a third of the population lived in a town or city with more than 10,000 inhabitants, but the impact of such rapid urbanisation – on those who remained in the country as well as those who made the move – was nonetheless significant, as new patterns of urban life emerged and communications between town and country improved.

At first, migrants to the cities were typically relatively young and single, and often expected to return in due course to their home villages to marry and settle down. They lived in boarding houses, factory dormitories or, as with the many who went to work as domestic servants, in someone else's home, receiving board and lodging and experiencing few opportunities to spend their limited earnings (part of which might well in fact have been paid to their parents) on anything other than the occasional little luxury. However, growing numbers never in fact went back to their villages, eventually marrying and setting up home in the city. They came to inhabit the tenement blocks that speculative landlords continued to build, often at first occupying tiny apartments without individual cooking or washing facilities. This left them reliant on the resources of the city – the cheap restaurants and street sellers of leftovers, the public baths (though these might actually be something of a luxury) and street entertainment. In due course, however, as urban families became more settled and better off, apartments with kitchen space became more common, and urban consumers began to be able to take advantage of the shops and markets, public transport and educational and leisure facilities becoming available in the cities. Meanwhile, the old urban professional and commercial classes, deriving their income from small businesses and crafts, were joined by white-collar workers from new forms of business and bureaucracy in utilising the shops, cafes and restaurants, parks and entertainment that the cities were increasingly able to provide.

[15] Taeuber 1958: 47–9.

Much of what was available to the growing urban population, in terms of infrastructure and facilities, continued to take forms inherited from pre-Restoration times – the tea-house, the public bath, the amusement quarters and the whole array of eating places and street food sellers. However, access to the fashions and technology of the industrial West, combined with the desire on the part of the government and business elite to 'catch up', resulted in a variety of additions to inherited structures. First the rickshaw and then the tram and suburban train offered new ways of getting about in the city. Public buildings constructed in the Western style – stations, hotels, post offices, the 'brick town' in Tokyo's Ginza district designed to bring modern shopping facilities to the capital – began to appear. Gas-lamps and, by the end of the century, electric lighting brightened up streets and homes. While older forms of entertainment and leisure activity – theatre in all its varieties, sumo, street entertainment, the pleasure quarters – continued to thrive, by the turn of the century the first cinemas and Western-style theatres, parks and baseball grounds were beginning to offer new alternatives.[16]

Meanwhile, although the cities, especially as they grew at their most rapid rates through the 1900s and the boom period of the First World War years, undoubtedly led the way in determining consumption patterns, the development of communications and infrastructure was also drawing the rural population – still just about in the majority up to the Second World War[17] – into the urban orbit. The rural elite, now clearly established as land-owners and landlords under the Meiji reforms, experienced widening opportunities to travel and to gain information, through their involvement in the new political institutions of local government, their reading of newspapers and so on. Many found their commercial enterprises – soy-sauce and sake breweries, textile workshops and dealerships, local banking and money-lending – prospering as the economy grew and were able to extend their houses, buy new goods and engage further in their chosen leisure pursuits and cultural hobbies.

At the same time, the establishment of national systems of education and local government, under the Meiji reforms, was drawing the mass of the rural population, as much as the urban, into a unified national culture – school meals and school uniforms as well as reverence for the emperor – while providing more and more of the population with the literacy and knowledge to engage with the wider world. Conscription

[16] For a vivid description of the transformation of Tokyo in this period, see Seidensticker 1983: ch. 2.
[17] Where rural is defined as living in a community of fewer than 10,000 inhabitants. See Hitotsubashi Daigaku Keizai Kenkyū-jo 1961: 34.

is widely regarded as having been a major factor in introducing young rural men to new patterns of food consumption and dress, as well as enabling them to experience life away from home in the cities and even overseas. Infrastructure investment brought electric lighting and the railway, along with better roads, telegraphic communications and the Western-style architecture of schools and public buildings, out from the cities into the countryside.[18] Although, since Tokugawa times, few villages had ever been completely isolated from their local towns and provincial capitals, the integration of the whole country into national networks of communications, goods and popular culture was significantly accelerated by the reforms of the Meiji era and the spread of the economic developments and new technologies that resulted from growing interaction with the Western world.

Shops and shopping

Urbanisation and the development of the communications system were also bound to affect the ways in which consumers acquired goods, although, as in the case of the production of consumer goods itself, it was largely through adaptations to existing forms, rather than the introduction of 'modern' retailing methods, that this took place. Through the turn of the century and beyond, travelling salespeople and stall-holders continued to represent the majority of retailers. They predominated in the sales of fish, fruit and vegetables, especially in rural areas, but also sold medicines and a whole range of handicraft products. In many cases, they came from households that produced the goods they sold, and retail activities were a common sideline for farming, fishing or craft-worker families. In Kyoto in 1910, Nakano Makiko, whose husband owns a pharmacy business, notes in her diary her purchases of fruit and vegetables from street vendors and the failure of the clam-seller to call (obliging her to use tofu instead in the soup); she is persuaded to buy kimono material from a travelling salesman from the Ryūkyū Islands – his cloth is reasonable and good quality and he has an interesting Ryūkūan name – and she is moved to tears, viewing the accessories and cosmetics on sale from a regular visiting peddler and realising that her mother is no longer there to buy such things as little presents for her.[19]

---

[18] By 1920, 7 million households, out of a total of 11 million, had an electricity connection (Partner 1999: 17).

[19] Nakano 1995 117, 147, 169. Makiko's diary for 1910 has survived and has been translated by Kazuko Smith.

Nonetheless, as the towns and cities grew, the numbers of permanent shops steadily increased. For obvious reasons, shops tended to congregate together and shopping streets began to emerge, sometimes planned, as in the case of the Ginza in Tokyo, sometimes naturally occurring. This process was encouraged by the enthusiasm of local authorities throughout the country for fairs or exhibitions, often in specially constructed exhibition halls, which they saw as a means to educate consumers and develop a modern consumer culture.[20] The success of an exhibition of goods from all over the country, staged by the Tokyo local government in Ueno Park in 1878, led to the establishment of a number of permanent 'bazaars' (*kankōba*) containing groups of individual stalls or shops, much in the manner of the shopping centres to be found throughout Japanese towns and cities today. Here shoppers could enter with their shoes on and view goods displayed with price tags – no haggling – at their leisure, as well as eat and be entertained (Fig. 4.1).[21]

In urban areas at least, such developments drew shoppers (or their servants) out of the house and brought them together in streets and markets where they could window-shop, compare prices and meet their neighbours. In the great cities, shopping continued to develop as a leisure activity and tourist attraction; strolling along the Ginza window-shopping and taking in the atmosphere eventually became a sufficiently well-recognised pastime to cause a word – *gimbura* – to be invented for it.[22] In the heyday of the bazaar around the turn of the century, the Ginza area boasted seven of them, as well as pioneering retailers of the products that symbolised, in the catch-phrase of the day, 'civilisation and enlightenment', such as the watch shop of the founder of Seikō, the pharmacy that gave birth to the Shiseidō cosmetics company and the famous Western-style bakery and confectioners Fugetsudō.[23] The first beer hall in the country was opened there in 1899, and in 1911, not far away, the first of the European-style cafés that were to symbolise the style and decadence of the pre-Depression years.

[20] Miyamoto and Hirano 1996: 32.
[21] Seidensticker 1983: 62, 113–14; Moeran 1998: 143–5. By 1902, there were twenty-seven bazaars in Tokyo and others in Osaka, but thereafter they began to disappear, as proper department stores took over their role.
[22] This was a compound of 'Ginza' with 'burabura', an adverb describing aimless wandering. It was from around the time of the First World War that *gimbura* became the really fashionable thing for smart young people.
[23] Seidensticker 1983: 200–1. The clock tower built by the Seikō founder over his shop at the Ginza crossroads has been the symbol of Ginza ever since.

Figure 4.1 A bazaar in the Ueno area of Tokyo, pictured in 1884.
Nitta, Tanaka and Koyama 2003: 23; courtesy of the Edo-Tokyo
Museum.

Nonetheless, although the number of shops increased sharply from
the late nineteenth century onwards and their growing range offered
new kinds of shopping experience for urban residents and tourists at
least, the vast majority of retail outlets, where most people did their day-
to-day shopping, remained very small and specialised. From the 1900s
onwards, a number of the famous old Edo-period dry-goods stores were
widening the range of goods they sold, expanding their floor space and
work-forces and becoming limited companies, thus converting themselves into what were, by the inter-war period, department stores on the
model of those to be found in the cities of the West (see pp. 112–15).
Nonetheless, by the 1930s, when small shops hit by the Depression
began to demand help and protection from the government, at least 70
per cent of all retail establishments were still small-scale/family enterprises employing no more than one or two people.[24] Many of these
combined production with retail of such things as tofu and miso, confectionery or *tatami* matting, while in every urban locality there were
greengrocers, hardware shops, pharmacies and ceramics sellers, and in
towns and cities, at least, shoppers would not have had to go far to find
highly specialised outlets for particular kinds of food product, knives,

[24] Miyamoto and Hirano 1996: 355–7.

Figure 4.2 Traditional-style, small-scale shops, still to be found selling souvenirs at Kiyomizu Temple in Kyoto.

combs, footwear and much more (Fig. 4.2). In the big cities, retailers of new products were also beginning to establish themselves: butchers and Western-style bakeries were appearing in Tokyo from the 1870s, and dairies, selling milk from shops and door-to-door, were apparently a favourite business venture for ex-samurai looking for new ways to make a living.[25]

In this environment, the bulk of households' purchases took the form of fresh or locally manufactured – often made-to-order – unbranded goods. However, as the first steps were taken towards factory production of both new and some existing types of consumer good, branding and advertising, by no means unknown in earlier times, as we have seen, became increasingly significant through the second half of the nineteenth century as the means of developing markets and encouraging sales. Rival cigarette producers competed with each other through posters and packet design, as they sought to encourage the switch from pipes to (their brand of) cigarettes.[26] As

[25] Nitta, Tanaka and Koyama 2003: 24–5.
[26] The tobacco industry was nationalised under a government monopoly in 1904, in response to incursions by foreign tobacco companies. However, the state tobacco

Figure 4.3 Advertisement for Sapporo Beer from 1909. The model headed a national poll to find the top geisha.

domestic beer production became established, brewing companies designed dramatic labels for their bottles and employed top geisha as models for their posters (Fig. 4.3). In areas ranging from cosmetics and pharmaceuticals, through Western-style confectionery and other processed food and drink, to basic household goods such as matches,

corporation continued to brand and advertise tobacco products on a large scale. See examples displayed in the Tobacco and Salt Museum in Tokyo.

Tokugawa-period precedents and styles were adapted and developed, sometimes but not always with the addition of 'modern' Western-looking elements, to create brands not a few of which are still names to conjure with in Japanese retailing.

'Civilising grain': food and drink in the emerging urban industrial world

In the period between the momentous events of the 1850s and 1860s and the inter-war years, Japanese people saw the infrastructure within which they consumed goods adapt and change in various ways. Meanwhile, as their numbers grew, with the population stability of the Tokugawa period giving way to the rising trend typically associated with urbanisation and industrialisation, an expanding proportion of them were coming to live in new urban settings, away from the home-grown produce and family customs of the countryside, and with access to the facilities that towns and cities were increasingly able to offer. As they shifted into new kinds of household structure and new forms of working life, and responded to the environment and consumer culture of the cities, they adapted their consumption patterns to their new circumstances and used the goods they acquired as a means to demonstrate and, as far as possible, enjoy their changing status within the urban industrial society Japan was becoming. Food and drink were central to this process, as new urban households and eventually also those in rural areas affected by industrial growth, devised their version of the 'civilised' diet once the prerogative of the urban elite.

Rice as self[27]

By the late Tokugawa period, many city dwellers had already come to regard food as much more than just subsistence and the 'rice plus side dishes' menu had become established as the form of civilised eating and the means by which food could be utilised as a source of status and enjoyment. In the countryside, the rural elite were gradually incorporating elements of the urban diet into their meals, as they experienced the wider world and as the commercial facilities for the acquisition of food products, and knowledge of them, expanded. Nonetheless, the

---

[27] The title of anthropologist Emiko Ohnuki-Tierney's examination of the role of rice in Japanese culture and identity-formation (Ohnuki-Tierney 1993). As will become clear, the 'consumer self', to whom rice stood as the 'civilising grain', is a somewhat different phenomenon from the distinctively Japanese self defined by the growing and eating of rice that Ohnuki-Tierney seeks to describe.

stews of vegetables and other ingredients and the mixtures of rice with other grains that rural families cooked, using predominantly home-grown produce, over their *irori* hearths remained the standard fare of the majority.

However, as the Tokugawa commercial economy gradually merged with the urbanising and industrialising forces of the Meiji era, the adoption of the 'civilised', white rice-based diet became feasible and increasingly indispensable for the growing numbers of households who found themselves able, both financially and logistically, to obtain the range of commercially supplied ingredients of which it tended to be composed. During the Tokugawa period, servants and other ordinary urban residents of the great cities had eaten white rice, as they shared the food prepared in their masters' kitchens or ate out in the array of cheap restaurants. By the late nineteenth and early twentieth centuries, as the cities swelled with new kinds of inhabitant, the white-rice habit was spreading rapidly among the growing numbers of industrial workers and tenement dwellers, coming to define what it meant to live a civilised life in the new urban-industrial Japan. Female workers in textile mills ate rice on its own in their canteens;[28] the army provided conscripted soldiers with three rice-based meals a day. Few who had experienced such 'luxury' could face the food of their rural families in quite the same way again.

For those who were coming to live independently and permanently in the towns – the single workers and the newly establishing urban families – the shift to a 'rice plus side dishes' diet was a necessary part of the move to an urban life. Few now lived within the kind of household that assembled round the hearth to dip into mixed-grain stews, while urban women lacked the time, space and equipment to make and store the ingredients of the rural diet. At first, those living in the newly constructed urban blocks relied on cooked rice bought from street vendors, but after the turn of the century many more became able to cook rice in the tiny kitchens now attached to apartments.[29] Meanwhile, neighbourhood shops, markets and peddlers provided access to commercial supplies of the fish, pickles, seasonings and processed foods that went with rice. Various surveys conducted around the turn of the century suggest that even the ghetto poor were eating diets largely composed of white rice, even if purchasing it meant they could afford little else.[30] By then,

[28] This was typically cheaper imported rice, which Japanese consumers regarded as not tasting right, but it was still enough to create a significant problem with beri-beri among mill workers (Hazama 1976: 31n14; Hunter 2003: 117).

[29] Uno 1993: 55–6.

[30] Chūbachi and Taira 1976: 414–15.

Tokyo residents apparently found the thought of rice mixed with other grains quite repellent, and urban brides making their first visits back to their rural families reportedly demanded that their mothers stop the practice of adulterating the pure grain.[31] While 'country cooking' held out in many rural areas, urban meal patterns, and the white rice served on its own that was central to them, became an increasingly essential symbol of the civilised way of Japanese life.

This is reflected in the rising per capita consumption of rice statistically observable once national-level data collection began, following the Meiji reforms (see Appendix, Table 5).[32] Through the second half of the nineteenth century, consumption of other grains, mainly wheat and barley, was also rising, as country dwellers used their improving incomes to enable them to eat more of the traditional grain mixtures, while demand for processed foods based on wheat, such as noodles and confectionery, was also growing.[33] When per capita consumption of wheat and barley peaked after the turn of the century, there were still wide regional variations in the share of rice in total grain consumption, which ranged from 70 or 80 per cent in the most developed and commercialised areas to 20 or 30 per cent in regions such as southern Kyūshū where other staples – in this case the sweet potato – were widely consumed.[34] By the inter-war period, however, rice's share was rising nationwide, and polished white rice had become irrevocably established as the central element in the diet of modernising, urbanising and industrialising Japan.

The increasing demand for rice produced by changing eating patterns, combined with rising incomes, put growing pressure on the supply. By the turn of the century, Japanese farmers were finding it more and more difficult, given available land resources and technology, to increase their output of the Japanese-type (*japonica*) rice that they grew and that Japanese consumers had come to regard as the only proper rice for Japanese cuisine. Imports of the long-grained (*indica*) rice grown

---

[31] Ogi 1999: 227.

[32] The figures in Table 5 show Shinohara's estimates of the net per capita supply of rice on the domestic food market. Other estimates derived from production figures in a less sophisticated way give a higher overall value for per capita consumption and indicate a rise from an average of 116.7 kg in 1876–82 to a pre-Second World War peak of 169.2 kg in 1918–22 (Kayō 1958: Table K-a-1). Comparable data for earlier times are hard to find, but Nishikawa estimates annual average per capita rice consumption in the fairly typical domain of Chōshū as standing at just over 100 kg in the 1840s, rising to 114 kg in 1887 (Nishikawa 1986: 435–6).

[33] Annual per capita consumption of non-rice grains (wheat and barley) rose from around 50 kg in the 1880s to a peak of around 65 kg in the late 1910s (Kayō 1958: Tables K-a-2 and 3).

[34] Umemura, Takamatsu and Itō, 1983: Tables 16 and 17.

in much of the rest of Asia began to increase but, being only a poor substitute for real Japanese rice, failed to stem the rising price of rice in the Japanese market. By the summer of 1918, the additional inflationary pressures produced by the First World War boom had pushed the price of rice up to record levels, triggering serious rioting in a range of rural and urban locations throughout the country.

Although the causes of the riots were not the same everywhere, the common underlying thread appears to have been the threat that the high price of rice posed to consumers' ability to buy what had become the sine qua non of a civilised Japanese diet.[35] The authorities blamed the riots not on hunger or general food shortage, but on the 'luxury' to which consumers had become accustomed. Their efforts to solve the crisis by importing more foreign rice and providing it at low prices or as aid met with resistance from those whose dietary patterns had now come to centre on Japanese-style rice boiled and eaten on its own. In the cities, most rioters were not the poorest recent or temporary migrants, but relatively long-term residents concerned to maintain the respectable urban lifestyle that the rice-based diet symbolised; the press was full of stories of white-collar households struggling to keep up appearances in the face of the skyrocketing price of rice.[36] Rural rioters came from areas affected by the growth in industrial employment, rather than from more remote agricultural areas, and were similarly protesting against the rice traders and speculators they saw as threatening the standard of living, represented by their rice consumption, that they had achieved. The Rice Riots stood as a symbol of the extent to which, by 1918, a dietary pattern that had once been an urban luxury had become an essential element in the lifestyles and identities of consumers in industrial Japan.[37]

Commercialising food: processed tradition and new treats

While bowls of white rice were becoming the central feature in the diets of the growing populations of Japan's cities, so that, for the urban poor, rice could account for 80 per cent or more of expenditure on food, the side dishes and accompaniments that went with it were also emerging as essential elements in meals, both nutritionally and to add taste to otherwise bland food. Soya beans and fish continued to

---

[35] For a detailed analysis of the riots, see Lewis 1990; for a summary, see Francks 2007: 157–8.

[36] Lewis 1990: 37, 118.

[37] For a French example – involving coffee and sugar – of a similar historical process and its relation to food riots, see Jones and Spang 1999.

represent the key sources of protein and were commonly consumed, alongside whatever fresh produce was available, in preserved forms as side dishes, pickles or seasoning. In the countryside, many households continued to make these accompaniments themselves, using home-grown ingredients, their own kitchen and storage facilities and recipes handed down from mother to daughter-in-law, although fish and other items were now more obtainable from village shops or travelling salespeople. In the cities, however, time and space were at a premium, while markets and shops were much more accessible. As a result, the market for processed food products steadily grew, and an expanding array of commercial versions or developments of what had once been home-made items became available. In their quality and variety, now emphasised by branding and advertising, they were before long integral to the food pattern establishing itself in the industrialising cities and beyond.

In particular, as meals based on plain white rice became more and more standard in urban life, miso and soy sauce became increasingly indispensable as seasonings and protein sources. While output and, to some extent, per capita consumption of both products rose steadily up to the inter-war years, more striking is the growth in the share of consumption taken up by factory-produced, as opposed to home-made, products, which, in the case of soy sauce, jumped from around 40 per cent in the 1880s to over 80 per cent by the mid-1920s.[38] The process went somewhat less far – from around 30 to over 60 per cent – in the case of miso: the ingredients for miso – basically soya beans and salt – were relatively easily available even in the cities, and those households that could often continued to make their own. Since these were likely to be the better-off, who had the space, the equipment and probably the servants to do the work – Nakano Makiko, for instance, was still organising the production of her own miso in Kyoto in 1910 – there seems to have remained some cachet to the home-made product.[39] However, a growing range of commercially produced products, differentiated by flavour and brand, became available in the cities. Although soy sauce gradually replaced miso as a flavouring in cooking, a bowl of miso soup continued to represent an essential element in a 'rice plus side dishes' menu, whether grand or basic, while numerous uses for miso as a preserving and flavouring agent remained.

[38] Shinohara 1967: Tables 54, 55, 56, 57.
[39] Nakano 1995: e.g. 213. In England in the seventeenth and eighteenth centuries, this seems to have been similarly the case with items such as butter and cheese, which better-equipped households could make for themselves (Overton et al. 2004: 63–4).

Meanwhile, soy sauce proceeded on its march from luxury seasoning to ubiquitous element in Japanese cooking and dining. Home-made
equivalents for bought soy sauce – unlike those for miso – were no match
for the commercial product, which could be brewed and matured over
a long period to produce something much more tasty and convenient. Its numerous uses within a 'rice plus side dishes' menu made it
eventually indispensable to 'civilised' eating patterns, and, although
it remained something of a treat for the less well-off in rural areas,
the urban population before long found it hard to do without. Soy-
sauce brewing remained a major industry, composed of the thousands
of small-scale breweries producing for the local market and the larger-
scale enterprises serving the mass markets of the big cities with increasingly branded and advertised products.

Miso and soy sauce were of course not the only accompaniments to
rice in the urban diet, and wherever possible fresh fish and vegetables
were included in the selection of dishes presented. Many items, though,
were frequently used in preserved or processed forms, and commercial production and retailing of such goods steadily expanded. Dried
and salted fish products, tofu in various forms, seaweed products and
pickles of many different kinds were available from local grocers and
specialist producers. Commercial production of vinegar and *mirin*, the
sweet rice wine used in much Japanese cooking, continued to develop
as a significant business. Noodles, which had always been largely commercially produced, though typically as a rural sideline, became more
widely available, and by the end of the nineteenth century mechanised
rollers and imported wheat flour were making larger-scale production
feasible.[40] In many respects, commercial products were more reliable
and convenient than their home-made equivalents might have been,
and they made a wider range of foods available to the growing numbers
able to afford them.

Finally, it became increasingly the case that no rice-based meal was
complete without green tea. Tea had already, by the late Tokugawa
period, become the standard accompaniment to 'civilised' meals, as
well as the refreshment to offer guests, even if poorer rural households
had had to rely on low-quality home-produced leaves. Consumption
of commercially produced tea, of a widening variety of qualities and
types, continued to grow through the late nineteenth and early twentieth centuries, reflecting rising incomes and the gradual universalisa-
tion of meal patterns within which tea played a key role.[41] The uses of

[40] Sasama 1979: 67–8.
[41] Real per capita consumption of tea increased more than six-fold between 1890 and
1920 (Shinohara 1967: Tables 73 and 74).

tea – as something to wash down rice, but also as refreshment poured from the endlessly refilled pot in workplaces and as the focus of the mysterious ritual and etiquette of entertaining visitors – began, in the urbanising and industrialising context of the time, to develop towards the forms still in operation in present-day Japan.

As larger numbers of urban households came to be able to eat three rice-based meals a day, commercially produced food items thus gradually colonised their menus, providing taste, variety and key nutritional elements. However, outside these meals too, a growing range of commercial food was becoming available to more and more consumers, in the cities at least. Sugar was a major element in many of these treats and snacks, as well as an increasingly popular flavouring in cooking, and although per capita consumption never rose to the levels reached in the United States and parts of Europe, the association between urban industrialisation and growth in sugar consumption does not appear to be an exclusively Western phenomenon. The opening of the ports made available much cheaper supplies of better-quality imported sugar, and the development of secure sources of sugar for the Japanese market was a major goal of the eventual colonisation of Taiwan after it was ceded to Japan in 1895. As a result, Japanese-style confectionery based on sugar became accessible to a much wider market as gifts, souvenirs and more everyday sweet things to enjoy with a cup of tea. Eventually Western-style sugar-based confectionery items – biscuits, chocolate, ice cream – came to be widely consumed as snacks and treats, but Japanese food culture was by no means without its own scope for the growing indulgence of a sweet tooth, as incomes rose and urban facilities developed.[42]

By the inter-war period, therefore, the commercialised version of the 'civilised', white rice-based diet had become the norm in the cities, even if 'country cooking' still provided the basis of the rural diet. Many of the varieties of processed food that Japanese people still consume today – and indeed many of the companies producing them – had their origins in the process whereby commercial versions of the everyday ingredients that went into the 'rice plus side dishes' menu were developed. While large-scale businesses like Kikkoman and confectionery and dairy-products producer Morinaga, branding their output and selling to a national market, began to emerge in the food industry, much of this process nonetheless remained in the hands of a myriad of small-scale producer/retailers manufacturing for a local market and to suit particular tastes. Such producers took advantage of whatever new technology

---

[42] See Sasama 1979: 26–7. For statistical estimates of per capita sugar consumption, see Francks 2009: 148–51.

was appropriate to them – mechanisation among commercial producers of miso, for example, made it possible, from the late nineteenth century, to speed up the otherwise slow fermentation process – but it would not be until well into the post-Second World War period that the commercialisation of food supply meant widespread mass production.

Food, drink and social life

The facilities now available in the cities made it possible not just for many more to eat rice and its accompaniments in the 'civilised' manner at their day-to-day meals, but also for other elements in 'traditional' food and drink to come to be used and enjoyed in new ways in the urban setting. This involved the consumption of food and drink in the changing social situations in which the inhabitants of the growing cities – and those affected by industrialisation elsewhere as well – now found themselves. The food and drink that they consumed in their social gatherings might have remained much the same, but the ways in which it was consumed were changing to reflect the new context of life in urbanising and industrialising Japan.

In the limited spaces of their new urban homes, nuclear families now gathered to eat rice-based meals as small groups, but the entertaining of larger groups of extended family or non-family members, which rural houses had often been able to accommodate, was circumscribed, instead often taking place in the many kinds of catering establishment that the cities now offered. For single men or those without cooking facilities, the noodle stalls and cheap eateries that had sprung up to feed the working people of the great Tokugawa cities continued to increase in number and range, while more expensive Japanese-style restaurants entertained networking businessmen like Nakano Makiko's husband – often recorded as taking business lunches or dinners in particular restaurants – and family groups on special occasions. As chefs trained in Western (typically French) cuisine began to emerge from the grand hotels that served the expanding number of foreigners in Japan, Western-style restaurants – equipped with tables and chairs, knives and forks, plates and glasses – began to appear in the cities, catering to those rich enough to be able to demonstrate their fashionable familiarity with Western dining.[43] Meat-eating was already a fad by the 1870s, and establishments serving a kind of beef stew (*gyūnabe*) sprang up as haunts for the trendy, while students hung out at *sukiyaki* restaurants that served meat in a Japanese way. In due course, cheaper restaurants

---

[43] See Cwiertka 2006: ch. 2.

offering adapted versions of something like English food became more common – there were around 1,500 in Tokyo by the turn of the century[44] – but restaurants serving Chinese-style food, lacking the aura of Western modernity that the times demanded, were not to be established in any numbers until Japan began developing its imperial link with China in the early decades of the twentieth century. 'Milk halls', precursors of later cafés and coffee shops, where patrons drank milk and read newspapers, enjoyed a brief spell of popularity, and open-air stalls selling ice cream or flavoured ice were common sources of refreshment on hot summer days in Tokyo by the 1890s.[45]

Meanwhile, patterns of social drinking were also adapting to the urban industrial context. Although Western-style drinks – most notably beer (see p. 127) – became available to Japanese consumers, at a price, following the opening to trade, sake remained far and away the most commonly consumed alcoholic drink throughout the period up to the Second World War, and per capita consumption of it remained on a more or less rising trend until the inter-war years.[46] However, both its nature as a product and the ways in which it was consumed continued to adapt to the changing circumstances within which people came together to drink. Home-brewed, unrefined sake was still produced in the villages for communal celebrations and as a pleasant source of calories, but the Meiji government's imposition of a national tax on sake led to much greater regulation of brewing, eventually relegating home-brewing to a more and more rare underground activity. In the cities, it was the refined product produced by commercial breweries, both small-scale and local and large-scale and eventually national, that was available to and preferred by consumers, who switched to it when they could afford to do so. Branding and product differentiation proceeded, along with attempts to link sake to regional locations, in the manner of wine. While connoisseurs drank expensive specialities, ordinary commercial products filled the sake flasks of drinkers everywhere.

The growing consumption of commercial refined sake reflected the changes taking place in the social contexts within which it was drunk. In the expanding towns as in the countryside, sake remained the drink

---

[44] Cwiertka 2006: 48–9. The food in such restaurants was always served with rice, however, and liberally doused in Worcestershire sauce, taken to be the Western equivalent of soy sauce.

[45] Nitta, Tanaka and Koyama 2003: 25–6.

[46] See Appendix, Table 5. Traditional spirits (*shōchū*) continued to be drunk, especially in more remote rural areas such as southern Kyūshū but, in the changing world that followed the Meiji Restoration, they took on an image as the means for the poor to get drunk quickly that was not really lost until *shōchū* was reinvented as a fashionable cocktail ingredient in the 1980s.

Figure 4.4 An inter-war period sake bar. Asahi Shinbun 1933: 18.

served at public festivities such as weddings, but it was also emerging as by far the most common accompaniment to smaller-scale and
more private social occasions, within the home or outside.[47] Nakano
Makiko, for example, serves sake to wedding guests and also to her
husband's employees on the occasion of the annual shop-cleaning, but
her husband drinks it with friends at restaurants and party guests in
her home get drunk on it. A visiting relative from the country, on the
other hand, insists on drinking sake with his breakfast, following rustic custom by now sufficiently unusual, in Kyoto in 1910, for Makiko
to remark on it.[48] Increasingly, small groups of (male) friends or colleagues drank sake together in bars and restaurants (Fig. 4.4), with
snacks or full-scale meals, while wives served it to their husbands with
their dinners at home. With its long-standing religious associations,
sake continued to hold an important place in the developing rituals
of the new nation-state – the send-offs for soldiers going to war, for
instance – but it also, until eventually overtaken by beer, represented

[47] This follows the pattern observed in, for example, urbanising and industrialising
Europe, whereby mass public drinking of rough, locally produced drinks gradually
gave way to the private consumption of refined, commercial products in the inns and
bars of the towns and cities. For some comparative analysis, see Francks 2009.
[48] Nakano 1995: 121, 221.

the everyday social drink of all classes in the changing environment of the late nineteenth and early twentieth centuries.

Clothes and household goods: fashion, novelty and changing tradition

While diets developed primarily along Japanese-style lines, this was not necessarily the case with other areas of everyday life, into which new goods could be incorporated more easily and with less disruption to prevailing tastes and ways of doing things. Nonetheless, although Western-style goods in these areas were coming to be bought – as novelties and accessories demonstrating trendiness or sometimes as useful additions to otherwise Japanese-style everyday lives – their most significant impact was felt rather through the ways in which they influenced demand for Japanese-style goods, encouraging changes in the design and production of the kinds of clothes and household goods that Japanese people had been utilising, whenever they could afford to, since the Tokugawa period. It was really only from the time of the First World War boom that Japanese people, and then largely only middle-class ones, began to get to grips with the modern lifestyle embodied in Western-style goods. Meanwhile, the mass of their compatriots selected from the array of new possibilities, as they adapted what they consumed to the changing conditions of their working, social and family lives.

Clothes

One of the strangest things about the foreigners who arrived in Japan in the 1850s must have been their outfits, from their haircuts and beards, through their uncomfortable suits – or, in the case of the few women amongst them, their voluminous dresses and complicated underwear – to their heavy shoes. Nonetheless, it was recognised among the elite that, on public occasions at least, it was necessary to dress in Western style if Japan was to be taken seriously in the world, and the upper echelons of society, including the emperor and empress, were wearing formal Western dress at ceremonies and banquets by the 1870s. The military and the police had adopted Western-style uniforms before the Restoration, and members of the bureaucracy were soon required to wear the civilian equivalent – the Western-style suit – in the office.[49] Symbolically, the national conscript army that defeated the 1877 uprising of disgruntled samurai known as the

[49] Seidensticker 1983: 97.

Satsuma Rebellion were dressed in Western-style woollen uniforms, while the rebels wore silk and cotton samurai outfits.[50] Postmen and railway staff wore Western-style uniforms, and Western-style school uniforms for boys – modelled on military outfits – were introduced in the 1880s.[51] Gradually Western-style dress became the norm for men in most white-collar work, although the manager of the Bank of Japan's Osaka branch still, after the turn of the century, had to order the staff of this quintessentially modern institution to wear Western suits – the Osaka business community still preferred Japanese style, it seemed.[52] Meanwhile, the head of a village in the north was still wearing formal *hakama* trousers when fulfilling his duties in the village office in the 1900s.[53] After the opening of the ports, elite women who came into contact with foreigners experimented with long dresses and hats, but by the 1880s a reaction had set in and kimono, in the regional colours and patterns of the Tokugawa period, became fashionable again.[54] Throughout, however, most women, along with the majority of men much of the time, continued to dress basically in Japanese style until the inter-war period at least.

This did not, however, mean that clothing did not change or was not influenced by contact with the wider world. First, what Western style did offer was a range of accessories and peripheral changes to overall outfits that would go with male or female Japanese-style clothes, as symbols of style and modernity or simply because they were convenient or useful. Men were quick to abandon the top-knot hairstyle (which involved fiddly shaving and hair-oiling and precluded hat-wearing), have their hair cut short and grow beards or moustaches, although only the most 'advanced' women had their hair done in Western ways before the inter-war period.[55] Women, first in the cities and gradually elsewhere, did give up blackening their teeth and began to use some elements of Western make-up. Western-style footwear – better for mobility and protecting the feet but a business to take off and on when entering and leaving Japanese-style housing – could be worn with Japanese dress and became more popular as public buildings began to be built in Western style.[56] But the most popular symbols of 'civilisation and enlightenment', to be spotted in rural towns and villages as well as out

---

[50] Nakagawa and Rosovsky 1963: 62.   [51] Jō 2007: 258.
[52] Metzler 2006: 191.   [53] Bernstein 2005: 30.   [54] Jō 2007: 258–9.
[55] Top-knots were actually banned in 1871 and sword-wearing in 1876. After the turn of the century, Chinese reformers, debating the wearing of the queue and Chinese-style clothing, recommended following the Japanese practice of cutting hair but continuing to wear traditional dress – ironically largely to aid the Chinese silk industry, which was suffering from Japanese competition (Gerth 2003: 86).
[56] Seidensticker 1983: 101.

on the streets of Tokyo, were small-scale accessories: the Western-style umbrella, the pocket-watch, the walking stick, the Western-style man's hat, the woollen shawl. Geisha in full kimono had their photos taken in elegant poses with black umbrellas;[57] rural gentlemen wore trilbies with their *hakama* trousers and *haori* jackets; trendy girl students tied their hair up with ribbons and wore Western-style shoes, to go with their distinctive brown kimono.[58]

More significantly, however, contact with Western textiles was to influence the manufacture of traditional textiles and generate fashions in Japanese-style clothing that spread widely and gradually changed what most people wore. From the supply-side point of view, most emphasis has been placed on the import of cotton textiles. At their peak in the 1870s, imports met about a third of the domestic demand for cotton cloth, and the availability of relatively cheap imported cotton was certainly a factor enabling more ordinary people to enter the market for purchased textiles. However, domestic producers of both silk and cotton textiles were also able to take advantage of the growth in the mass market for clothing material, responding through the production of new varieties of the harder-wearing, better-quality cloth that Japanese consumers preferred for their everyday clothing to the thin white cotton ('shirting') that was available from abroad.[59] They shifted to silk/cotton mixes, soft and lustrous but relatively cheap, and even the craft weavers of high-class silks in Kyoto adopted the Jacquard mechanism – and eventually the power-loom – and began producing a wider range of differentiated products in lower-quality silks and silk/cotton mixes that reached new markets beyond the old samurai and merchant elite.[60] Textile-producing regions in various parts of the country innovated with machine-spun, sometimes imported, yarn, chemical dyes and brighter colour schemes that met the demand for relatively cheap but still high-quality goods.

Meanwhile, woollen cloth, first imported and snapped up as a fashion good in the 1850s, was also creating new demands and markets. Wool met the still quite limited demand for material for most Western-style clothing, such as men's suits, but, more significantly, light woollen fabrics came to be widely fashionable in winter accessories worn with kimono, such as short overcoats and shawls; by the 1900s worsted was even being used for kimono themselves. Although wool was a good deal more expensive than cotton, imports of lighter wool fabrics and wool/silk mixes continued to grow, demonstrating to Japanese textile

[57] Seidensticker 1983: 94.   [58] Jō 2007: 259, 29.
[59] Saitō and Tanimoto 2004: 287–94.   [60] Hareven 2002.

producers the scope of the market, among ordinary as well as urban elite consumers, for what were essentially Japanese-style fashion goods. In 1881 a technique was developed for dyeing worsted in Japanese-style patterns, and after the turn of the century a domestic wool-spinning and -weaving industry began to be established.[61]

The widening choice of materials and the fashions that this made possible spread from the city to the countryside and from rich to ordinary consumers through the second half of the nineteenth century, and new styles, not just in special kimono but also in everyday wear, were clearly being transmitted among men but especially among women all over the country. In the city of Nagano, before the coming of the railway in 1888, people dressed in the style prevalent in the rather remote regions of the 'wrong', northeastern side of the country, wearing sleeveless jackets instead of the *haori* sported in the sophisticated urban centres of the south and west, but thereafter both men and women adopted Tokyo fashion, undergoing 'a complete change in appearance'.[62] Even a rural bride could include in her trousseau a *furoshiki* wrapping cloth in imported printed calico – a highly desirable luxury item among the urban rich and the height of *iki* chic.[63] The designer handbag of its time had made it into the provinces too.

Household goods

Despite the large-scale changes in their working lives and social conditions that many Japanese men and women experienced through the second half of the nineteenth century and into the twentieth, the domestic environment within which they lived retained continuity with earlier forms in important respects. Although they might now live in a cramped urban tenement instead of a rural farmhouse, Japanese families still ate with chopsticks from bowls placed on trays or low tables and slept on the floor under futon. They might go to work, by train or tram, in a factory or workshop, instead of walking to the fields or setting up a household loom, but they still came home to rice-based meals, drank sake with their friends and relaxed in the public bath. In the changing economic environment of the time, households were able to acquire more of the equipment with which the better-off had long surrounded themselves, though increasingly manufactured in new ways or from new materials that helped to make them accessible to the growing mass market. New goods entered their lives as and

[61] Nakagawa and Rosovsky 1963.
[62] Ericson 1996: 93.   [63] Tamura 2004: 230.

when they usefully and conveniently fitted in or added a touch of class to home decoration, but the evolving pattern of consumption centred around the everyday goods long associated with Japanese home and social life.

With the changes consequent on urbanisation and industrialisation, many new houses were built, or old ones refurbished, and many urban families lived, initially at least, in newly constructed tenements with no more than one or two rooms plus a kitchen area if they were lucky. However, as urban housing developed, it adapted many of the architectural features that prevailed in rural housing, with *tatami*-floored rooms that could be opened up to create larger spaces when needed. The distinction between the formal, masculine areas of the house, in which guests were entertained, and the feminine regions, where the family ate, slept and amused themselves, was maintained to whatever extent possible and even the tiniest houses were constructed with *genkan* hall spaces, where shoes were taken off and tradesmen or insufficiently superior visitors quarantined from the rest of the house. Such houses needed only the kinds of movable furnishings – trays, cushions, chests – and formal decoration – vases of flowers, hanging scrolls – that had always amassed in better-off houses and offered little scope or space for larger items of furniture, draperies or decoration. Heating continued to take the form of braziers (*kotatsu*) that heated the person rather than the room, supplemented by padded clothing. Kitchens with *kamado* stoves (or smaller-scale equivalents) and sinks became increasingly common, but the utensils to be found in them were more and better versions of the rice-cooking pots, knives and ceramic or lacquer bowls that the emerging dietary patterned required.

Nonetheless, amidst the accumulation of everyday Japanese-style items, some new goods were finding their way into homes across the board, while the better-off were picking up the kinds of Western-style object that could be used to demonstrate their 'civilisation and enlightenment'. Useful small-scale items, such as matches, bars of soap, tin buckets, aspirin and other Western-style medicines, were soon being manufactured in Japan and becoming universal purchases. Books and newspapers began to reach much wider audiences, as new production methods were adopted. Children acquired toys, sometimes of traditional Japanese types but now also in new forms, using new materials, so that the toy-making industry, largely composed of small-scale businesses in Tokyo, developed the basis for its subsequent export success. The one large-scale item that significant numbers of households came to own at this stage was the bicycle. These were at first imported and expensive but by the turn of the century more likely domestically produced and cheaper, so that by the time of the First World War the bike had ceased to be just a rich man's toy and become a major means of everyday transport.[64]

Meanwhile, the better-off – the emerging middle classes of the towns and cities and the rural elite of land-owner/businessmen – splashed out on the more expensive items that came to embody the modern world to which Japan aspired to belong. Rural businessmen came back from trips to the cities bearing clocks and watches, walking sticks and umbrellas, glass vases, lamps, photographs they had had taken of themselves (and eventually cameras of their own) and pairs of spectacles, alongside Western-style clothes and accessories (hats, shirts, shoes and socks, handkerchiefs) and materials. By the turn of the century, many such items were available locally, as were the clock repairers, tailors and so on necessary to service these new possessions.[65]

By the 1920s, even the household of a poor tenant farmer in a relatively out-of-the-way region had come to possess purchased items that included 'pots and pans, umbrellas, books, utensils, braziers, a bicycle, paraffin lamps and a sewing machine'.[66] Although household interiors retained many of the basic features that had characterised rural and urban housing as far back as the Tokugawa period, causing modernising reformers in the 1930s to recoil in horror at their unhygienic lack of 'rationality', they nonetheless contained more, and sometimes different, contents that reflected both rising incomes and the material requirements of life in an increasingly urban and industrial society. The equipment needed to cook and eat a 'civilised' diet, to get to work, to equip your children for school, not to mention to enjoy new leisure and educational possibilities, thus gradually began to accrue within *tatami*-floored, wooden-walled houses designed and structured along the most familiar of lines.

Consumer goods and the path of economic development

The increased contact with the technologies, markets and material cultures of the Western industrial world that the opening of the ports ushered in undoubtedly helped to accelerate the growth of output in

---

[64] Takeuchi 1991: ch. 4. Bicycle parts production and assembly, though carried out for the most part by small-scale enterprises, constituted a major industry in pre-Second World War Japan, with important backward linkages to metal-working, machine-building, and so forth.
[65] Nakanishi 2000.   [66] Partner 2004: 25.

Japan and to bring about urban industrial expansion. By the beginning of the twentieth century, Japanese producers were able to manufacture ships, iron and steel, chemicals and industrial equipment in relatively large-scale plants modelled on those of Britain, Germany and the United States. Assorted Western-style consumer goods, initially imported, were also soon being manufactured by domestic producers, so that, with the exception of some cotton textile products, imports of consumer goods remained limited (and imported goods relatively expensive), despite the fact that Japan did not regain tariff autonomy until 1911. Japanese tailors made Western-style suits; Japanese factories and workshops produced the matches, watches, umbrellas, toothpaste and cigarettes that Japanese consumers, richer and poorer, began to find themselves unable to do without; Japanese breweries were soon brewing Japanese beer, even if the technology they used was German.[67] Nonetheless, most producers of consumer goods did not choose to go down the road of large-scale factory production, opting instead to use new techniques and inputs, where appropriate, to respond to consumer preferences for the differentiated, often still location-specific, products that small-scale producers, frequently co-operating together, were best placed to produce.

As a result, while modern textile mills, using machinery imported from Lancashire, employed increasing numbers of factory girls in the spinning and weaving of textiles mainly destined for export markets, the smaller-scale silk and cotton weavers who supplied cloth in the forms and patterns that suited Japanese-style clothing developed their own ways of utilising water, and eventually electric, power, adapting their equipment to produce more of the higher-quality and differentiated textiles demanded in the domestic market. Cotton weavers switched to better-quality imported cotton yarn and chemical dyes, but continued to produce growing amounts of cloth in kimono widths and designs, innovating on the basis of their existing skills in mixing colours and threads to produce a huge variety of regionally specific designs and colour schemes which could be utilised to create fashion within the

---

[67] This being the case, and given that there was only limited direct foreign investment into Japanese consumer-goods industries, the 'nationality' of consumer products does not seem to have been as contentious an issue as it was to become in China (see Gerth 2003). Although the wider moral and cultural implications of the adoption of elements of a 'Western' lifestyle were matters of concern by the 1930s (see ch. 5), goods that had initially been imported had by then become sufficiently domesticated not to raise the same production-side issues of national identity as in China. In fact, imports of Japanese-made consumer goods were to be a major factor in stimulating the movement to promote Chinese 'national products'. For further discussion of this issue, see ch. 8.

forms and tastes embodied in Japanese-style clothing.[68] In the food-processing industries, while some larger-scale facilities for producing new items, such as beer and Western-style confectionery, were gradually being set up, soy-sauce and sake brewers, rice polishers, tofu and miso makers all continued to expand output of their differentiated local products, introducing elements of new technology where appropriate. Ceramics makers developed new lines of production, including Western-style tableware for the export market, but also manufactured growing amounts of Japanese-style bowls, dishes and sake flasks in the designs associated with their particular localities.[69] While the new shipyards, steel mills and chemical plants, producing heavy industrial and military goods on the basis of imported science and engineering, attracted the greatest attention, local small-scale makers of paper products, lacquer-ware, bamboo furniture, *tatami* mats, Japanese-style footwear, toys and much more did not die out.

In fact, small businesses also outperformed large ones in the manufacture of all sorts of 'modern' consumer products, for export as well as for the home market, ranging from soap, through brushes and buttons, to bicycles and their parts.[70] The small-scale sector, now often utilising appropriate forms of new technology, such as the electric motor, and new organisational forms based on local networks of producers, continued to account for a large part of national output/employment, with much of its output directed towards the domestic consumer market.[71] In the production of, for example, most of the food and drink items that Japanese people continued to enjoy, there was no ready-made superior Western technology to import, but in clothing and household goods, where there might have been, small-scale producers continued to offer a range of highly differentiated products suited to particular market niches, even where the product concerned was not a 'traditional' Japanese one. It was small-scale producers who could supply the right food for the season, the appropriate accessories to match the right Japanese-style outfit for every occasion and dishes of suitable sizes and designs for all the different kinds of side dish making up a Japanese meal. As it turned out, they could also make each of the many parts that go to make up a bicycle or the twenty-nine different kinds and qualities of shell button for use in Western-style clothing such as uniforms, which a network of household producers in the Osaka area was able to offer, and

[68] See Tanimoto 1992.
[69] Yamada 2006.   [70] For examples, see Takeuchi 1991.
[71] Around 60 per cent of all workers in manufacturing in 1920 were employed in, or owner-operators of, workshops with no more than five workers (Tanimoto 2006b: 6).

they could respond to changing fashions in Japanese- or Western-style goods in quick and inventive ways.[72] The persistence of the small-scale business sector in Japan is thus intimately tied up with the developing nature of demand for consumer goods.

At the same time, the particular pattern of demand and supply in the market for consumer goods came naturally to be reflected in a retail structure dominated by the small local shops, markets and travelling salespeople who could provide their customers with the specialised, differentiated, fresh and local products and services that they sought. The persistence of the small shop in Japan, demonised as a wicked trade impediment by 1980s trade negotiators from an Anglo-American background, though a much less bizarre phenomenon to continental Europeans, has been explained in many ways.[73] Regulatory barriers to the construction of larger-scale shops date back to the late 1930s, and the protection of the small shop has been seen as a surreptitious form of social security, providing employment for the elderly in particular in the absence of adequate pension provision. However, it has also been attributed to the apparently strange preference of Japanese consumers for the experience of neighbourhood shopping and buying fresh food regularly in small amounts. Underlying this is the historical link between the small-scale producer and the small-scale retailer, forged in the form of products highly differentiated and specialised by function and by the ways in which they fit into the lives and wider material culture of Japanese consumers. The interconnections between the pattern of consumer demand and the retail structure – products of adaptations on both the supply and demand sides, as urbanisation and industrialisation changed everyday life – were to live on to cause 'frictions' in the process of Japan's incorporation into the world economy through the second half of the twentieth century and beyond.

By the end of the First World War, Japan had been accepted as an industrial power (albeit a rather junior one) with military forces to be reckoned with and a growing empire of its own. The political and economic developments that lay behind this had produced sometimes dramatic change in the infrastructure of Japanese people's daily lives and in the structures and institutions within which they lived and worked. Growth and change in the material goods that they consumed, on the other

[72] On shell buttons and bicycles, see Takeuchi 1991: chs. 1 and 4.
[73] See ch. 6. For an interesting comparison, discussing the issues surrounding the clash in inter-war Europe between the small shop and the 'modern', 'rational', 'Americanised' distribution system, see de Grazia 1998.

hand, are harder to discern and have generally only received attention when they involved new, Western-style goods that obviously contrasted with otherwise 'traditional' Japanese lifestyles. This is, however, to ignore the many more subtle ways in which Japanese consumers, as their incomes rose and their working, family and social lives changed, used their growing and changing consumption to enable them to adapt to their new conditions and to demonstrate and enjoy their status as citizens of an industrial power.

Hence, even in the case of the expensive, elaborate and undoubtedly 'traditional' *obi* sashes woven by the Nishijin craft weavers of Kyoto, 'a Taisho-period [1920s] *obi* looks very different from a Meiji-period *obi* or from a contemporary one'.[74] The kimono in which Japanese women got on trains and went to work in factories or offices were made of different materials, cut in different ways and reflective of different fashions from their earlier predecessors. The meals these women ate with their families when they got home took the 'rice plus side dishes' form of the elite urban cuisine of the Tokugawa period, but they were not what ordinary families would have eaten then and their ingredients – branded soy sauce, processed seafood, imported sugar – would not have been available to the cooks of the past. The kitchens within which these meals were prepared and the rooms in which they were eaten may have been small urban adaptations of rural predecessors, but they contained both many more of the utensils that Japanese cooking and eating require and a range of sometimes new, convenient and even consciously smart and modern items and accessories.

The production and distribution of the goods with which the consumers of industrialising Japan surrounded themselves sustained a large and significant part of the manufacturing and services sector of the economy through the years up to the Second World War (and indeed beyond).[75] The majority of the businesses involved in the supply of consumer goods and services remained small in scale, but adapted their methods and products to the changing demands of households experiencing not just rising money incomes, but also the shifts to new patterns of work and social life. This meant continuing to produce the kinds of food and drink products, clothes and household goods that better-off consumers at least had used in the past, but in changing varieties that reflected new technical possibilities and the widening and diversifying consumer market. Product differentiation – by function,

---

[74] Hareven 2002: 31.
[75] See Appendix, Tables 1 and 2, for a statistical indication of the significance of consumption expenditure within the macro-economy.

quality, region, season and also changing fashion – continued to create niches for small-scale manufacturers and retailers, even as some found opportunities to engage with the new products that consumers were also beginning to fit into their everyday lives.

By the inter-war years, Japan's industrial strength and involvement with the rest of the world had reached a level such that the consumers brought up in this complex world of differentiated products and evolving Japanese-style fashions were finally confronted, on a scale not experienced before, with the possibilities opened up by modern goods and all that went with them. Their responses to these possibilities are the subject of the next chapter.

5   Living with modernity: the emerging consumer of the inter-war years

> With the changes in society that have accompanied the progress of civilisation, the problems of actual home life have become increasingly complex. What sort of house to live in? What sort of food to have? And what sort of clothes to wear? The problems of the home are matters of food, clothing and shelter, as they have always been, but the food, clothing, and shelter of the new era must naturally be something different from those of the old.[1]

In Japan, as in many other parts of the world, the inter-war period was a time of political and economic instability, characterised by financial and economic crises and growing discontent among civilian and military groups, leading to attempted coups and deepening military influence over the elected government. As the Japanese army extended its control over northern China, establishing its puppet state in Manchuria in 1932, the prospect of military conflict, not only with China but also with the Soviet Union, the United States and the major European powers, began to loom, just as the rise of Nazi Germany was pushing Europe towards war. By December 1941, when the order was given to launch a pre-emptive strike on the United States Navy at Pearl Harbor, Japan's economy was firmly on a war footing and its society mobilised. As more and more of the male labour force was conscripted into the forces and more and more of the country's economic resources were diverted into military production, rationing was introduced and Japanese people experienced an increasingly severe struggle to subsist. By the summer of 1945, US bombers, by now able to attack the Japanese mainland at will, had destroyed much of the infrastructure of major cities, and homelessness and starvation threatened the millions of families who, in the pre-war years, had begun to enjoy the benefits of urban industrial life.

At the same time, again as in many other parts of the world, the early decades of the twentieth century saw growing numbers of people coming

---

[1] Advertisement in the newspaper *Kokumin shinbun* for a 'Home Exhibition' that it organised in 1915; translated and quoted in Sand 2003: 165.

to grips with the potential and the challenges that industrialisation and urbanisation brought. In the United States in particular, the mass production of manufactured goods, ranging from processed-food items to cars and other consumer durables, was opening up consumption possibilities for growing sections of the population, while the expansion of cities out into the suburbs created the space for new forms of domestic life. As architects built the skyscrapers in which the urban middle classes were coming to work, shop and amuse themselves, engineers and industrial designers explored the ways in which science and mass production could provide the means to save time and enhance lifestyles, and new giant corporations set about utilising the expanding media to inform consumers of what they could now buy and enjoy.

In Japan in the inter-war years, the techniques that lay behind mass manufacture, and the institutions and lifestyle that went with them, encountered a society already experiencing rising living standards on the basis of patterns of consumption originating in the urban culture of the Tokugawa period and formed in the context of the relatively rapid industrialisation of the late nineteenth and early twentieth centuries. While the superiority of large-scale, 'scientific' technology in the production of heavy industrial and military-related goods – iron and steel, chemicals, ships and warplanes – was obvious, the application of such methods to the ordinary consumer goods which constituted the material culture of Japanese society was more problematic. Manufacturers, intellectuals and the government, as well as the emerging middle classes of the cities themselves, all confronted the challenge of finding ways in which the potential of industrial design and mass production could be utilised to the benefit of everyday lives within the structures and institutions of Japan's economy and society. The outlines of a modern Japanese everyday life were beginning to emerge in the cities and their suburbs just as war-time austerity kicked in. While it was to re-emerge once recovery from the effects of war had been achieved, thence to become established throughout Japanese society as the economic miracle of the 1960s proceeded, its origins in the choices and adaptations made by consumers responding to the modernising possibilities of the inter-war years are not hard to discern.

Cities, suburbs and shopping

By the inter-war period, Japan was experiencing the development of many of the infrastructure features taken to characterise 'modern life' in the West – commuter suburbs, department stores, the systems of mass advertising and so on. In many respects, these features provided the framework within which a growing urban middle class sought to obtain and accommodate new consumer goods derived from the West and the lifestyle embodied in them. Nonetheless, the adaptation of the infrastructure of modern mass consumption to Japan's historically conditioned realities was far from straightforward or one-way: in the emerging world of modern consumption – the urban and suburban environment, the shopping and leisure facilities, the techniques of mass marketing – was born the Japanese version of modernity that continued to play itself out in everyday lives long after the upheavals of the inter-war and war-time years were over.

Urbanisation, suburbanisation and the new middle class

The years up to and including the First World War boom had seen a steady acceleration in the growth of Japan's urban population, as migrants from the countryside sought industrial employment and changing social patterns produced rising birth rates in the cities. Urban growth continued through the inter-war years – the population of the six great cities almost doubled between the censuses of 1920 and 1940[2] – as members of rural households continued to set out for the towns and cities in pursuit of off-farm employment. But the period was also one of consolidation in urban life, as incomers came to accept that their futures lay in the city and that they and their children would not be returning to the countryside. This opened up long-term prospects for investment in the infrastructure and services that urban families could utilise, so that, while national and local governments launched programmes to improve urban housing and public utilities, private investors set about developing the transport, retail and leisure facilities that met new and growing demands. Meanwhile, given the continually developing communications network, the still large rural population could not remain unaware of the bright lights and new possibilities of the cities. As perceived rural/urban inequality became a more and more fraught political issue, the integration of rural households into the emerging national lifestyle, via infrastructure investment, institutional developments and the widening network of markets and communications, took on growing significance for the state and for private-sector businesses and reformers.

At the same time, with the emergence of larger-scale business organisation and the professionalisation of jobs in fields such as local and national government, teaching and medicine, a larger number of urban

[2] Taeuber 1958: 154.

families were coming to base their lives on stable, salaried, white-collar employment. Such families constituted a 'new middle class', in some ways distinct from the 'old middle class', whose livelihoods derived from small businesses or crafts, land-ownership, traditional kinds of teaching and so on. This new status was based on educational qualifications, earned through the new national school and higher-education system, and on command of the skills required by modern business, professional and bureaucratic life. Alongside the expanding ranks of 'salarymen' employed in bigger businesses and government were the doctors trained in Western medicine, the architects, artists and designers, the journalists and writers, the school and university teachers whose social and economic positions were firmly grounded in the modern urban industrial world.

The consolidation of urban life, and the emergence of the new middle class alongside both the new industrial working class and the persistent small-business and services sector, brought about significant shifts in the geography and infrastructure of the cities. In the central districts of the great metropolises of the Tokugawa period and the new industrial cities, housing conditions were changing, as incoming migrants married and had families on the basis of more stable employment opportunities. Although something like the dormitory-style row-houses inhabited by groups of single men have persisted to this day in the slum areas of cities where day-labourers congregate, growing numbers of urban families found themselves able to rent apartments and small houses with more than one room and their own kitchen, toilet and washing facilities. Public utilities began to supply widening areas of cities not only with improved water supply and sewerage facilities but also with gas and electricity. Although most urban inhabitants continued to live in small dwellings, the greater security and utility of their houses enabled them to acquire more goods of their own, to cook their own meals and to live a family life in the city.

Meanwhile, the cities were also spreading outwards, as new suburban developments emerged in conjunction with the expansion of the suburban rail network. In Tokyo, new suburbs sprang up to the west and south, particularly after the major earthquake of 1923 had destroyed large areas of the old city; in Osaka, private developers opened up residential areas to be served by the new commuter rail services in which they were investing. The construction of suburban housing, principally aimed at new middle-class home-owners who would commute to white-collar jobs in the city, provided a clean slate on which architects and property developers could attempt to design the dream homes which modern urban husbands and wives might desire. Freed from the constraints of traditional housing design and construction methods, the new breed of architects, influenced by an eclectic range of Western domestic architectural styles, created estates of individual houses, faced with clapboard or concrete stucco and decorated with assorted Western-style detail, in which nuclear families could live independent, modern lives. Whereas the traditional house was built in wood by craftsmen using standard designs and methods and focused on the entertainment of guests and the accommodation of larger social groups, the suburban house incorporated features such as individual bedrooms for married couples, bathrooms, floored kitchens and dining rooms where parents and children could eat together round a table. Although such a house remained a dream for most pre-war urban families, it represented a model of the domestic surroundings of life in urban industrial Japan that the post-war economic miracle was to make realisable for a great many more middle-class households.[3]

Most of those establishing themselves in the expanding cities of the inter-war period, however, adapted their living environments to their new ways of life within the constraints of existing forms of housing. New urban couples were often free to set up their own homes away from their parents' houses – and the entertaining and other obligations that rural family and village life imposed – and unencumbered by the furniture and fittings that they would have inherited had they stayed in the country. The newly constructed or refurbished urban houses and apartments ideally contained improved kitchen facilities and possibly a room that could be furnished in Western style, as a dining room, study or sitting room. They thus offered scope for the acquisition of more and sometimes new kinds of furniture and equipment. Typically though, behind the smart, but probably uncomfortable, Western-style room, were Japanese-style rooms for everyday living, so that the *tatami* matting, Japanese-style sleeping facilities, *genkan* entrance halls and *tokonoma* alcoves that had characterised earlier housing styles remained standard, in new houses and old, for almost all who could afford them. The compromise between the fashionability and convenience of Western style and the comfort and familiarity of Japanese living arrangements was to represent a continuing theme running through the Japanese response to modernity.

Shopping and leisure

The expansion of the suburbs and the emergence of the commuting life were closely linked to the changing infrastructure of facilities for

---

[3] For a detailed study of homes and housing in inter-war Japan, see Sand 2003.

consumption in the cities. The property developers who constructed the suburban housing estates were typically one and the same as the suburban railway companies aiming to profit from the growing numbers of commuters. Meanwhile, they were also investing in shopping and leisure facilities at the central stations where commuters came together to get their trains out to the suburbs. The Hankyū railway company in Osaka led the way in this form of development, eventually opening the Hankyū department store at its Umeda station in 1929. Similar projects were also underway in Tokyo, where the points at which commuting workers changed trains – Shinjuku, Shibuya, Ikeburo – were beginning to emerge as shopping and leisure centres, establishing a pattern of association between stations and shopping complexes. As the new Shinjuku station was completed in 1925, Mitsukoshi opened a branch of its Ginza department store there and the Keiō railway company, whose trains terminated at the station, set up the forerunner of its present store.[4] Hankyū in Osaka also pioneered other ways of increasing its railway passenger business, constructing an assortment of leisure facilities – a zoo, a hot-spring resort, the Takarazuka revue theatre, a baseball stadium (and team) – on land along its lines.[5] In Tokyo, the Keiō rail line advertised itself on the basis of the scenic spots to be viewed by down-train users and the department-store shopping to be enjoyed by up-train ones.[6] As the railway network and the suburbs expanded together, so too did the opportunities for the urban population to enjoy shopping and outings.

Investment in new facilities for consumption was not, however, confined to railway companies and station precincts. The most famous department stores were set up in what became the smartest shopping streets of the big cities – Ginza in Tokyo, Dōtonbori in Osaka – but their lesser brethren sprang up in town centres throughout the country. Much attention has been focused on the department stores of the interwar years for two reasons. First, from the turn of the century, large stores had been converting their premises to facilitate modern forms of shopping (Fig. 5.1). They put in shop windows and glass display cabinets and installed wooden flooring, so that shoppers could walk in off the street without removing their shoes and freely view the merchandise. They used innovative forms of advertising and marketing, from poster campaigns at stations to gift vouchers and mail order and delivery services.[7] Secondly, although department stores sold a whole range of goods, including high-class Japanese-style clothing, ceramics, food products and so on, they also offered Western-style goods not available

---

[4] Tipton 2000: 124.   [5] Ericson 1996: 363.
[6] Nitta, Tanaka and Koyama 2003: 78–9.   [7] Moeran 1998: 145–51.

Figure 5.1 The interior of the 1914 North Building of the Mitsukoshi department store at Nihonbashi in the Ginza district of Tokyo.

elsewhere and took on something of an educative role (not, of course, unfavourable to their sales) in introducing consumers to new products. They sought to be leaders of fashion and taste, sponsoring exhibitions and artistic events and offering a range of experiences beyond just shopping, as they competed to provide rooftop gardens, equipped with menageries, skating rinks and children's playgrounds, alongside a wide choice of restaurants.

In fields such as Western-style clothing, food, furniture, gadgets and even art, the department stores were, in due course, to take a major share of the new middle-class market in the big cities.[8] Nonetheless, most consumers in urban, and even more so rural, areas continued to rely on small-scale local shops, travelling salespeople and street markets for most of their everyday needs and even for major purchases of new modern goods. The Singer Sewing Machine Company in Japan instituted a system of instalment credit on sales of what became a very widely purchased item, and, although the department stores considered consumer credit beneath them, by the 1920s it was possible to

---

[8] The first national census of the distribution industry, carried out in 1939, found that shops with more than fifty employees accounted for 22.2 per cent of retail sales. However, 91.9 per cent of retail establishments still fell into the one- to four-employee category. See Miyamoto and Hirano 1996: 356.

buy many larger-scale items – pianos, furniture, men's Western-style suits, ceramic- and lacquer-ware – by means of instalment payments organised by visiting sales representatives or local retailers.[9] While the department stores offered a window on to 'modern life' and accelerated the development of shopping/window-shopping as a leisure activity in the great cities, much of the real business of buying things – both new and 'traditional' – remained the preserve of the small-scale retailers who had been establishing themselves since Tokugawa times.

Meanwhile, shopping was not the only consumption activity for which inter-war urban growth provided an expanding infrastructure and new opportunities. The cities had of course been offering a range of facilities for eating and drinking outside the home since the Tokugawa period, and fancy restaurants, tea-houses, noodle stalls and sake bars continued to prosper, serving much of the need for fast food, special-occasion meals and social drinking of the populations of cities, towns and even villages. Alongside them, by the inter-war period, various kinds of Western-style restaurant were becoming well established in the main urban centres. Eating places selling Chinese-style food, from cheap noodles to superior cuisine, also grew more popular, as China loomed larger in Japan's consciousness. By 1923, there were estimated to have been 5,000 Western-style restaurants in Tokyo. Re-building after the earthquake in that year provided a further opportunity for more establishments to switch to tables and chairs or counters.[10] The number of purveyors of Chinese-style food similarly grew rapidly after the turn of the century.[11]

Some of the factors underlying the growth in popularity of non-Japanese restaurant styles emerge from the results of a turn-of-the-century survey, bringing out the attractions of Western-style catering for informal social eating in the context of modern urban life: meals were simpler and better adapted to a wider range of accompanying drink; you could eat what you liked, rather than being faced with a set array of beautiful, but not necessarily tasty, small dishes and you could avoid all the expensive and restricting trappings – the right plates and bowls; kimono-clad waitresses trained in the proper ritual; a private and appropriately decorated room – of a formal *kaiseki* meal.[12] Department-store restaurants, where one could eat in Western style and keep one's shoes and coat on, enabled working women and house-wives to eat out at ease.[13] The Hankyū department store in Osaka gave over two of its five floors to restaurants and cafeterias, serving relatively

---

[9] Gordon 2006.   [10] Ishige 2001: 158–9.   [11] Cwiertka 2006: 138–48.
[12] Watanabe 1964: 281.   [13] Tipton 2000: 123.

Figure 5.2 The interior of the Lion Beer Hall in Ginza, constructed in 1934.

cheap hybrid Japanese/Western meals, including as much as you could eat of rice, pickles and 'sauce' for five sen (¥.05).[14] Meanwhile, from the turn of the century onwards, new Japanese beer companies were setting up beer halls, where beer could be bought by the glass (usually a German-style tankard) and consumed at tables and chairs in Western-style surroundings (Fig. 5.2). By the 1920s, beer halls had spread out from Tokyo to other urban industrial centres where beer was beginning to become a more familiar and popular drink for men on their way home from work or groups of colleagues socialising.[15]

The most talked-about new form of catering establishment, how-ever, was the café.[16] Cafés were definitively modern: they had exotic English or French names; they sold Western-style drink – beer, wine, spirits – and food such as sandwiches, consumed to the sound of jazz; they advertised themselves with neon lighting and their interiors daz-zled with mirrors, aluminium and stained glass.[17] But above all, unlike the European cafés they were supposed to be modelled on, they were

---

[14] Takemura 2004: 96.   [15] Kirin Bīru 1984: chs. 2 and 3.
[16] The first famous cafés in Tokyo, Café Printemps and Café Lion, were set up in 1911. The first apron-clad waitresses appeared at Café Tiger in 1912 (Uchida 2002: 42). By the early 1930s, according to police surveys, there were around 30,000 cafés and bars nationwide, employing over 100,000 waitresses (Tipton 2000: 122).
[17] Tipton 2000: 125.

staffed by waitresses who, with their fashionable clothes, make-up and hairstyles and their bold and flirtatious ways, symbolised the changing nature of women within the world of urban consumption.[18] The many thousands of young women who worked as café waitresses in the cities in the 1920s and 1930s, deriving their incomes from tips, introduced their patrons to the eating and drinking of new kinds of food and drink in a Western-style setting and, perhaps more significantly, to eating, drinking and free conversation between men and women in a public place as an expression of style and modernity. The growing association of cafés with decadence, and of café waitresses with prostitution, led to government attempts to restrict and regulate them and to the metamorphosis of many of them into establishments ranging from respectable restaurants to brothels. Nonetheless, café culture survived to be reborn in the huge numbers of coffee shops (*kissaten*) and Western-style hostess bars that flourished in the booming cities of the post-Second World War period.

The development of the cities and their transport links also facilitated the emergence of a range of other new leisure activities and consumption opportunities. Train travel made it possible, for the better-off at least, to take holidays: new seaside resorts grew up along the rail routes out of Tokyo, but equally popular were trips to hot-spring resorts (*onsen*) which rising middle-class incomes and the train brought within reach of a wider public. The Seibu railway company developed mountain resorts at Hakone and Karuizawa, where visitors could ski, swim in a pool and play golf or tennis.[19] Sea-bathing was a mass summer activity in the Osaka area by the 1920s – rather more exclusive around Tokyo – with trains taking holiday-makers to the beaches at Sakai or to 'camping villages'.[20] Nearer home, for those with less time or money, amusement parks were being constructed to rival the traditional pleasure quarters where fortune-tellers, puppet shows and storytellers had congregated. The commercialisation of sporting activity, both new and old, proceeded apace: professional baseball teams played in large new stadiums – the Kōshien baseball stadium in Osaka was completed in 1924 to hold 50,000 spectators[21] – while those with the means to attempt to be smart and modern joined clubs and took up tennis or golf. Sumo wrestling became an institutionalised competitive sport with the establishment of the championship system, heavily sponsored by newspapers and radio.[22] In the poorer areas of the cities,

---

[18] Café waitresses typically continued to wear kimono, even if accessorised in Western style. For more on kimono fashion, see pp. 129–31.

[19] Young 1999: 58.   [20] Takemura 2004: 94.

[21] Takemura 2004: 95.   [22] Thompson 1998.

billiard halls competed with mah-jong parlours for the leisure time of
the working man. By 1940, there were 2,363 cinemas in the country,
with film viewings working out at an annual average of almost six per
person,[23] while the entertainment quarters of the great cities offered
theatres, producing everything from nō and kabuki, through serious
modern plays (Japanese and translated Western) to the hugely popular
all-girl Takarazuka review, alongside street entertainment to suit a wide
range of tastes and pockets. What emerged, Jeffrey Hanes argues, was
less 'mass culture' than a diversified and differentiated culture industry
seeking out the niches and segments of a market that stretched from
Westernised intellectuals, through 'modern' boys and girls and aspiring
salarymen, to the working classes, old and new.[24]

Nonetheless, while commercial, consumer-oriented leisure activities were increasingly available to the new urban public, divorced from
their traditional communities and yet to form new ones within their
emerging work organisations, community-based activity remained central to social life in provincial towns and villages, and even some of
the older areas of big cities. Village banquets and parties continued to
represent the main form of social recreation for rural people, even if
now fuelled by bought-in rather than home-made sake, and local festivals still offered the opportunity to dress up, eat and drink, and be
entertained.[25] Village group outings might now involve baseball games
or city sightseeing rather than pilgrimages to shrines and temples, but
they still represented opportunities to travel and to bring back souvenirs. The cinema was reaching provincial towns by the inter-war period
(Fig. 5.3) and other venues for modern leisure and social activity were
beginning to spread out with the railway network, but it was still not
until the post-war advent of television that most rural people ceased to
rely on their own communal resources for all but exceptional moments
of entertainment and relaxation.

Imagining the modern life: advertising and the housewife

In Japan as elsewhere, the inter-war growth in the consumption of more
and different things depended on the provision not just of the infrastructure through which to purchase them, but also of the information
and images by means of which consumers came to desire, and to learn
how to use, the multiplicity of new goods coming within their reach.
The development of techniques for the mass production of consumer

---

[23] Gordon 2007: 7.   [24] Hanes 1998.
[25] For examples, see Embree 1964: 99–110; Dore 1978: 219–20.

Figure 5.3 Schoolboys queue for the cinema in Saga City in Kyūshū in 1938. Saga, well off the beaten track, had four cinemas by the 1920s. Furukawa 1979: 76.

goods, which began with the mechanised factory production of textiles in northern England, came to be symbolised by Henry Ford's vehicle production lines that made cars – albeit only black ones – affordable for more and more American families. Mass production made the American suburban lifestyle possible, and mass advertising, in ever more sophisticated forms designed to take advantage of new media opportunities, idealised and promoted that lifestyle in its efforts to sell the goods in which it was embodied. Outside the United States, local small-scale production and retailing continued to supply the majority of the everyday consumption goods obtained by most households, while craft producers still created differentiated luxury goods for the rich. Nonetheless, it was American goods and the glamorised American lifestyle, observed worldwide in media such as the cinema, that came to represent what was 'modern'. Where their parents had coveted English tailoring and French confectionery, the smart young things who hung out in the trendy cafés of inter-war Tokyo were being converted to baseball, steaks and the gadget-filled individual home where the happy housewife welcomed her husband back from the office.

However, anything resembling US-style mass production would have been hard to find in the parts of the economy that supplied the domestic consumer market in inter-war Japan. Ford and General Motors had already spotted the potential market for mass-produced passenger vehicles and set up assembly plants in Japan, only to find themselves forced out, in the 1930s, by government regulations favouring domestic manufacturers. Nissan and Toyota responded by establishing themselves as vehicle producers, but their main markets were in military vehicles. In some areas of the food industry, companies using larger-scale manufacturing and marketing techniques had already become established by the inter-war period and some Western-style but ordinary consumer goods had been produced using larger-scale imported technology from the start. But most consumer goods, ranging from clothes through a huge range of processed-food items to ceramic and lacquer household goods and children's toys, continued to be produced and marketed by networks of small businesses, increasingly aided by appropriate new technology, such as the electric motor, and advances in design. After the First World War as before it, variety and differentiation remained the hallmarks of many areas of the consumer-goods market, as tofu and noodle sellers made their own produce, local dressmakers sewed kimono and made up Western-style fashions, and the *tatami* maker, the carpenter and the local futon shop provided most home furnishings.

In those areas where larger-scale production for the mass market did emerge, however, so did branding and its associated advertising. Japan's dominant advertising agency, Dentsū, had been founded as far back as 1907.[26] By the 1930s, commercial design was a thriving area of activity, creating images associated with major brands ranging from Kaō soap and Shiseidō cosmetics to Sapporo beer and Hero cigarettes. Department stores advertised the latest kimono fashions and even the government employed the techniques of the advertising industry to promote savings campaigns and eventually war-time drives against waste and 'luxury'.[27] Smaller businesses advertised too, as they had always done, adapting to the new age the pictures of pretty geisha and actresses that their Tokugawa predecessors had used.

The main vehicles for advertising were newspapers and magazines, together with posters and other street displays. Circulations expanded, and a whole range of specialised publications emerged.[28] Particularly significant from the point of view of consumer education and advertising

[26] Ivy 1993: 242.
[27] On the emergence of commercial design, see Weisenfeld 2000; on savings campaigns, see Garon 2000.
[28] The *Asahi* and *Mainichi* newspapers both had circulations of over a million by 1924 and various monthly magazines also reached mass readerships (Gordon 2007: 4).

were women's magazines, of which a number of national titles existed, with large circulations, by the 1920s.[29] The focus of magazines such as *The Housewife's Friend* (*Shufu no tomo*) was largely on good housekeeping – economical and 'rational' ways to make and use things – but they also aimed to educate readers in how to use new products, including, for example, recipes for dishes involving meat which would not offend the palates of Japanese husbands or break the bank.

Such magazines assumed a literate female readership, now often educated through the school system to act as managers of household consumption, capable of feeding and clothing their families in efficient ways that combined what worked in the context of Japanese tastes and resources with the benefits of new goods. For the better-off, higher-level schooling for girls offered training in the techniques required of the modern wife and mother. The patriarch from the rural north (see earlier chapters) sent all his children to be educated in Tokyo, buying a house there to accommodate them: the boys went to schools preparing them for entrance to universities where they would study medicine, law and veterinary science; the girls entered women's colleges where they majored in the home economics subjects that would prepare them for their roles as modern wives and household managers.[30] Armed with tools such as the sewing machine – to be deployed, according to the women's magazines, in everything from sewing up cotton kimono to creating little Western-style mats and curtains to add a smart touch to a living room – housewives with appropriate education were increasingly viewed by the media, advertisers and the state as the agents through whom the Japanese version of a modern lifestyle might become an everyday reality (Fig. 5.4).

By the inter-war period, therefore, Japanese cities at least were equipped with much of the infrastructure of modern consumption activities – the transport, the shops, the leisure facilities, the media – and rural towns were developing their own, perhaps smaller-scale and less glamorous, versions of them. These facilities certainly allowed for the consumption of new, Western-style goods: the department stores would teach you how to wear Western-style clothes before selling them to you; the cinemas would transport you to dream worlds filled with new goods; beer halls would enable you to drink beer with colleagues on the way home from the office; and cafés would sell you sandwiches and enable you to converse with 'new' women. Above all, newspapers and magazines would

[29] See Sato 2000.   [30] Bernstein 2005: ch. 5.

Figure 5.4 Cover of a dressmaking magazine from 1936.

educate you in everything from sewing techniques to table etiquette, while advertising all you would need to lead a modern life.

However, facilitating the spread of new products and lifestyles was only part of the way in which the infrastructure of modern life changed the consumption patterns and everyday lives of Japanese people. It also played its role in the continuing process whereby Japanese material culture itself changed and modernised. Department stores sold not only Paris fashions but also the latest in kimono colour schemes; they offered branded sake and miso from the best production regions, as well as exotic Western tinned food; trains enabled more and more people to enjoy trips to hot springs, as well as transporting them to leisure parks and baseball stadiums; posters and magazine advertisements extolled the virtues of brands of tea, sake and soy sauce, as well as beer and cigarettes. As we turn now to the actual practice of everyday life in the inter-war years, it will become clear that 'modernisation' was a much more complex and historically conditioned process than simply coming to consume what Americans had.

Everyday life in the modern world

In the context of inter-war Japan, it was of course the modern and new – hence to a large extent the imported or Western-style – which was exciting, fashionable and newsworthy. However, most Japanese people lived within a world of consumption that had been developing and changing since the Tokugawa period in response to rising incomes and changing social and economic conditions, but in which the modern goods of the West played only a peripheral role. As Japanese consumers came to establish their ways of life within an urban industrial environment that now often involved the features of the modern city worldwide, they did begin to find ways to use and enjoy the items that mass production and industrial design were making more and more available. However, this was only by means of a process of selection and adaptation that altered both the nature of the imported product itself and the home-grown material culture within which it was consumed. Through this process – applied to their food and drink, the clothes they wore and the household goods with which they surrounded themselves – the pioneers among Japanese consumers in the inter-war years laid down the outlines of the consumption patterns of all those who were able to join the 'middle masses' created by the post-war economic miracle.

Food and drink

By the inter-war period, the 'rice plus side dishes' pattern was firmly established as the proper form of meal among the urban population, and households were increasingly well equipped with the cooking and eating utensils that it required. Anything else was 'uncivilised' and, although many households in the countryside continued to eat mixtures of grain for a variety of reasons – when the rice harvest was poor, as in the north in the disastrous years of the early 1930s, there was little choice, but other factors, such as the availability of appropriate cooking facilities and ingredients, must also have played a part – this was coming to be regarded as evidence of rural poverty and backwardness. A constant refrain running through the memories and records of those who lived through the inter-war years in the countryside is dislike of the grain mixes it was necessary to eat and it is clear that the ratio of other ingredients to rice in the mixes was seen as a measure of poverty. Rural teachers inspecting the packed lunches of their pupils during the Depression of the early 1930s were horrified to find only rice/barley mixes, while the children were ashamed to reveal them; the housewives of Suye Mura, the village studied by American anthropologist John Embree in the 1930s, claimed not to like the rice mixes that represented their everyday staple and never served them to guests.[31] For the rural population as for the urban, eating the 'rice plus side dishes' meal pattern had come to mean living the civilised lifestyle of modern Japan.

It was therefore within the framework of the rice-based diet that the continued development and 'modernisation' of Japanese eating patterns took place. For urban consumers in particular, commercialisation and technological developments in food processing continued to open up an expanding range of side-dish ingredients, pickles and flavourings, to be eaten alongside the fresh items that local grocers, markets and door-to-door sellers provided. These included both the standard elements of rice-based cuisine – soy sauce, vinegar, dried and salted fish products, pickles, seaweed and so on – and newer items, such as sugar-based confectionery and adaptations of Western-style sauces and flavourings. Meat became cheaper and more easily available, and the range of fruit and vegetables widened to include new items such as cabbage and tomatoes, while Japan's expanding empire supplied tropical produce such as bananas and pineapples, as well as much cheaper sources of sugar and soya beans. The development of large-scale fishing techniques, alongside the industrial production of ice, brought fresh fish to many more consumers.[32]

However, by the inter-war years it had been recognised that the heavily rice-based diet did result in nutritional deficiencies, leading in particular to beri-beri, the incidence of which rose steadily as more and more people ate more and more rice. Western-style foods, in particular those involving meat and fats/oils, were widely regarded as nutritionally superior to Japanese ones, and for other practical reasons – supplying cooked rice to the military in the field was logistically difficult, while bread was much more convenient; the Rice Riots had demonstrated the limits to expansion in the supply of Japanese-style rice, encouraging diversification into other grains – the authorities were keen to

---

[31] K. Smith 2001: 72; Embree 1964: 38.   [32] Watanabe 1964: 287–90.

promote their consumption. Consumers, on the other hand, appear to have had little taste for meat and bread – still relatively expensive items obtainable only from specialist retailers – on a day-to-day basis, and their kitchen and dining equipment and facilities were designed for a kind of meal pattern into which Western-style dishes did not fit straightforwardly. If new items were to be consumed at an everyday level, they would have to be adapted to existing dietary patterns.

One way to do this was to leave foreign cooking to the experts and to allow the growing number of Chinese- and Western-style restaurants to provide the means to consuming more meat and oil. In fact, most Chinese restaurants came to sell Chinese-style noodles (*rāmen*) cooked and served in a Japanese fashion and Japanese-Chinese cooking (*chūka ryōri*) emerged as the distinct genre, with its own characteristic dishes, that it is today. Similarly, all but the smartest Western-style restaurants – typically those opened by Western-trained chefs from the big hotels – served rice with whatever was their particular speciality and offered adapted dishes that could be eaten in a Japanese way – rice with pieces of chicken or pork added, omelettes, deep-fried fish or prawns and so on. Curry-rice, modelled on the English version using curry powder and containing one or two pieces of meat if you were lucky, proved to be one of their most enduring inventions. The fusions of Japanese and foreign cuisines thus produced their own distinctive forms which could be fitted into or used to supplement the standard 'rice plus side dishes' diet.

Meanwhile the middle-class urban households in receipt of the exhortations of women's magazines and the government's message about healthy eating did their bit towards incorporating nutritious foreign items into home cooking too, in ways that fitted their tastes and resources. Bread could be bought from bakeries in the cities but remained an exotic treat eaten, for example, for special Sunday breakfasts. Meat remained relatively expensive and was typically only eaten in the form of the 'three big Western foods' – curry-rice, potato croquettes (with a small amount of minced meat inside) and cutlets (*tonkatsu*) involving thin slices of pork – which made a small amount of meat go a long way (Fig. 5.5). These were to become firm favourites but were never going to raise per capita consumption of fresh meat to anywhere near the level of fish.[33] Factories were set up to produce ham and other tinned meats, but demand remained limited. Milk was largely regarded as something to be endured for medicinal purposes, and dairy produce in general was little consumed before the 1970s, except in the form of ice cream.

[33] Takemura 2004: 107.

各種お持ち帰りできます

当店カレーNO.1
エビフライカレー　600円

ビーフカレー　480円
魚フライカレー　550円
玉子カレー　550円
ブロッコリーカレー　550円
チキンカリカリカレー　600円
カツカレー　600円
ミックスカレー　700円
・カレー各種大盛　100円UP

600円　480円　600円

【期間限定】
カツ煮定食

Figure 5.5 Two of the 'three big Western foods' of the inter-war period – curry-rice and cutlets – still available in Osaka in 2007.

Nonetheless, new products that could be consumed in ways that did not conflict with the Japanese meal pattern – as snacks, for instance – did come to be much more widely purchased and enjoyed in the modernising context of the inter-war years. Chocolate and other kinds of Western-style confectionery such as biscuits became common treats, and the major Japanese confectionery producers established themselves and advertised widely. Cafés served coffee, black tea and fizzy drinks. Tomato ketchup and the Japanese version of Worcestershire sauce became standard elements in Japanese/Western fusion dishes.[34] However, perhaps the most significant Western-style product to establish itself as part of the Japanese lifestyle was beer.

[34] For more on the incorporation of Western-style items into Japanese meals, and in particular on the role of military catering in the process, see Cwiertka 2006: ch. 3.

Imported bottled beer had been available in Tokyo and in the ports where foreigners congregated from the time of the opening of the country in the 1850s. For Japanese consumers it continued to be an expensive product, drunk only by the modernising bureaucratic and military elite and strongly associated with eating Western-style food. By the late nineteenth century, however, Japanese breweries (such as Sapporo, Kirin and Asahi) were being set up on the basis of imported German brewing technology and beginning to sell their product by the glass in beer halls and cafés. Beer retained something of an association with the modern: it was sold on trains and at stations; it seems to have been the drink of choice in the military and at 'modern' public occasions, such as the opening of bridges or the return of soldiers from the Russo-Japanese War. Consumers in the cities and new industrial towns, but also village officials and teachers in rural areas, were made more familiar with it through advertising and other kinds of publicity, and, although beer remained quite expensive, relative to sake, consumption of it grew rapidly.[35] Beer was fast becoming part of the lifestyle of white-collar workers, enjoyed with colleagues in bars after work, drunk even with more or less Japanese-style meals in cafés and canteens, and served by housewives to tired husbands returning from the office. With the spread of 'middle-class culture' to the mass of the population in the postwar years, it was beer, rather than sake, that was to become the indispensable accompaniment to everyday social activity.[36]

The inter-war years thus saw established a pattern of Japanese food consumption centring for the most part on commercialised versions of the fresh and processed foods that had accompanied rice in the urban diet of the Tokugawa period. The range of side dishes and accompaniments was expanded by the inclusion of some Western- and Chinese-style elements where these fitted in, and restaurants offered a growing variety of types of food, even if typically adapted to be served alongside rice. Like *sukiyaki* earlier, curry-rice, *tonkatsu* and *rāmen* emerged as standard Japanese ways to accommodate meat and other elements of supposedly nutritionally superior cuisines. It remained, however, chiefly in the form of treats, snacks and drinks that new products entered into the lives of food consumers: sugar, chocolate and coffee – along with tea the 'drug foods' of the consumer revolution in Europe – came to be adopted as sources of comfort and relaxation, while beer began its relentless progress towards the dominant role in masculine social life that it now occupies. While the less well-off continued in rural areas to

---

[35] See Appendix, Table 5.
[36] For more on the story of beer consumption, see Francks 2009 or Kirin Bīru 1984.

eat mixed-grain stews and in the cities large amounts of rice with whatever side dishes they could afford, the new middle classes were busy
laying down the structure of the more diversified and commercialised
pattern of food and drink consumption that almost all were to adopt in
the post-war years.

Clothes

Most photographs of city street scenes in inter-war Japan show the
majority of men dressed in Western style and the majority of women in
Japanese style. This impression is confirmed by the numbers collected
when contemporary journalists and sociologists went out counting.[37]
Nonetheless, within this broad pattern, outfits were very far from being
uniforms, as both Western and Japanese dress offered a widening and
sometimes bewildering range of variations through which image and
fashion could be expressed. Dressing in a 'modern' way was far from
being simply a matter of wearing what Westerners wore, and inter-war
Japanese people continued the process of learning to live with and enjoy
fashion within the world of the kimono, as much as that of the skirt and
the suit.

For men in urban white-collar jobs, the Western-style suit proved not
just a symbol of modernity but also more convenient and functional, in
the context of offices in which shoes were worn and people sat on chairs
at desks. By the 1920s, mail order was bringing the salaryman's suit
even to distant outposts, such as the colonies, without tailors or department stores.[38] Nonetheless, there were all sorts of ways in which a suit-
based outfit could be varied: the sociologist Kon Wajirō, conducting
'scientific' observations of Tokyo street life in the 1920s, categorised
men according to the ties – bow ties, 'bohemian' ties and so on – and
tie-pins they wore; hats and shoes offered considerable scope for styl-
istic variation, as did overcoats, waistcoats and watches.[39] Moreover,
most men who wore suits to the office continued to wear Japanese-
style clothes on other occasions: for example, at home, where they were
more comfortable and convenient for shoe-less *tatami*-based living, or
when out and about with wives and daughters wearing kimono. The
outer garments worn on such occasions typically remained plain and
conservative, but fashion and modernity could still be expressed by
means of undergarments and linings decorated with war scenes, planes,
trains or skyscrapers.[40] Manual workers in town and country continued

[37] Ogi 1970: 156.   [38] Takemura 2004: 101–2.
[39] Silverberg 1992: 37–9.   [40] Van Assche 2005: 27.

to wear Japanese-style work clothes, although those required to wear uniforms – soldiers and sailors, railway staff, schoolchildren and many more – usually had Western-style outfits.

On the other hand, most women, even those with modern jobs in the cities, continued to wear Japanese-style outfits in and out of the home. By the 1920s, girls' school uniforms were Western-style – basically the same unflattering pleated skirts and 'sailor suit' tops as are still often required in Japan today – and something of a status symbol at a time when not all families could afford to keep their daughters in school, but most girls reverted to kimono once they had graduated.[41] Western-style uniforms went with certain kinds of job, such as nurse or bus conductor, and department stores famously required their female assistants to wear Western-style outfits following a number of fatalities among female staff who, so the story goes, refused to jump from a burning department store because their kimono outfits had not necessitated underwear. But those required to wear Western-style frequently commuted in kimono and changed for work.[42] The modernity implied by the wearing of Western-style dress was clearly not something most women outside the cosmopolitan rich or intellectual elites wished to display. Girls from 'nice families' did not wear dresses or skirts unless they wanted to make a point and demonstrate rebellion or independence.

However, the wearing of a kimono did not preclude, any more than it had ever done, the making of a fashion statement. New kimono styles continued to emerge, with design features that made them more practical for modern city life, such as more narrowly cut sleeves. The spread of chemical dyes and electric equipment among smaller-scale textile producers reduced costs and made it possible to offer new patterns and designs to a widening market. In particular, the inter-war period saw a spectacular boom in production and sales of the machine-made, stencil-dyed silk known as *meisen*, originally made from waste silk and relatively cheap, but still soft and lustrous like much more expensive fabrics.[43] *Meisen* silk had been produced since the Tokugawa period in Gumma prefecture, just to the north of Tokyo, as a cheap but strong kimono fabric in traditional striped patterns. However, by the time of the First World War, production was being mechanised to meet a growing demand for the fabric in striking new designs which could be consistently reproduced to create good-quality, fashionable, but not too expensive, kimono, and by the 1930s the use of synthetic fibres was bringing the price down further. *Meisen* made it possible

[41] Ogi 1970: 154–6.   [42] Ogi 1970: 156.
[43] Nitta, Tanaka and Koyama 2003: 54–76; see also Van Assche 2005: 25, 214.

Figure 5.6 Fashions in *meisen* kimono for 1930, as shown in a women's magazine. Nitta, Tanaka and Koyama 2003: 74; courtesy of the Edo-Tokyo Museum.

for Tokyo department stores to design and commission, and for many more ordinary consumers to buy, a regular stream of changing designs, many of them incorporating Western influences, such as art nouveau and art deco, alongside traditional motifs. Department stores advertised this season's fashion in women's magazines and used *meisen* kimono to create striking displays in-store (Fig. 5.6). The combination of technological development among traditional textile producers with department-store sales strategies enabled many more women – often now, in the cities at least, earning some money of their own and freer to make their own spending choices – to dress up and step out in what was visibly the latest fashion.[44]

At the same time, dressing in Japanese style did not rule out the use of a whole array of more or less Western-style accessories to demonstrate

[44] In 1930, over half of the output of silk cloth in Japan was *meisen*; 51 per cent of the women observed by Kon Wajirō walking on the Ginza in May 1925 were wearing *meisen* (Nitta, Tanaka and Koyama 2003: 62, 64). It is possible to see the *meisen* boom as paving the way for the development of contemporary street fashion in Japan, providing a vehicle not for high-fashion *haute couture*, but for the day-to-day enjoyment of fashion as *o-share* – dressing up and going out to walk about and be seen (Nitta, Tanaka and Koyama 2003: 76).

image and fashionableness. Western hairstyles – flapper-style bobs, plaits, perms, swept-up arrangements with flowers or art deco hair-clips – became more popular;[45] although too much make-up was considered 'provincial' by city sophisticates, cosmetics companies such as Shiseidō, importing the techniques and products of Western-style cosmetics manufacture, achieved large national markets.[46] Western-style sportswear demonstrated a middle-class ability to engage in fashionably healthy pursuits such as sea-bathing or hiking, while Western breeds of pet dogs were 'symbols of comfortable domesticity'.[47] Panama hats for men and toques for women were key 'modern' accessories, along with Harold Lloyd glasses,[48] and Western-style shoes, gloves and handbags were easy to combine with kimono and more practical for city life than their Japanese-style equivalents. Shawls and mufflers in lace or brocade provided warmth around the open neck of the kimono, while fox-fur collars and tippets on kimono overgarments were defining symbols of 'Taishō chic'.[49] Equally, though, the detachable kimono collar (*han-eri*) was a key battleground for the fashion-conscious – embroidered, threaded with gold lamé, decorated with coral, pearl or even diamonds and sometimes more expensive than the kimono itself.[50]

Meanwhile, outside the realms of fashion and city life, adaptations continued to take place to fit clothes to the changing demands of modern life. The spread of the sewing machine enabled women to make, mend and adapt clothing to suit their families' needs much more easily than in the era of hand-sewing, and women's magazines were full of instructions on how to make practical items such as Western-style children's clothes, which were promoted as cheap and practical.[51] The all-encompassing white apron, designed to keep sleeves and all other parts of a kimono out of the way while doing housework, was nationally adopted in the inter-war years as a symbol of the hygienic modern housewife's profession (Fig. 5.7).[52] Those devoted to the 'rationalisation' of everyday life encouraged women to make and wear the *appappa*,

---

[45] By 1939, there were 850 hair salons in Tokyo offering perms. War-time governments disapproved of perms (*pāmanento*) but women continued to have them, even if under a Japanese pseudonym such as *denpatsu* (electric hair) (Brown and Minichiello 2001: 20).

[46] Seidensticker 1983: 43.

[47] Jō 2007: 262; Brown and Minichiello 2001: 20, 54.

[48] Kon Wajirō observed that 34 per cent of the men walking on the Ginza were wearing glasses (Nitta, Tanaka and Koyama 2003: 52).

[49] The Meiji emperor died in 1912. The Taishō period (1912–26) was the reign of his successor.

[50] Nakamura 2005: 76.   [51] Sand 2003: 211.

[52] Sand 2003: 71–3. Café waitresses also wore distinctive versions of the apron (Nitta, Tanaka and Koyama 2003: 50).

Figure 5.7 A housewife in her apron advertises a branded camphor-based insect repellent in a 1936 magazine.

a standardised cotton shift dress promoted as cool for summer and a kind of bridge into Western-style clothing. As war approached, however, Japanese-style austerity demanded that women, of whom increasing amounts of manual work within and outside the home were being required, dress in *monpe*, the baggy trousers in traditional patterns that rural women had worn while working in the fields.[53] Women

---

[53] *Monpe* were generally disliked as ugly and old-fashioned. It eventually became unpatriotic to express such a view, but it was possible to dress your *monpe* up a bit, as a little show of resistance (Ogi 1970: 163–4).

in headscarves and *monpe*, in fields and factories, mending roads or clearing up after air-raids, were to provide the iconic image of the female contribution to war work.

Household goods

The persistence of Japanese-style house design, along with Japanese cooking and eating patterns, sleeping arrangements and facilities for entertaining guests and spending free time, demanded a certain continuity in the kinds of goods that were acquired and used around the house. Nonetheless, by the inter-war years, growing numbers of urban households, including many in public housing and rented row-houses, had their own kitchens, toilets and washing facilities, hence the capacity and incentive to accumulate more in the form of plates and bowls, cooking utensils, futon, small-scale furniture and so on.[54] In rural areas, and in the older parts of towns and cities, new acquisitions were more constrained by existing housing structures and stocks of goods owned or inherited, but even here more and new goods could often be accommodated without disrupting the underlying pattern of everyday life. The degree to which new goods symbolised a rebellious modernity or rather a more comfortable and efficient version of the Japanese lifestyle was up to the consumer.

Many of these new goods were reflections of the use of new materials to produce cheaper and more convenient items. Glass, for instance, became much more common with the spread of beer and other drinks that were not served in ceramic cups; versions of Japanese-style household goods, such as *bentō* boxes, in aluminium or synthetic materials began to come on the market. The bicycle was the one larger-scale item widely owned by the inter-war years, while sewing machines, cameras and some small-scale electrical items, such as heaters, fans, irons and radios, were beginning to spread, though they were still mainly confined to the relatively well-off.[55] The larger-scale electrical goods, such as fridges and washing machines, that were beginning to fill suburban American houses, not to mention the cars that made the suburbs possible, were unattainable luxuries for all but the richest in Japan.[56]

---

[54] See Appendix, Table 5, for estimates of the growth in expenditure on such items in total.

[55] By 1930, 8 million bicycles were in use among the 14 million households in the country. The Singer Sewing Machine Company had 800 shops throughout the Japanese empire by then, but still probably fewer than 5 per cent of households owned items such as sewing machines or radios (Gordon 2007: 5–6).

[56] Kendall Brown and Sharon Minichiello reproduce a Taishō-period folding screen portraying the three daughters of the founder of Hitachi, all in luxury kimonos but

At the same time, however, for the emerging middle classes, and especially the housewives among them, the purchase of household goods was not just a matter of raising levels of comfort and convenience, but also of coming to terms with the potential uses and meanings of an expanding range of goods and the scope that they offered for the expression of evolving lifestyles. The decoration of the traditional Japanese house had been largely a male preserve, a matter of selecting artistic items – which might nonetheless range from the cheap and ordinary to the most expensive and exquisite examples of craftsmanship, taste and fashion – from the household's collection for display at appropriate times of the year. The new single-family suburban houses, on the other hand, were the domain of the housewife – 'places of consumption and female labour'[57] – and their décor could express the middle-class lifestyle she desired to create out of possibilities opening up to many more outside the elite classes. For the media, this meant a growing concern with the idea of *seikatsu*, literally 'life', but taken to imply, as Jordan Sand defines it, 'the material life generated by modern capitalism, a world of new commodities to be negotiated'.[58]

This reflected the fact that devising a furnishing strategy for what were still small and predominantly Japanese-style houses and apartments was not a simple matter. Those consumers who aspired to what became known as the 'culture life' (*bunka seikatsu*) sought furnishings that were modern but also suited to their own Japanese tastes and structures. Bamboo and rattan furniture – vaguely 'oriental' but fulfilling the functions of Western-style items – became popular for proper or 'converted' (by means of, for example, rugs over *tatami*) Western-style rooms. Rather than using hierarchically arranged individual trays, modern middle-class families came together to eat around a single table, but this was usually low and designed for those sitting on cushions on the floor (Fig. 5.8).[59] Instead of traditional scrolls, 'culture' households should display Western-style paintings, which department stores were keen to promote in their exhibition spaces but, since Japanese architectural styles and building methods did not create large areas of solid blank wall, artists developed lines in small, oblong, Western-style oil paintings that would fit the wall spaces above sliding doors and panels.[60] Relatively cheap items such as shelves or lamps in art nouveau-type

posed around a glamorous car and sporting a Leica camera as an accessory (Brown and Minichiello 2001: 46–9).

[57] Sand 2003: 164.   [58] Sand 2000: 116.

[59] In fact, Sand suggests, working-class families probably adopted single tables earlier than better-off ones, as they were more convenient for smaller spaces (Sand 2003: 36).

[60] Sand 2003: 123–4.

Figure 5.8 The family of a factory-employed mechanic eating round
their single table. Asahi Shinbun 1933: 37.

designs could be used to give a modern touch to otherwise Japanese-
style rooms.

In many ways the most significant part of the house for the new
middle-class housewife was, however, the kitchen. The provision of
gas, electricity and piped water, in the towns and cities at least, opened
up the possibility of cooking on a gas ring, washing up in a sink and in
general creating a kitchen with work tops and storage space designed
for use standing up. Such kitchens were widely promoted by the proponents of 'rationalisation' and, although possibly of greatest benefit
to the live-in maid whom most middle-class households still employed,
became a standard symbol of efficient, hygienic, modern household
management. The 'culture houses' that architects designed for the
modern suburban family were all equipped with such a kitchen, alongside the obligatory Western-style study and reception room and the
Japanese-style living and sleeping rooms where, one suspects, the family still felt most comfortable.[61]

By the inter-war years, therefore, household consumer goods were
becoming a key element in defining the respectable, modern, middle

[61] See surviving examples in e.g. the Edo-Tokyo Open-Air Architectural Museum.

class – the middling sort, as they were termed in eighteenth-century England.[62] This was increasingly, though, a definition in terms of the kinds of goods acquired, rather than the quantity or cost, and many of those who aspired to middle-class status, on the basis of their educational qualifications and white-collar jobs, did so armed with only modest salaries. The ideal middle-class home, as Sand describes it, was comfortable, efficient and simple: 'a tidy suburban house and garden with running water and gas in the kitchen and a few electric appliances, ideally with a Western room containing rattan chairs, a set of one-yen books, a radio or a gramophone, or better still, a piano or organ; a clean change of Japanese clothes in the evening and Western clothes in the morning for the breadwinner, a white *kappōgi* apron and silk kimono for his wife, and Western clothes for the children'.[63] Such a home, furnished with the goods that defined middle-class comfort and respectability, was to remain the ideal throughout the post-war decades, though one achievable by many more families in the expanding middle class created by the economic miracle.

Attitudes to modern consumption

By the inter-war years, Japanese people were confronting a range of goods that was broadening to encompass not just the food products, clothing and household goods on which they had honed their skills as consumers and the fashionable Western-style accessories and gadgets that they had been enjoying since Meiji times, but also now the everyday goods that embodied the modernity of the West. Nonetheless, the clear dichotomy between 'Japanese' and 'Western' or 'American', beloved of later theorists and epitomised in Edward Seidensticker's concept of the 'double life' – the need to lead, and switch between, a Japanese-style and a Western-style life – does not appear to have been so very problematic for inter-war consumers, who constructed their everyday lives out of an eclectic mixture of 'traditional', 'modernised Japanese' and 'Western' goods and leisure activities.[64] Although department stores and the media undoubtedly sought to 'educate' consumers in the desirability and superiority of new Western-style goods, consumer use of such items was selective and adapted to particular needs and tastes and to the physical and social infrastructure within which consumption

---

[62] Furnishings and household goods – chairs and tables, mirrors, china, draperies – had similarly served to define the respectable middling sort in eighteenth- and early nineteenth-century Europe and North America. See e.g. Shammas 1990.

[63] Sand 2003: 225–6.   [64] On this point, see Silverberg 1992.

took place. More significant, perhaps, than the new goods themselves was the impact of modernity on the production and marketing of the Japanese-style goods that continued to dominate everyday consumer life.

Nonetheless, the burgeoning array of goods – some of them undoubtedly 'foreign' in their uses and connotations (though relatively rarely in their manufacture) – and the choices that it presented to consumers did oblige both the political and intellectual elites to confront the issues that the emergence of the modern consumer raises. Although consumers themselves generally seem to have got on with enjoying the growing variety of goods available to them and experimenting with new possibilities, the government became increasingly concerned about the implications of consumption growth both for the capacity to save and invest and for national identity, while media commentators debated the best ways to direct consumption towards rational, efficient and moral ends. The question of how it might be possible to be a good Japanese citizen while wanting and enjoying the material goods associated with everyday life in the Western nations with which Japan was now coming into conflict exercised Japanese intellectuals and political leaders, just as similar issues have exercised their counterparts in, for example, China in the past and the present. Whether their agonising had much effect in the long term, when confronted with, on the one hand, the forces of global modernity and, on the other, the capacity of consumers to devise their own versions of modern everyday life, is perhaps open to doubt. In the short term, however, the road to war created conditions under which frugality, rationality and patriotic consumption (and saving) were the order of the day.

The state and consumption

It is surely the case that Japanese governments have never had much interest in enabling the population to spend more on consumption. The Tokugawa regime's attempts to control consumer activity through sumptuary laws had broken down in the face of the rising incomes and fluid social trends of the first half of the nineteenth century. Thereafter, however, the Meiji government, although recognising that the 'civilisation and enlightenment' that they pursued might sometimes be embodied in the kinds of consumer goods that would impress Western visitors, essentially concerned itself with raising investment in the industries and infrastructure that formed the basis of economic and political power in the late nineteenth-century world. This meant trying to maximise savings and taxation, and if necessary discouraging spending on consumption as far as possible. The incomes of the majority rural population were taxed relatively heavily via taxation on land; the tax on sake was frequently raised, to the chagrin of local brewers throughout the country; and little policy consideration was given to the kinds of small-scale industry that produced most everyday consumption goods. The political reaction to this generated some shift in national and, more significantly, local government policy towards 'traditional' manufacturing, largely of consumer goods, but for the most part such local industries found their own ways of developing technologically and responding to consumer demand.[65]

Saving, on the other hand, was positively encouraged, along with the frugality and sensible, if necessary deferred, consumption on which it depended. The Post Office savings system had been established as early as 1875 to provide small savers, in town and country, with a secure and easily accessible vehicle for their savings, while savings banks and local mutual savings groups, some with a long history, continued to enable ordinary rural and urban households to save what they could for emergencies, weddings/dowries and small-scale investments. By the 1920s, the authorities were running sophisticated campaigns to promote savings, using a wide range of modern advertising techniques as well as a network of community groups and activists employing 'moral suasion'.[66]

By this time, however, with the majority of the population now heavily reliant on a market that offered an ever widening range of goods, it was much harder to draw the kind of straightforward luxury/necessity dividing line on which campaigns to economise and save might once have been based. Spending on some kinds of goods, while not strictly essential for survival, might now be necessary from the point of view of leading the kind of civilised lifestyle appropriate to the modern Japanese family. The state, along with the civil society groups linked to it, was therefore coming to distinguish between the 'rational', 'efficient' consumption of modern goods, which was educational and good, and the 'irrational' consumption of traditional goods – elaborate dowry collections, eating and drinking at local festivities and so on – which was 'wasteful' and bad. The modern housewife/household manager should plan the family's budget, obtaining new goods where they contributed towards a healthy and efficient lifestyle and the long-term capacity to save. To this end, she should keep an account book

---

[65] For Meiji-period examples, see Pratt 1999: ch. 6. See also various cases in Tanimoto 2006a.
[66] Garon 1998.

and cut out 'wasteful' expenditure, but buy a sewing machine, if necessary on credit, on which to sew Western-style clothes for her children
and make sure her husband ate (economical amounts of) meat. Savings campaigns may thus have had less effect in damning consumption
and glorifying frugality as such than in validating a particular kind of
middle-class lifestyle.[67]

Given this, there is not a lot of evidence that, in the pre-war period,
such campaigns had much success in constraining consumption expenditure for the macro-economic goals the government espoused. Overall
savings rates appear to have been quite volatile but not on average especially high, and consumption expenditure continued to grow.[68] Over
the pre-Second World War period as a whole (from 1887), on average
60–70 per cent of the overall growth of expenditure in the economy was
accounted for by growth in personal consumption, and, although this
proportion did decline over time, it was only in the depths of the inter-
war depression that investment or exports contributed more to growth.[69]
Growing expenditure on sake and beer, tobacco and all sorts of processed-food products, as well as on a whole range of leisure activities,
suggests that consumers themselves were determined on the immediate
enjoyment of at least part of their rising incomes, and not necessarily in
the 'rational' ways that the great and the good prescribed.

Nonetheless, during the difficult times of the inter-war years, and
especially as the government pursued the deflationary policy necessitated by its (ultimately unsuccessful) attempt to return Japan to the
gold standard, officials and businessmen alike railed against consumers'
pursuit of 'luxury' and 'waste' and urged economy and frugality. In
the spirit of the times, as Mark Metzler points out, major businesses
did not appear to see domestic consumption demand as significant for
economic growth and regarded Japanese people 'more as their workers
than their customers', while the finance minister could urge the people
to 'cultivate the beautiful customs of self-control and saving'.[70] Inoue
Junnosuke, the chief proponent of the return to the gold standard as a
solution to the macro-economic and financial difficulties experienced
by Japan (along with many other countries) in the 1920s, was particularly critical of women, as the guardians of the nation's purses, arguing
that 'women's sin' of 'unreasonable consumption' was the major cause
of the problem.[71]

[67] For this argument, see Garon 2000.
[68] See Appendix, Table 1, and Horioka 1993: 259–64.
[69] See Appendix, Table 2.   [70] Metzler 2006: 140, 154.
[71] Metzler 2006: 206. According to Inoue, 'women's understanding in regard to the
economy is extremely slight'.

By the 1930s, there were voices arguing against this moralising view of consumption spending as a wicked indulgence of 'luxury'. The journalist and future post-war government minister Ishibashi Tanzan, influenced by the contemporary writings of J. M. Keynes, argued that consumption demand generated increased production and economic growth and should be promoted as the solution to the Depression.[72] Within government itself, Inoue's successor as finance minister, Takahashi Korekiyo, who took Japan off the gold standard in 1931, had long believed that increasing ordinary consumption was both central to the growth of the economy and a key goal of economic policy.[73] His instinctive prefiguring of Keynes' understanding of the role of consumption expenditure within the macro-economy provided the basis for policies that lifted Japan out of Depression in the early 1930s considerably earlier than most other economies and might have set the country on a different course from the one pursued so disastrously by his successors. However, following his assassination in 1936, those advocating increased military expenditure, on the basis of limiting consumption, moved into the ascendancy. Thereafter, the moral belief in the ability of the Japanese people to save and to endure hardship became more and more central to the strategy of the government and military leadership as war approached; Ishibashi's vision of a mass consumption society was to remain, for the moment, ahead of its time.

Hence, with the onset of war-economy conditions, resources were increasingly re-allocated to military-related production, supplies of consumer goods dwindled and household savings grew. Although war-related spending was largely financed through more or less voluntary economies and savings on the part of the population, strict rationing and all kinds of social and institutional pressure on households to save for the nation clearly played a major part in this. It may be, as Sheldon Garon argues, that war-time austerity drives combined with the cumulative effect of pre-war 'anti-luxury' and savings campaigns going back to the turn of the century to generate the positive attitude to saving (and conversely ambivalence towards consumption) of

[72] 'We still want to wear good clothes and to live in good houses, we want good furniture, we want pianos and violins, we want better radio sets, we want to see plays and go to movies ... such desires are limitless. To properly satisfy these desires, if we encourage consumption, production will necessarily increase accordingly' (translated and quoted in Metzler 2006: 243).

[73] As Richard Smethurst shows, Takahashi had taken on board the views of Maeda Masana, one of his mentors in the 1880s, as to the importance of raising ordinary people's living standards and promoting local-level production of consumer goods. For a full account of Takahashi's remarkable life and economic understanding, see Smethurst 2007.

the post-war years.[74] At any rate, though such campaigns may not, in the long run, have done much to quell Japanese people's need and desire for the material goods that the industrial economy can produce, they certainly helped to establish the model of the efficient, housewife-run, middle-class home, combating 'waste' and 'irrational' spending, that was to condition the pattern of consumer activity through the economic miracle and beyond.

Debating modern life

Meanwhile, the Japanese state was by no means alone in worrying about the implications of increasing consumption of an ever widening range of goods. Like their counterparts in other parts of the world, the inter-war Japanese media and intellectual elite debated, and tried to influence, the ways in which consumers utilised the growing abundance of goods and the meanings that might be embodied in modern everyday life. On a practical level, women's magazines and department store publications sought to educate consumers in the appropriate use of new products, while architects competed to design homes in which the 'culture life' could be lived. But behind this lay difficult issues to do with, on the one hand, the relation of goods to social and family life – gender roles in particular – and, on the other, conceptions of Japanese cultural identity in the face of new goods that might embody 'Western values'.

For the new middle classes, the purchase and use of new goods formed an integral part of the 'modern life' to which many aspired. Suburban 'culture houses' were designed to be inhabited by modern couples, enjoying romantic privacy in their own bedrooms and eating together at their single tables. There might be space for a maid and eventually children, but not for accommodating parents or entertaining wider kinship groups and community networks. The knowledge and skills that mother had passed on to daughter and daughter-in-law – preserving food, sewing and patching kimono, knowing what gifts to give to whom – were rendered obsolete by commercial goods, and it was the young wife, with her education and training in modern ways, who now knew what to buy and how to use it. The equipment and decoration of the house became matters for her personal choice, rather than reflections of household tradition.

Modern goods and their surroundings therefore embodied threatening implications for existing structures of power and authority within the family. The fact that modern houses had lockable doors, enabling

---

[74] Garon 2000.

women to go out during the day rather than perform their traditional roles of guarding the house and entertaining visitors, was regarded as liberating by some women's magazines, but bemoaned by other commentators concerned with the undermining of family values. The fear that the conjugal intimacy made possible by separate bedrooms would compromise extended family relations and dangerously liberate female sexuality was reflected in police moves to ban the term 'double bed' from advertisements for houses and hotels.[75] While men were expected to appreciate the freedoms made possible by Western-style clothes, the same was not true for women – only the rather scary 'modern girl' dressed in Western-style when she did not need to.

Nonetheless, in some situations modern goods were increasingly unavoidable, as well as rational, efficient and indeed sometimes desirable, and for most people it was necessary to find a compromise way round the dilemmas that modernity posed. For many in the authorities and the elite, part of the solution lay in emphasis on the new role women could play as modern housewives, remaining within the home, of course, but developing the skills necessary for the scientific management of a healthy and happy household and its goods and finances. This chimed in with the 'good wife, wise mother' ideology that the inter-war state was applying to women's issues, but added a layer of professionalisation – embodied in the uniform apron and the account book – that recognised the new roles that modern goods gave to married women. As food choices expanded and began to include new items, menus had to be thought about and new ways of cooking learnt; instead of directing the home production of miso and pickles and organising the giving and receiving of gifts in kind, the modern housewife needed the skills to keep her account book up to date, recording the expenditures on goods that modern life involved. Although women continued to make up a significant part of the labour force outside the home and to contribute to production alongside their husbands and fathers in a whole range of small-scale businesses, it was their role as housewives and mothers that was emphasised in the media and government propaganda. The growing abundance of goods and gadgets was not to liberate them from household chores, but rather to demand of them a professional commitment to the rational and scientific management of the everyday life of their families. The dangerous aspects of consumerism could be neutralised if such features of it as the availability of instalment-plan consumer credit could be used to nurture 'disciplined female saver-consumers who might pursue pleasure, but whose impulse to shop was balanced by the obligation to pay and whose purchases were likewise valued for building the national economy'.[76]

For some, however, this was not enough to combat the threat that modern goods, and the lifestyle they embodied, posed to the essential nature of Japanese society. As conflict with 'the West' intensified through the 1930s, intellectuals became concerned to try to define what was distinctive about 'Japanese civilisation' and to provide a philosophical basis for the values, traditions and 'beautiful customs' that it involved. In their efforts to define a Japanese way of 'overcoming modernity', American-style consumerism was seen as the enemy of the true and eternal Japanese understanding of, and relation to, the material world: 'the twentieth century had witnessed the emergence of a consumer culture satisfied only with the possession of plenty rather than with the quality and beauty of scarcity and restraint. American democracy, therefore, had as its real substance the satisfaction of the masses with trivial goods produced in large quantities, a condition that had permeated Japanese life as well.'[77]

One possible response to this threat lay in a return to the purity and simplicity of rural life close to nature, and a new respect was accorded to the skills and crafts that produced traditional goods and underlay community activity. Traditional arts and pastimes were revived but, in the modern world of the inter-war years, even they represented something new and different: the tea ceremony enjoyed growing popularity, no longer as the elegant pursuit of country gentlemen, but rather as a training in etiquette and deportment for middle-class young women. Traditional pottery and textiles became *mingei* (people's art), inspiring new schools of artists and craftsmen who exhibited in galleries and designed expensive furniture and houses. By the 1930s, it was no longer possible for the 'rural' and 'traditional' to be anything other than fashion choices for those who lived within the consumer culture of the urban world.

In such ways, people coped with the possibilities and dilemmas posed by life in the modern material world. New goods might be challenging in many ways but, by the inter-war years, beer-drinking and baseball were already too much embedded in Japanese life to be extirpated as 'foreign' – all one could do was invent Japanese terms for them and

---

[76] Gordon 2006: 155. See also Gordon 2007: 10 describing advertisements – in this case for sewing machines – that promoted such 'rational' purchases on the grounds that they opened up opportunities for more leisure and shopping.

[77] Najita and Harootunian 1988: 766.

imbue their practice with Japanese values. With the onset of the rural depression of the early 1930s, reformers, policy-makers and rural leaders became more concerned with improving standards of living in the countryside than with preserving the moral values inherent in rural crafts and festivals. Urban philanthropists, horrified at the state of rural kitchens, set out to train village women in the business of hygienic and efficient housekeeping,[78] while the mass-circulation magazine of the national organisation of agricultural co-operatives provided recipes and sewing tips alongside technical advice for farmers and patriotic and uplifting news and stories. Meanwhile, in their everyday lives and consumption choices, 'new middle-class' families continued to aspire to elements of the 'modern', 'rational', 'scientific' and in many ways Western-style life that they read about in newspapers and magazines and saw in the cinema, while at the same continuing to consume the Japanese-style goods and services that had come to constitute the symbols and substance of a 'civilised' Japanese way of life.

With rising incomes coinciding with the development of improved production and marketing techniques in fields such as Japanese-style food and drink, clothing and household goods, more and more people were able to enjoy, through the inter-war years, 'mass market' versions of what had once been the privileges of the rich, while adapting and enjoying Western-style goods as and when they fitted in. The state of war, which was beginning to affect everyday life by the late 1930s, ultimately reduced the emerging consumers of the inter-war period to bartering and begging for the means of subsistence. Nonetheless, they had by then already laid down the basis for the Japanese version of the middle-class lifestyle that, once the horrors of war were over, the post-war economic miracle made a feasible goal for the majority of Japanese households.

[78] Partner 2001.

6   The electrical household: consumption and the economic miracle

[Y]our National washing machine will clean your washing beauti-fully. The mechanism is scientifically set to protect fibers, and to use only a small amount of soap and electricity. Housewives, please use the superb National electric washer to keep yourselves ever young and beautiful, and to have plenty of time for self-improvement and leisure.[1]

During the later stages of the Second World War and the aftermath of Japan's surrender in August 1945, Japanese people who had lived through the war on the mainland, together with the 6 million or more returning from battlefields and colonial territories elsewhere in Asia, faced near-starvation conditions. Japan's subsequent occupation and government by a US-dominated coalition of forces brought aid and the gradual revival of domestic production, so that by 1952, when the Occupation formally ended, pre-war levels of output had largely been re-established. Thereafter, Japan's economy entered the period of inter-nationally unprecedented high-speed growth that is generally known as the economic miracle. By the early 1970s, when a series of 'external shocks' triggered the end of miracle growth, Japan had entered the top division of industrialised countries and was home to some of the world's most competitive producers of manufactured goods ranging from ships, cars and motorcycles through to the transistor radios, televisions and all manner of household electrical goods that transformed everyday life in the post-war world.

Except in as far as it is treated as 'export-led', the Japanese eco-nomic miracle is typically regarded as a 'supply-side' phenomenon. The standard picture views it as driven by investment, technological improvements and rising labour productivity, aided and abetted by gov-ernment policy and effective business organisation, and it is as savers

---

[1] A 1960s radio advertisement for National washing machines, preceding a pro-gramme sponsored by the manufacturer Matsushita; translated and quoted in Partner 1999: 171.

that Japanese households are seen as playing their major part in the process. In fact, however, although it can be argued that rising export potential was eventually to become a significant stimulator of economic growth, the share of exports in Japan's overall output has remained small, compared with that observed in many other industrial countries. The domestic consumer market, on the other hand, grew to be massive (see Appendix, Tables 1, 2 and 4), despite the high rate of saving, and continued to be central to the activities of most Japanese producers, so that it was there, from the 1950s onwards, that the big names of post-war Japanese manufacturing learnt their trade. The desire of consumers to acquire the goods that came to represent the comfortable family life of the Japanese middle-class household was the necessary condition underlying the investment decisions of Japanese firms. It was by means of this investment that new technology was embodied in ever expanding production facilities and that output grew, in turn generating the rising incomes that enabled households to realise the dream known as *mai hōmu* (my home).

From war and occupation to economic miracle: state, society and mass consumption

The period that saw Japan immersed in war, at first on the Asian mainland and then more widely in the Pacific, was for many years afterwards bracketed off as the 'dark valley', a disastrous but aberrant deviation from the pre-war path towards economic growth and democracy to which the nation returned after defeat and occupation. More recently, however, it has become possible to look again at the war-time period and to re-evaluate its influence on subsequent developments. The institutional structures put in place in the effort to mobilise for war are now seen to have survived to play a part in promoting the economic miracle, so that, for example, the systems through which the state sought to manage consumption and encourage savings continued to influence the ways in which ordinary consumers spent and saved. Within this framework, as economic growth and urbanisation resumed at unprecedented rates, growing numbers of households were able to conform to the pattern of middle-class life that had started to emerge in the inter-war years. As they began to surround themselves with the post-war versions of the goods in which the comfortable but modern middle-class lifestyle was embodied, these 'middle masses' carried out the consumption expenditure that drove the growth of Japanese industry and established Japanese consumer-goods producers as world-beaters in their fields. Nonetheless, as a 'mass market' they retained and developed the characteristics that had been forming over the long consumption history that Japan had already experienced.

Rationing and regulation in war and peace

Japan's economy was increasingly being placed on a war footing through the first half of the 1930s, and full-scale military operations in China began with the Marco Polo Bridge Incident in 1937. From then until the surrender in 1945, military production was prioritised in the allocation of the dwindling resources of labour and raw materials, and supplies of consumer goods, including food, became more and more scarce. The state came to play a determining role in the allocation of production inputs and final output. Rationing of basic food items began in 1940, and people became used to obtaining much of what they needed, or at least could get, through neighbourhood associations, mobilised by the state to provide the organisation and management of the distribution of goods, as well as much else.[2] Shortages were to continue after the surrender, though mitigated by means of goods supplied, formally and informally, by the American officials and troops based in Japan as part of the Occupation. High rates of inflation nonetheless persisted through to the drastic application of deflationary measures – the so-called Dodge Line – in 1949, necessitating continued price controls and rationing. To a significant extent, therefore, how much and what households could consume came to be determined by the state, leaving a legacy of state intervention in and regulation of consumption – but also of resistance and circumvention – that was to persist long after the end of war-time conditions.

This is exemplified in the history of what came to be known as the Food Control System. As the war progressed, farm households began to struggle to maintain agricultural output in the face of the conscription of rural workers and shortages of fuel, fertiliser and equipment.[3] Under legislation that culminated in the 1942 Food Control Law, the output of rice and other key food crops was requisitioned by the state at low prices and allocated to meet the needs of the military and the civilian population. By the closing years of the war, the rations available to urban households had become small and erratic: sweet potatoes largely replaced rice, and it was necessary to apply considerable ingenuity to the cooking of the increasingly unpalatable vegetables and

---

[2] Scherer 1999: 108; Havens 1978: ch. 5.
[3] In fact, food production held up until the final phase of the war and no one starved. Nonetheless, there were huge problems with the food supply and distribution system, caused by factors such as the collapse of imports, poor-quality produce and so on.

bits of fish that were all that could be had.[4] Once the war was over, priority was given to the revival of agricultural production, and this, along with food aid from the United States, helped to restore food supplies. Nonetheless, the Food Control System, under which, theoretically at least, the entire rice crop was acquired by the state's Food Agency and marketed at controlled prices by state-regulated dealers, remained in place, as the state retained responsibility for the supply of the 'staple food'.

In due course, the Food Control System became the chief mechanism whereby the state provided support and subsidy to farmers, and in general the widespread regulatory intervention in the economy known as 'industrial policy' – much of it originating, in many ways, in pre-war and war-time mobilisation and control measures – is seen as aimed at supply-side goals.[5] In the push for economic growth, consumption was subordinated to investment in industrial capacity, just as it had earlier been to the military build-up. Rules and regulations might be justified on the grounds of consumer protection, but their influence on consumers' lives was more significantly felt through their impact on what could be bought, where and at what price. Long after the end of war-time and Occupation rationing and price controls, regulatory restrictions – on imports, on retail provision, on consumer credit, on the degree of competition between domestic producers – continued to influence what consumers could buy, while state promotion of saving continued. As a result, consumer prices remained high, relative to world-market levels, and one day, when business investment ceased to be able to drive the growth of the economy, economic policy-makers were to reap the whirlwind of their less than enthusiastic attitude towards consumer spending.[6]

Nonetheless, the scope and persistence of state control and regulation of consumption were throughout only one side of the story, as Japanese consumers consistently found ways to buy what they needed or wanted. Through the war and beyond, black markets were ubiquitous, and most households acquired at least some of their food and other goods via technically illegal channels, since in practice it was more or less

---

[4] For contemporary accounts of the struggle to acquire edible food, see Yamashita 2005.

[5] For the seminal history of industrial policy, see Johnson 1982.

[6] For this argument, see Katz 1998: ch. 8. It should be pointed out, however, that taxation of consumer spending remained limited or non-existent; it was not until the 1980s that the Japanese government seriously attempted to grasp the political nettle of a consumption tax (value-added tax). The lack of a broad-based consumption tax in the state's armoury was reflected in low levels of government spending in areas such as welfare provision; see Akaishi and Steinmo 2006.

impossible to survive on the erratic food rations available.[7] Direct sales and bartering with farm households were commonplace, and members of urban households travelled long distances, by train or whatever means they could find, in response to tip-offs that food products might be available somewhere in the countryside. Faced with the low prices paid by the state for its quotas of agricultural output, many rural households succumbed to the temptation to engage in private sales or barter food for the valuables accumulated by once superior urbanites. Meanwhile, shopkeepers were in a strong position to short-change customers and divert supplies, while reported cases of ration-fiddling were clearly only the tip of the iceberg. Those with money or, more importantly, the right connections were able to obtain goods that existed for most only as mouth-watering memories of pre-war consumption, and resentment at perceived unfairness and corruption in the distribution of food and other goods certainly existed.[8] Large amounts of police time were spent trying to catch black marketeers, but to little avail in the face of such widespread, small-scale and often necessity-driven law-breaking.[9] By the end of the war huge differences had emerged between free-market and government-stipulated prices, largely undermining the government's attempts to control prices and ration goods.[10]

With rationing and shortages continuing under the Occupation, opportunities for black-market activity became even more rife. Large-scale illegal but tolerated markets emerged in particular areas of big cities, and struggling urban families relied on them for many basic household goods and clothes otherwise unobtainable. The markets came to be controlled and organised by *yakuza* gangs who used them as the economic basis for their later diversification through the post-war period.[11] The goods sold included food bought up privately in the countryside, the products of the many small factories that had lost their former military market and supplies appearing, one way or another, out of the American bases. The markets were jungles for traders and shoppers alike, ruled by the strong arm of the *yakuza*, but their descendants have survived in more legitimate and regular forms, metamorphosing

---

[7] A survey of 2,000 city families carried out in 1943 found half admitting that they bought black-market food, even though most could barely afford the prices charged. By 1944, surveys in Tokyo and Osaka concluded that households were acquiring on average at least a quarter of their food via the black market, considerably more of their fish and vegetables (Havens 1978: 94, 125–6).

[8] For examples, see Yamashita 2005.   [9] Scherer 1999: 114.

[10] Kuroda 1993: 35; Havens 1978: 94.

[11] According to a report by the Public Safety Division of the Occupation authorities, *yakuza* groups controlled 88 per cent of the 45,000 stalls in Tokyo in the late 1940s (Dubro and Kaplan 1987: 65).

Figure 6.1 Stalls sell electrical parts in Akihabara in Tokyo today, as they did under the Occupation.

into the concentrations of small shops and stalls – Tokyo examples include the Ameyokochō area around Ueno and the Akihabara electrical goods district (Figs. 6.1 and 6.2) – operating largely outside the restrictive retail distribution system of the later post-war years.[12]

The experience of scarcity in the war-time and immediate post-war periods thus accustomed consumers both to experimentation with new goods and to a distribution system that combined an outward face of heavy government regulation of legal supply channels with a reality made up of informal ways of getting hold of goods. American food aid came principally in the form of wheat, and just as, during the war, the sweet potato had been perforce adopted as part of the diet outside its traditional areas in the southwest, so now consumers found ways to incorporate bread and noodles into their meal patterns in acceptable and enjoyable ways. But the Americans of course brought much more than just food. The arrival of large numbers of American troops – who

[12] Partner 1999: 48–9. Akihabara has its origins in stalls selling radio components, supplied somehow or other out of military stockpiles and surplus stocks from the US bases, in the immediate post-war years when everyone's radio had gone wrong and parts were in very short supply.

Figure 6.2 The Ameyokochō district of Tokyo, a black market during the Occupation era and still thriving as an area of stalls and small shops.

turned out not to be the monsters portrayed in war-time propaganda – opened up many opportunities for fraternisation, by means of which the money and goods of the richest nation in the world were disbursed among the deprived survivors of war-time Japan.

Prominent among the recipients of this largesse were the many young women positively encouraged by the Japanese authorities to fraternise with the Americans. John Dower cites an estimate that over half of the many millions of dollars laid out on 'recreation' by the Occupation forces went on payments or gifts to the so-called *pan-pan* girls who consorted with the troops. Little luxuries, such as chocolate, cigarettes, lipsticks and nylons, provided an escape from the hardships of post-war life and enabled the *pan-pan* girls to set a style – bright Western-style clothes, conspicuous make-up, high heels, cigarette in hand – amidst the prevailing austerity. As Dower puts it, 'no-one surpassed them as the harbingers of a hedonistic, materialistic, American-style consumer culture'.[13] The areas of Tokyo where concentrations of foreign military personnel lived, in particular Roppongi and Harajuku, emerged as the centres of Americanised consumerism that they have remained for the young people of the city.[14]

Meanwhile, for the majority of those, mainly women, who struggled to feed and clothe their families, the challenges posed by post-war short-ages, like war-time rationing and economising before them, continued to help to validate their role as household managers and controllers of consumption. Those who, from the 1920s onwards, had pioneered a greater political role for women as housewives and consumers – as distinct from male roles as workers and producers – had utilised war-time conditions as a means to involve women in public life, co-operating with the state in turning consumption from a private activity into some-thing of significance for national goals.[15] The post-war years were to see no blurring of the division of labour between men and women within the household, but did witness continued growth in the influence of women's organisations that emphasised the social significance of con-sumption. Following a rally in 1948 to protest at the poor quality of the household matches available under the rationing system, women's leaders who had been heavily involved in the war-time state's organisa-tion of consumption established the Housewives' League (Shufuren) as a pressure group; other women's support organisations followed. Such groupings, following ideas that were formed in the pre-war and war-time period, continued to promote the distinctive role and interests of the housewife and to draw attention to the aspects of consumption that impacted on the life of the community and the nation in the new world of the modern consuming household that was to emerge out of the ashes of defeat.

By the end of the Occupation, Japanese people were well on the way to recovering the standard of living they had come to enjoy before their tragic descent into the 'dark valley'. However, war and occupation left a lasting impact on the goods that went into that standard of living, on the distribution routes whereby such goods were acquired and on the approach of both the state and consumers themselves to the growing material abundance which the economic miracle was to make possible. The experience of war-time regulation and the black market produced a widespread acceptance of more or less legal means of getting round the system and of the role of personal relationships in securing con-sumer goods. It also consolidated the influence of those who stressed

---

[13] Dower 2000: 138.   [14] Yoshimi 2006: 69–72.   [15] See e.g. Narita 1998.

the significance of consumption activities, and the housewives who managed them, for national and community life. The Food Control System itself was eventually to be undermined by the growth in 'private' and technically illegal sales of the best-quality and tastiest rice varieties, creamed off by farmers and rice dealers from the mass of state-purchased rice. Despite the best efforts of the bureaucrats, who continued to believe that the long-term benefits to Japan as a whole of prioritising investment and supply-side interests outweighed the short-term costs to consumers, consumption was to remain a potent and sometimes subversive force in the economy.

Nuclear families, salarymen and urban growth

Following the end of the Occupation, recovery and growth in the Japanese economy picked up speed, receiving a significant boost from the expenditure of the United Nations forces, chiefly American, fighting in the Korean War (1950–3), many of whom were based in Japan or at least obtained their supplies from Japanese producers and enjoyed their rest and recreation in Tokyo. Such 'special procurements' were paid for in US dollars, which could then be used to acquire from abroad the equipment and technology that Japanese businesses needed to re-establish themselves and expand production. Employment in industry began to grow and household incomes recovered and expanded, as those who had come through pre-war and war-time education and experience found jobs in new factories and workshops. While heavy industrial producers expanded to meet the rising demand for steel, chemicals and the whole range of industrial raw materials, opportunities also opened up for the consumer-goods industries, as more and more households found themselves in a position not just to return to their pre-war consumption patterns, but also to begin to enjoy the growing range of consumer goods that formed the basis of the urban middle-class lifestyle.

In fact, however, it was rural households who were first to benefit from the post-war recovery. Food was the top priority for government planners and consuming households alike in the post-surrender period, and farmers received priority allocations of the inputs they needed for agricultural production, as well as subsidies and state investment in irrigation facilities and rural infrastructure. Meanwhile, the Occupation authorities set about implementing the land reform, which transferred ownership of most tenanted land to its cultivator and thereby redistributed rental income to the mass of small-scale, former-tenant farmers. Former munitions producers converted their factories to the manufacture of agricultural equipment – in particular the power tiller that became ubiquitous in the Japanese countryside in the 1950s – as rural households used their gains from high food demand and government support to invest in the means both to produce more and to ease their agricultural workload, freeing time for other forms of employment. With rising incomes and improving rural infrastructure and communications, they began the process of transforming villages composed of rambling, thatch-roofed, wooden houses-cum-workshops into the collections of neat, tile-roofed, family dwellings – equipped with modern kitchens and often more spacious than their urban equivalents – that dot the countryside today.

For most, however, it was in the recovering cities that the opportunity of a job and a new life was to be found. As economic growth speeded up, the devastated areas of the great metropolises of the pre-war period were hastily re-built, while new industrial facilities generated rapid expansion in the populations of cities such as Nagoya and Fukuoka, well placed for raw materials and market opportunities. As a result, the urban population more than tripled between 1945 and 1970, by which time over 70 per cent of the population lived in an urban area, with more than 40 per cent concentrated in the most densely populated belt stretching along the Japan Sea coast from Tokyo to Osaka.[16] The provision of housing, both for those needing to rebuild or renovate their pre-war houses and for the massive influx, presented an enormous challenge. This was met in part by the continuous construction of blocks of flats and apartments – typically, in earthquake-prone Japan, relatively low-rise – and by the steady expansion of suburbs composed of the small, detached houses that represented most families' ideal. The suburban rail network spread ever wider, with lines ripping through residential areas, so that the sound of the level-crossing bell came to represent the unnoticed background music to urban life.

As a result, most people lived of necessity in newly constructed buildings providing living space on average smaller than that typical in the United States and some parts of Europe at least and lacking the solidity and privacy common in housing in the West. For those who entered the post-war period housed in hastily constructed 'barrack' huts or in the wooden one-room apartment buildings that still constituted 38 per cent of Tokyo homes in 1968, the chance to move to a flat in a concrete block on one of the *danchi* housing estates being constructed by public authorities and companies for their workers was a dream.[17]

---

[16] Mills and Ohta 1976: 680, 682; For discussion of the changing post-war definitions used to measure the urban population, see *ibid.* 741–3.

[17] Yoshikawa 1997: 29, 62.

Figure 6.3 The kitchen and living room of a late 1950s *danchi* apartment. Kubo 1991: 36.

Such flats were typically equipped with bathroom and kitchen facilities far superior, in convenience and cleanliness, to those found, if at all, in typical pre-war urban housing (Fig. 6.3). At the same time, planners and house-builders, alongside city dwellers, reacted against what now seemed like the backward, patriarchal and unhealthy, not to say immoral, design of pre-war housing, with its focus on accommodation for guests of the household head, rather than family life, its communal sleeping arrangements and its multi-purpose everyday space. The demand now was for 'modern' housing, with separate bedrooms for parents and children and designated dining areas floored with wood or vinyl and suitable for tables and chairs.[18] Post-war housing therefore offered scope for, and encouraged, a private family life – even if enclosed in a small area and not terribly well sound-proofed – rarely possible in pre-war housing.

The rapid expansion of urban industrial conglomerations, largely unplanned and unregulated, led to the environmental destruction and pollution that was recognised by the early 1970s as a cost of miracle economic growth. The polluted atmosphere, the lack of urban public space and social amenities and the seemingly endless sprawl of crowded, poorly constructed, ugly and unimaginative buildings created a stressful and unattractive urban environment. While the rail network functioned magnificently as a means of transporting the urban millions to and from work, the road construction that might have made it easier to get around in town and country lagged. The nationwide provision of electricity and telephone, much by means of overhead cables that criss-crossed the view of the sky, was rapidly achieved, but mains drainage and sewerage systems – much more costly and difficult public investments – were slower to spread.[19] The re-built and hugely enlarged cities offered little in the way of space and facilities for public social activity, and the lives of newly settling families and individuals tended to focus on homes and workplaces and on the establishment of a secure and comfortable domestic life, after the upheavals and horrors of their recent experience.

As a result, as Japanese families grew better off, through the 1950s and 1960s, more and more of them came to live the kind of urban or suburban lives that the emerging middle classes of the pre-war period had begun to define. Those who migrated to the cities in pursuit of work found, as the economy grew, that they were able to establish urban households of their own, marrying and bringing up children on the basis of long-term careers in offices or factories. Such families were able to move up the housing ladder, from public or company apartment blocks to bigger rented flats or small houses and eventually, if things went well, to something they could afford to buy (with a hefty mortgage) for themselves. While many families ended up caring for elderly parents, and children typically remained resident in their parents' homes until

[18] See Waswo 2001: ch. 4.
[19] In 1968, only 4.1 million dwellings, out of a total of 24.2 million, had a flush toilet (Mills and Ohta 1976: 708).

they themselves married and set up new households, the extended family and community ties of rural areas or traditional urban neighbourhoods were not re-created in the new suburbs and apartment blocks. Although by no means everyone followed the same pattern of living arrangements – multi-generational households and close local communities persisted, especially in the countryside, while independent single people lived alone and day-labourers without families lodged in dosshouses in slums – it was the urban nuclear family that represented the model of domestic life within which the ideal forms of consumption in the Japan of the economic-miracle period were to be delineated.

In the still large sectors of the Japanese economy in which small businesses continued to prevail – on farms but also in many small manufacturing enterprises, shops and restaurants – husbands and wives worked alongside one another and of necessity shared in the process of housekeeping. In the model urban household, however, husbands/fathers typically spent long hours away from home, commuting, at work and in company-based after-work activity. While many wives continued to undertake paid employment in some form, opportunities for rewarding work for women remained limited, with the majority employed part-time, if at all, in relatively basic office, factory or service jobs. In the absence of their husbands, therefore, the day-to-day management of the household tended to fall to women, along with responsibility for child-rearing and education, and it was as housewives and mothers that women were seen as playing their part in national life. Women typically managed their household's finances and savings and took major expenditure decisions, as well as shopping and cooking, clothing the family and organising transport and leisure for the whole family. The organisation of gift-giving, a crucial element in the cementing of business and social relationships and a major item in overall expenditure, also became an important part of a housewife's work.[20]

If men left day-to-day household expenditure largely in the hands of women, they at the same time left much of their discretionary spending on entertainment and leisure to their work organisations. The after-hours socialising which was held to bond work groups together; the wining and dining of clients, government officials and representatives of subcontractors and collaborating businesses; the company-sponsored golf outings and trips to hot-spring resorts – all were expense-account activities that sustained the growth of the zones of cities given over to bars, eating places, massage parlours and hostess clubs. Companies ran

---

[20] For a description of women's role in home life in the late 1950s, see Vogel 1963: e.g. ch. 9.

holiday resorts and leisure activities for their employees; sports facilities were largely company- or school-based. Opportunities for family leisure were relatively limited: tired fathers might be dragged out on Sundays to trail round department stores or visit crowded beauty spots, but otherwise work and school kept parents and children occupied for much of the time. Students went out drinking together, young couples might go to the cinema, but in general leisure activity not related to work tended to be individual and solitary: an hour unwinding on a golf range or playing pachinko slot machines; a whisky on the way home from the station, while pouring out one's troubles to the bar's Mama-san; a sit-down and a chapter of a novel or a manga in a coffee shop.

The pattern of economic growth that underlay the miracle undoubtedly conditioned the environment within which people consumed in many ways, but equally the consumption expenditures that people chose to make played a significant role in generating that growth. Expenditure on the goods that would help to create a modern home was fundamental to the market on which Japanese manufacturers depended, while the demand for food and clothes was largely determined by housewives feeding and clothing their families. As household incomes rose, so too did the desire and capacity to obtain the electrical goods, furnishings, food ingredients, appropriate clothes and eventually even the car for family outings, all of which came together as the props to a modern, middle-class home life, lived out in the new urban environment that miracle growth produced. Meanwhile, the business organisation and human-resource practices of the companies that made the miracle helped to generate the market for the millions of small-scale service and leisure establishments in which salarymen pursued the entertainment and relaxation their work lives required. While the household saving that went to fund industrial investment was certainly an integral part of the process of building the desired home life, so was spending on the goods and services in which it was embodied. Although consumption was declining as a share of gross domestic product over the miracle period, it still grew at almost 8 per cent per annum, producing a tripling in real consumption expenditure per person (see Appendix, Tables 1, 2 and 4). Without the huge home market thus created, Japan's economic miracle could never have been sustained.

Shopping, advertising and the world of mass consumption

Miracle growth affected not just incomes and the kinds of things that people wanted to buy with them, but also the ways in which they came to know about and acquire goods. With the rapid growth of the economy, Japan entered the era of mass consumption with a vengeance, but the conjunction of consumption patterns and tastes developed during the pre-war period with inherited and protected retail structures produced a consumer market that continued to baffle foreign suppliers and to demonstrate that the infrastructure of mass consumerism was not necessarily the same the world over.

In pre-war towns and cities, most everyday goods had been bought in local small shops and markets or from door-to-door sellers, and this continued to be largely the case through the economic miracle and beyond. Each urban neighbourhood supported a set of relatively specialised small shops, ranging from fishmongers, tofu makers, confectioners and greengrocers, through pharmacies and hardware suppliers, to makers of *tatami* matting, futon bedding and furniture. There would be a bookstore, a liquor store, a tobacconist, a ceramics store and clothes shops, and as demand for new types of good grew, these too tended to be sold in small local shops. Electrical goods were marketed by small-scale retailers tied to particular big-brand manufacturers; photographic equipment was to be found in the local franchises of Fuji and Sakura. As a result, data for the early 1980s show Japan as still having twice as many shops in general per person as Britain or the United States and four times as many food stores.[21]

Nonetheless, the rapid expansion in the volume of goods being bought was opening up spaces for other kinds of retail outlet able to meet the new kinds of shopping need that were beginning to emerge. Local convenience stores, supplying the instant food and drink that the returning commuter or solitary student needed, along with his manga and packet of cigarettes, began to appear on the roads radiating out from the stations. By the second half of the 1950s, the first self-service supermarkets were being established: the Aoyama (Tokyo) branch of the upmarket chain Kinokuniya claims the record as the first to be set up, in 1953, but cheaper rivals, such as Daiei, Itōyōkadō and Seiyū, followed. However, their branches were typically located in town centres rather than suburbs and did not specialise in fresh food, instead selling clothes and household goods alongside processed food, so that they did not really compete with the small local shops that continued to meet the need for fresh produce and personal service.[22] At the same time, the private sector did not have a monopoly on retail provision, and manufacturers and retailers were able to make increasing use of the many local organisations that came through the war and continued to provide links between local groups and the wider world. In rural areas, many consumer goods were

[21] Flath 2000: 293–4.   [22] Kikkawa 1998: 111–16.

marketed through the agricultural co-operatives, which also provided households with the financial services by means of which they could pay for them. Women's groups were offered demonstrations and factory tours through which to learn about electrical products,[23] and the first consumer co-operatives (*seikyō*) were being set up.

The city-centre department stores that had come to dominate high-end retailing before the war meanwhile continued to develop and expand the role they had carved out for themselves as the delineators of fashion, especially in foreign goods, and the focal points of shopping as a leisure activity. Branches of the big-name stores – Mitsukoshi, Isetan, Seibu – continued to spring up in the station complexes through which commuters passed daily, as well as along the smart shopping streets to which every town or suburb aspired. With their restaurants, galleries, children's playgrounds and rooftop gardens, they offered scope for a complete day out, surrounded by luxury goods beautifully displayed, and – even for those who could not afford to buy – an education in the possibilities of consumption. Under their wings, smaller shops offering more specialised ranges could draw customers, creating a succession of fashionable shopping areas in the big cities.

As they had before the war, department stores and their entourages of expensive boutiques continued to promote foreign goods and to educate customers in how to use them and exercise discernment over them. However, they also continued to sell upmarket Japanese-style goods – kimono, ceramics, high-quality food and drink items – and to provide the kinds of service associated with traditional retailing practice – impossibly polite, uniformed sales staff wrapping the smallest purchase to perfection. While promoting Christmas and Valentine's Day, department stores were also instrumental in the institutionalisation of gift-giving in the traditional mid-summer and New Year seasons, giving over whole floors to service desks providing advice and ordering facilities for appropriate gifts. In so doing, they helped to define the distinctive ways in which the growing quantity, quality and variety of goods was fitted into the changing patterns of Japanese life.

The retail system was thus beginning, as the economic miracle developed, to diversify and to open up new shopping opportunities for consumers as they grew better off. Nonetheless, it was still dominated by the small shop, with the result that day-to-day shopping remained a more labour-intensive and personalised activity than it typically was in, say, the United States. Housewife shoppers could pride themselves on their judgement in selecting what to buy and in the relations they

[23] Partner 1999: 160.

developed with retailers: the relationship between a household and its rice dealer, for example, could determine whether or not it had access to the prized varieties of rice that somehow slipped through the official rice distribution network.[24] The small-scale retailers who sold most electrical goods frequently made use of home visits and demonstrations of items, such as televisions, with which potential customers were often unfamiliar, especially in rural areas.[25] Despite the explosion in the availability of goods, and the steady rise in the quality, quantity and variety of everyday consumption that miracle growth made possible, most shopping remained a local and social experience for the millions of women building new lives for their families in the cities.

As a result, by the 1970s, as miracle growth was coming to an end and Japan's expanding trade surplus was beginning to generate 'trade friction' with Europe and the United States, foreign trade negotiators fixed on what they regarded as the still 'backward' Japanese retail system, and the regulation that seemed to protect it, as an important factor limiting the ability of foreign producers to market their goods in Japan. In particular, legislation requiring a long and tortuous application procedure of anyone seeking permission to construct a store over a certain size was seen as restricting the development of the supermarkets and large-scale retail chains that might have stocked imported goods. The complex and many-layered wholesale network by means of which goods reached the numerous local retailers was difficult to penetrate and raised the prices consumers faced in the shops. Against this, Japan's geography and the small scale of most houses undoubtedly mitigated against forms of shopping that depended on the car and on domestic storage space for items bought in bulk. The housewife/household manager was typically in a good position to shop daily for fresh food and to deal with the local tradesmen who supplied individualised items for the home, while she was often restricted in the cupboard space available to her. The costly distribution system, meanwhile, was in part at least a reflection of the complexities involved in distributing goods, many of them required to be absolutely fresh, within the densely packed networks of Japanese cities.[26] By the 1980s, as a result of both foreign and domestic pressures, the retail landscape of Japan was beginning to change, increasingly opening up the market to the impersonal self-service store and supermarket chain, but up to then the distribution of the products of miracle growth had largely been achieved through the persistent but changing small shop.

---

[24] See Francks 1998: 7.   [25] Partner 1999: 158, 183.
[26] For detailed economic analysis of the retail system, see Flath 2000: ch. 14.

Meanwhile, the shopping that did take place in the expanding and diversifying department stores and shopping centres, driven, as it was, by fashion and novelty, of course depended on product differentiation and branding, hence on the power of advertising to create images and desires. Japan's advertising industry duly expanded with the rest of the economy: expenditure on advertising increased dramatically over the later 1950s and continued to grow at a rapid rate through to the end of the miracle.[27] The advertising of branded food and drink products and household goods – soy sauce, beer, chocolate, cigarettes, cosmetics and so on – by means of newspapers and magazines, posters and the radio picked up where it had left off in the pre-war period, though now enhanced by the emergence of a number of large-scale producers in these fields. However, much everyday shopping continued to involve the products of the local confectioner and tofu maker, furnishings and fittings made to order by local suppliers and unbranded fresh food. It was therefore rather in the marketing of new products, such as electrical goods, in which it was necessary to create demand and 'educate' consumers rather than just compete with other producers of familiar goods, that advertising developed in scale and sophistication and moved into the new medium of television.

Much of what advertisers sought to sell, therefore, as they discovered and embraced the marketing techniques – market research, brand development, corporate image creation – initiated in the United States, was the 'bright new life',[28] and the image conveyed was heavily based on the American lifestyle with which Japanese consumers came into contact, through the Occupation and via films, music and popular culture in general. This bright life was embodied especially in kitchen gadgets and household electrical products and central to the image of it was the housewife and her efforts to manage an efficient household by means of rice-cooker, toaster, fridge and washing machine. In line with pre-war and war-time campaigns to promote 'rational' consumption, the emphasis in advertising was placed less on time saving and more on the ways in which electrical equipment could contribute towards health, efficiency and economy, enabling women to play the role of the modern, and not unattractively overworked, housewife. Healthy,

---

[27] Partner 1999: 153; Kōdō Seichō o Kanagaeru Kai 2005: 110. Partner points out that Matsushita Electric, for example, was spending much more on advertising than on research and development in the 1950s.

[28] 'Akarui seikatsu' in Japanese, as translated by Ezra Vogel in his 1961 study of the emerging Japanese middle class and discussed further by Partner 1999: 137. The term was widely used in the media and advertising and 'akarui' (bright, cheerful) has very positive, optimistic overtones in Japanese culture and morality.

smiling housewives in their white aprons beamed out from magazine advertisements and posters, as they demonstrated how clean and happy their washing machines made their families.[29] The complete set of electrical goods embodied the 'culture' by means of which the mass of ordinary families could pursue the 'culture life' that only a few had been able to enjoy before the war.[30]

Advertising therefore helped to create the image of what the ideal middle-class home life, presided over by the housewife, would look like. It was a nuclear-family life lived in a small suburban house and based on the growing abundance of the desirable, but not necessarily mass-produced or mass-marketed, everyday goods of the pre-war middle classes, such as unadulterated white rice. But it was also a life in which new goods – in particular the mass-produced electrical items that seemed to characterise the rich life of the American suburbs – could be mobilised in the interests of comfort, efficiency, middle-class status, education and national identity. What Japanese consumers made of this image, through the purchases that they actually pursued, is the subject of the next section.

Consuming the bright life

For the mass of Japanese households, the economic miracle meant a changing work and home environment, a rising income and a growing quantity and variety of goods with which to create a comfortable and appropriate lifestyle. Alongside the elements of the 'civilised' and modernising Japanese-style way of life that had been established in the pre-war cities, there appeared a growing variety of 'foreign' and Western-style items, ranging from household electrical goods, large and small, to doughnuts, instant Chinese noodles and whisky. Out of these items, consumers constructed patterns of consumption in which differentiated goods fitted into particular niches in their changing day-to-day lives. By the time that the miracle came to an end, Japanese families, more or less across the board, found themselves not just consuming much more for the benefit of their health, comfort and enjoyment, but also deploying an expanding repertoire of goods, quite a few of them initially unfamiliar, according to circumstance and situation. The

---

[29] The radio advertisement quoted at the beginning of this chapter summarises the whole message. Advertisers, including Matsushita, had used women in their promotions in the pre-war period as well, but typically to convey the modernity and glamour of their products rather than as symbols of housewifely domesticity (Yoshimi 2006: 77–8).

[30] Kōdō Seichō Ki o Kangaeru Kai 2005: 68, 82–3.

resulting complex and sophisticated consumption patterns created the markets within which Japanese manufacturers learnt their trade and created the miracle.

Food and drink

Japanese people emerged from the war years undernourished and deprived of almost all the food and drink items they had come to enjoy in the pre-war period. They had learned to make what they could of sweet potatoes, vegetable stalks and leaves and every part of a none-too-fresh fish, but they had not forgotten what pure white rice and beautifully prepared fresh vegetables and fish tasted like. As they had struggled to get hold of their rations and the essential black-market supplements, they had dreamed of New Year *mochi* rice cakes, freshly caught fish and *matsutake* mushrooms.[31]

The end of hostilities did not, however, enable these dreams to be immediately realised. Severe shortages of rice and many other foods persisted through the second half of the 1940s, necessitating the continuation of rationing until Japan's agriculture recovered and the foreign exchange to pay for food imports became available. In the meantime, households continued to make do with whatever they could find, supplemented by the substantial amounts of food aid provided by American official and charitable organisations. Much of this came in the form of wheat flour, along with powdered milk, canned meat and other Western-style food items, and is often argued to have been a significant factor in accustoming Japanese consumers, in particular by means of the school meals programme that it supplied, to a diet including bread, milk and meat. At the same time, some of the thousands returning from China unemployed after the collapse of the empire made use of the availability of wheat flour to introduce Japanese consumers to the Chinese-style dumplings, known as *gyōza*, that are now an essential Japanese favourite.[32] Nonetheless, nothing succeeded in overcoming the desire for rice and its tasty side dishes and, as the domestic food situation improved and incomes began to rise, the meal pattern that had come to symbolise the civilised life in urban industrial Japan re-established itself. Through the 1950s, it became standard across the ranks of increasingly comfortable households, even if it continued to incorporate, as it had done before the war, adapted elements of other, non-Japanese cuisines.

---

[31] Food is a constant preoccupation for all the war-time diarists translated in Yamashita 2005.

[32] Cwiertka 2006: 140.

As a result, as rice production recovered and yields increased, bowls of white rice once again came to provide the basis for the majority of meals, and the practice of mixing rice with other grains became a memory of a poorer rural past. The Food Control System, which the government continued to maintain, ensured farmers of a market for however much rice they could produce and consumers of a secure supply at an initially subsidised price, and per capita consumption maintained a rising trend through to the mid-1960s. Thereafter, however, it began to decline, as Japan's increasingly better-off consumers followed the path of their counterparts throughout the developed world and diversified their diets away from grain staples – even the 'luxury' grain that rice had been – and into a widening range of meat, fruit and vegetables and processed foods (see Appendix, Table 6). Some of this diversification did indeed involve Western-style ingredients, especially wheat flour, meat and oils/fats: many households switched from rice to toast – convenient to make in their new electric toasters – for breakfast and to sandwiches with ham or cheese for quick lunches. But the 'rice plus side dishes' format remained the norm for the majority of proper meals, with diversification and the shift away from staple-grain consumption taking the effective form of a rising proportion of side dishes to rice.

As in the pre-war period, therefore, the increasing range of food items that growing incomes opened up to consumers was incorporated into people's diets by adapting them to fit into standard meal patterns, rather than through any wholesale Westernisation of the diet. Fresh produce bought from local shops continued to figure largely in menus, although housewives were now able to afford more and different varieties of fish, fruit and vegetables. As elsewhere in the industrialised world, the share of processed foods in household budgets steadily grew but, although some of these took the form of Western-style products such as biscuits or instant coffee, many were processed versions of more or less traditional pickles, seasonings, seaweed, dried and salted fish, tofu and so on. Curry, cutlets and croquettes, always eaten with rice, remained the main vehicles for greater meat consumption, steadily losing their aura of Western-style modernity and becoming, in their processed and packaged forms, as fixed a part of the Japanese diet as sushi or sashimi. 'Instant *rāmen*', first produced in 1958 as a home version of the noodles sold in Chinese-style restaurants, also became hugely popular.[33]

With rising incomes and a greater variety of fresh and processed foods available in the shops, catering for the family became a more challenging task for housewives increasingly bombarded with advertisements

[33] Cwiertka 2006: 145.

from food manufacturers, nutritional advice from official bodies and all manner of recipes in women's magazines. Technology to some extent came to their aid, however, most significantly in the form of the refrigerator, although the electric rice-cooker revolutionised a process that had formerly been regarded as close to an art, while toasters and small oven-grills were the essential vehicles for the introduction of various more or less Western-style food items into the menu. Although the full-scale gas or electric cooking stove has never found a place in Japanese home kitchens, housewives in the confined spaces of their new urban apartments learnt to perform small daily miracles with a couple of gas rings, a rice-cooker and a grill, so that the restrictive and time-consuming art of cooking with a *kamado* was gradually lost.

Meanwhile, spending on eating out also steadily rose along with incomes. This was related in part to the emerging work culture of the company, frequently taking the form of work-related social eating in restaurants and snack-serving bars, or the salaryman's wolfed-down bowl of noodles on the way home too late for a meal with the family. Tiny restaurants serving meals based on noodles or rice met the demand for quick lunches away from the office (Fig. 6.4), while women out shopping or meeting friends made use of the growing provision of department-store restaurants and coffee shops. American-style burger and doughnut chains were establishing their first Japanese outlets by the early 1970s. The increasing profusion of eating places was based on clear demarcations between the types of food offered, the restaurant environment and the social occasions to which they were appropriate: restaurants offering traditional Japanese food – typically rather expensive, exclusive and aimed at the expense-account market – always served to customers sitting on cushions on the floor and eating with chopsticks from bowls; Western-style eating places, serving coffee and snacks, sandwiches, pasta and other kinds of faster and more casual food, were furnished with tables and chairs and provided cutlery. Japanese-style Chinese food, which took off from its relatively limited pre-war base to become completely indigenised on the basis of standard menus, is always served in large, brightly coloured bowls with Chinese-style spoons and chopsticks.

Meanwhile, the consumption of drinks continued to develop along the lines it had begun to follow before the war, though, like that of food, diversifying to incorporate certain 'foreign' drinks where they fitted into the emerging pattern of social practice. Sake was still drunk with Japanese food and in Japanese-style drinking places, but eventually began to lose ground in terms of per capita consumption (Appendix, Table 6). Beer, on the other hand, was increasingly mass-produced and

Figure 6.4 A *rāmen* (Chinese-style noodle) restaurant in central Tokyo, photographed in 2007 but much as it might have been in the 1950s.

became the affordable accompaniment to work-related socialising, as well as to father's meal at home, completely losing any vestiges of its foreign origins. Wine can be made from Japanese-grown grapes, but neither home-produced nor imported varieties caught on and neither did most foreign-style spirits. The exception of course was whisky, which had not been widely drunk before the war, but which rapidly carved out its niche, during the miracle years, as the drink to accompany male business-related socialising in hostess bars, clubs and other more expensive and exclusive venues. Imported Scotch was the most prestigious, but Japanese-made substitutes became widely available and were much cheaper. Meanwhile, the consumption of bottled and later canned soft drinks – Coca-Cola and other franchised foreign products, but also domestic alternatives – continued to expand and before long no one was ever far from a soft-drinks vending machine. Coffee (and to a lesser extent English-style black tea), not widely drunk before the war, came to be consumed everywhere in the Western-style environment of the coffee shop, although Japanese green tea continued to be drunk with meals and as the essential pick-me-up in office and home.

The food and drink consumption patterns that became established as Japanese people set about using their steadily rising miracle-period incomes had clear precursors in the approaches of the emerging pre-war middle classes to the modernity embodied in the expanding range of eating and drinking possibilities opening up to them. The basic 'rice plus side dishes' meal that had become synonymous with civilised living, and to which the institutions, facilities and equipment of eating and drinking had all been adapted, became the norm for the vast majority of families who now thought of themselves as middle-class. Such a meal pattern easily gave itself to the incorporation of larger quantities and greater variety of side-dish ingredients, eventually at the expense of the amount of rice consumed, and the growing availability of processed items, as well as the development of electrical kitchen gadgets, enabled busy housewives to prepare more elaborate and varied menus for their families.

At the same time, rising incomes and widening knowledge of different food cultures opened up alternative options, mostly in the form of eating and drinking out, but sometimes also in home-cooking, which could be employed as and when appropriate. The spread to a much larger proportion of the employed work-force of the big-company work practices that had applied to only a minority before the war placed many more in situations where different forms of eating and drinking – Japanese-style, Western-style, Chinese-style – in restaurants and bars were part of company life; meanwhile women, whether housewives or employees, found more occasions to use restaurants and coffee shops that served their own particular varieties of food and drink. As a result, new foods and ways of eating – *rāmen* in a cheap and cheerful Japanese–Chinese café, coffee and a doughnut in Dunkin' Donuts, tea and cake or an ice-cream 'parfait' at the top of a department store, whisky and water served by a hostess in a plush Western-style bar, 'pot noodles' or 'packet' curry sauce on a bowl of rice at home – entered the lexicon of possibilities, alongside more or less grand and formal rice-based Japanese-style menus. As far as food and drink were concerned, miracle economic growth, far from simply 'Americanising' Japanese eating, instead continued the pre-war process of opening up the range of culinary options consumers employed as they adjusted to their rising incomes and the changing patterns of their work and family lives.

Clothing

By the inter-war years, a significant proportion of Japanese men – most predominantly those in urban white-collar jobs – had adopted the Western-style suit as their daily uniform. The same had not been true of women, amongst whom Western-style dress had largely been confined to the cosmopolitan rich, the defiantly modern and those obliged to wear it because of the nature of their jobs. Resistance to Western-style clothes for women, on grounds of immodesty and, increasingly, anti-Westernism, continued through the war years, even as more and more men became used to Western dress during their time in uniform. All this was to change after the war: although there remained some occasions – relaxing after a bath, for instance – when men wore Japanese-style garments at home and male workers in some craft and manual occupations still adopted traditional working clothes, full-scale Japanese-style male outfits only came out for weddings and funerals; meanwhile, although it was still possible to spot older women wearing everyday kimono in 1970s Tokyo and female workers in more traditional occupations, such as waitresses in Japanese-style restaurants, continued to wear them, the vast majority of women, whether going out to work or being housewives, packed their kimono away for special occasions and faced the world in blouses and skirts.

The reasons for this were clearly complex. Clothes and clothing material were in short supply after the war, and it was possible to run up Western-style dresses on a sewing machine more quickly and cheaply, especially as man-made fibres became more widely available, than to restock with Japanese-style clothes.[34] The Occupation and the subsequent influx of American films and other media confronted Japanese people with a world of Western-dressed men and women that had been glimpsed only distantly in the pre-war period. Moreover, anyone who has ever tried to dress in a kimono will recognise that, in the modern world where women need to sit on chairs, get on and off trains and be at the office on time, Western-style clothes are more convenient to wear, easier to maintain and take up less storage space – kimono could not be put in the washing machines that more and more households were buying, nor just folded up in chests of drawers. At the same time, Japanese-style clothing tended to be relatively expensive and long-lasting, and, although fashion in kimono had never by any means stood still, it could never move with the speed of trends in the globalised world of Western-style fashion. The adoption of Western-style dress enabled the mass of Japanese women, as their incomes rose, to acquire a growing variety of clothes and to utilise them more easily to express the images

---

[34] Sewing schools represented a boom area of the post-war economy (Kōdō Seichō Ki o Kangaeru Kai 2005: 136).

that they wanted to convey.[35] The inconveniences of the kimono were not necessarily inherent in the garment itself, and by the 1980s fashion designers were returning to it, as a source of inspiration at least. But the cheap, mass-produced, easy-to-wash kimono never seemed to appeal, either to the producers of Japanese-style textiles, who had survived and even prospered before the war, or to the emerging mass of post-war women.[36]

As a result, although the kimono remained part of the clothing repertoire of most women, the occasions on which it was worn became increasingly only the most formal. Dresses and skirts, blouses and jumpers, along with all the appropriate underwear, footwear, hats and coats, took their place for most everyday work or leisure attire. Almost all households came to possess a sewing machine, and many items of women's and children's wear were home-made, but Western-style clothes were often bought ready-to-wear, unlike the kimono and made-to-measure suits of the pre-war period. The numbers of retailers specialising in all the different elements of Western-style outfits and accessories grew dramatically, as expenditure on Western-style clothing rose, so that the shopping malls being constructed above and below ground in towns and cities everywhere were soon lined with clothes shops.[37] Women gradually built up their wardrobes of Western-style items suitable for varying occasions, although most men left their clothes-buying to their wives, and any aberrations from the universal grey, synthetic-fibre, two-piece suit for work, and slacks plus polo-shirt combination for leisure wear, were largely imperceptible, to the foreign observer at least.[38]

Unlike the case with food, therefore, in their clothing, post-war Japanese consumers for the most part restricted their options to Western-style items. The prevalence of work uniforms, for men and women, in many more occupations than was typically the case in, say, Britain, also limited the scope for choice, variety and fashion. Nonetheless, before long, the fashion trends of Europe and North America were finding their way to Japan, via the media and in particular the large women's magazine market, even if the still relatively lower incomes

[35] Vogel suggests that, for the middle-class housewives he observed in the 1950s, Western-style clothes offered a relatively affordable way of looking smart, whereas a good kimono was too expensive and a cheap one looked cheap (Vogel 1963: 82).
[36] The direction suggested by the boom in *meisen* kimono in the inter-war period thus proved to be a dead end, even though it had been the vehicle by means of which many more women became engaged with fashion. By the time of the 1980s 'retro boom', pre-war *meisen* kimono were selling well in antique shops – and nowadays on e-Bay.
[37] Kōdō Seichō Ki o Kangaeru Kai 2005: 141–2, 137–8.
[38] Vogel was as unable to distinguish quality/status differences in men's suits as I was (Vogel 1963: 82).

of Japanese consumers reduced the speed of change. The Dior 'New Look' of the early 1950s was quickly picked up in Japan, and by the 1960s Japanese girls were adopting the mini-skirt en masse. Japanese adaptations of imported ideas included the *heppusandaru*, modelled on the high-heeled sandals worn by Audrey Hepburn in *Roman Holiday* – an early example of the universal must-have item – while 'Calypso style', 'Elvis style' and 'Ivy League style' all had their day, as the 1950s gave way to the 1960s.[39] By then, however, growing numbers of trends were emerging from indigenous sources: popular Japanese films generated their own fashions; the future crown princess gave rise to the 'Michiko style' around the time of the royal wedding in April 1959;[40] department stores engaged in large-scale campaigns to promote 'Italian blue' or 'sherbet tones' or whatever was that season's trend. By the 1960s, street fashion was also beginning to reassert itself against the media-driven universal trends, as *zoku* (tribe) groups started to dress up in their own particular styles to assemble in Ginza and Harujuku.[41] Western style may have overtaken the kimono but, as soon as they were able, Japanese consumers were to apply to it the same serious consideration of what clothing meant, in terms of image, status and identity, as they had devoted to their Japanese-style outfits for a hundred years and more, though now within the context of the more rapid and cosmopolitan fashion cycle that their rising incomes and adoption of Western dress made possible.

Household goods

The economic-miracle period is often portrayed as the era of electrical household goods, with the consumption patterns to which households aspired being defined in terms of symbolic sets of electrical appliances of increasing sophistication. However, the large-scale movement of people into new forms of urban accommodation, and the establishment of more and more nuclear-family households, involved the purchase of far more in the way of household goods – by no means all electrical or even 'modern' – in the creation of the home environment within which the widening range of electrical equipment was used and enjoyed. Following the path blazed by the inhabitants of the suburban 'culture houses' of the pre-war period, families setting themselves up in their

---

[39] Nitta, Tanaka and Koyama 2003: 120; Jō 2007: 270–5.
[40] Particularly popular, apparently, were versions of the white V-necked sweater that Michiko was wearing when she was famously introduced to the crown prince on the tennis court (Jō 2007: 273).
[41] Jō 2007: 275.

newly constructed flats and small houses employed to the full the mix of adapted Japanese- and Western-style goods that came to define the comfortable middle-class life lived out in *mai hōmu*.

The largest disjunction with the typical pattern of pre-war furniture and fittings came in the area of kitchen and dining facilities. Although it remained far from uncommon for families to eat round a low table, seated on cushions in a *tatami*-floored room, most new housing was constructed to include a dining–kitchen area (always known as a DK) with a hard floor, and a table-and-chairs set for this area was a common early household purchase. Kitchen areas, though often small, were supplied with stainless-steel sinks, draining boards and work surfaces, as well as some storage space, and provided scope for the storage and use of a growing range of kitchen equipment, both Japanese-style – ceramic bowls, knives, woks – and Western – forks and spoons, flat plates for Western-style dishes, glasses, plastic bowls – while vacuum jugs (in which to keep water for tea) in vivid floral designs added a touch of colour.[42] Into this bright new kitchen arrived the refrigerator, a large-scale purchase for many households and bought on instalment if necessary.[43] It clearly transformed food storage for the ordinary household, as well as making the cold beer an everyday possibility, and chilled or frozen food products offered a new level of convenience. This did not, though, overturn the priority afforded to freshly bought food in Japanese cuisine – no one makes sushi or sashimi from frozen fish.

In the rest of the house, the invasion of Western-style furniture and fittings was more gradual. With rising incomes and improving housing conditions, individual bathrooms became standard elements in houses, but designed along the same lines as traditional private and public baths, with a tiled-in area in which to wash before entering the bath itself for a long hot soak. The newly acquired washing machine might fit into a space by the bathroom, but was otherwise relegated to the balcony or patio area. Most families continued to sleep on the floor on futon that were put away in their purpose-built fitted cupboards during the day. Every few days, these had to be aired outdoors or over balcony railings, so that visibly good-quality bedding was a status symbol costing significant amounts of money and typically still bought from the local futon-maker.[44] Sofas and armchairs, standing on rugs over *tatami* if necessary, and desks and bunk beds for schoolchildren began to appear,

---

[42] Nitta, Tanaka and Koyama 2003: 126.
[43] For statistical data on ownership rates for consumer durables, see Appendix, Table 7.
[44] Vogel 1963: 82.

in sizes adapted to the space available in Japanese rooms, while coffee tables, bookcases, small cabinets and chests of drawers started to clutter living and guest rooms. What with sliding partitions and fitted cupboards, wall space for purely decorative items was restricted, but some houses retained the *tokonoma* alcove – often eventually proving a convenient spot for the television – and ash-trays, table-mats, ornaments and cushions offered scope for the display of individual tastes. Through the miracle years, therefore, 'the once sparsely appointed interior of the Japanese dwelling would become filled with objects'.[45]

Amongst these objects, electrical goods did undoubtedly occupy the most significant practical and symbolic place. Before the war, there had been quite widespread diffusion of the sewing machine, radio and electric iron, along with the bicycle the only consumer durables that any significant number of households could afford. By the 1960s, many more items of household electrical equipment – the washing machine and fridge as major items, along with the rice-cooker, toaster, vacuum cleaner, electric fan and heater – were being widely diffused (Appendix, Table 7). By no means all were straightforward replicas of their American counterparts: the automatic rice-cooker, first launched by Toshiba in 1955, was designed to produce cooked rice in the form eaten in Japan and, with the addition of a timer, enabled housewives to serve rice for breakfast without getting up hours before everyone else; electric versions of the *kotatsu* heater were constructed to fit into pits in the ground or under tables, like their solid-fuel predecessors; eventually electric futon airers would obviate the need to display one's bedding over the balcony rail.

Where the uses of electrical gadgets were unfamiliar, though, an army of salesmen undertook home visits to explain how they worked and why households might need them, and the electrical-goods shops that sprang up throughout the suburbs, often as tied outlets for the major manufacturers, put on displays and demonstrations, while advertisers provided the image of the healthy, happy and efficient household made possible by electrical goods. Electrical items were marketed as gifts and as obvious destinations for the twice-yearly bonuses (equivalent to several months' salary) that many employees received (Fig. 6.5). Whatever their practical value in terms of saving time and improving the performance of cooking, washing, heating and so on, electrical goods came to be viewed as central to the middle-class, housewife-run lifestyle to which growing numbers of households could now aspire.

[45] Waswo 2001: 63.

Figure 6.5 Electrical goods advertised as gifts within various price ranges. A 1956 newspaper advertisement reproduced in Kōdō Seichō Ki o Kangaeru Kai 2005: 79; courtesy of Nihon Edeitā Sukūru.

Equally if not more important to this lifestyle, though, were electrical goods that provided information and entertainment, including the radio, the record-player and, most importantly, the television. Japan's first television entrepreneurs took the decision to try to establish TV in Japan in the early 1950s, at a time when most experts concluded that incomes were still too low to permit the widespread diffusion of sets necessary to justify the costs of establishing national-level mass broadcasting.[46] The experts were proved wrong: by the end of the decade, with manufacturers bringing out ever cheaper, smaller and better-quality models, almost half of all households had come to own a black-and-white set; by the mid-1960s virtually all did (Appendix, Table 7). Public interest in events such as the royal wedding in 1959 and the 1964 Tokyo Olympics provided a catalyst, but TVs seem often to have been impulse buys, desired initially for their novelty/status-symbol value and eventually just for the fun and entertainment they provided. More TVs were bought at earlier dates than washing machines, and, while the purchase of useful appliances was carefully and 'rationally' planned, bonuses would be blown on a TV, the chance to watch the national sumo tournament alone justifying the extravagance.[47]

As early as 1955, a magazine was able to categorise households into 'classes', according to their ownership of electrical goods, the lowest of the seven classes owning only radios, irons and toasters, while the

[46] Partner 1999: ch. 3.
[47] Partner 1999: 162–6. By 1960, 9 million Japanese households had bought a TV, compared with 6 million a washing machine and only 2 million a fridge, even though a TV cost three times as much as a washing machine.

top classes owned fridges, washing machines and, most high-class of all, a TV.[48] By the end of the 1960s, virtually all households possessed the 'three sacred treasures' – black-and-white TV, washing machine and fridge – and a new set – colour TV, car and air-conditioner – was to be defined for the 1970s. The export successes of Japanese consumer-electrical manufacturers were based on the experience and technological mastery gained in the rapidly expanding home market of the miracle years, which enabled them to meet the exacting demands of foreign consumers, already more than familiar with electrical appliances, for reliable, high-quality and innovative products. For the Japanese consumers whose demand shaped the nature of the electrical and electronic products that were in due course to conquer the world, they were the embodiment of newfound comfort, security and enjoyment and the defining symbols of the 'bright life', amidst the accumulating and eclectic contents of their homes.

By the time that the 'shocks' of the early 1970s signalled the end of miracle growth, most Japanese households had achieved a standard of living comparable to that enjoyed in the rest of the developed industrial world. But as their incomes had risen, the strategies they had employed in amassing and using the vastly increased quantity and range of material goods available to them had varied across the different areas of their consuming lives and had by no means always followed the path laid down by the mass consumers of the United States and the rest of the West. While their electric toasters enabled them to eat toast, spread with margarine and jam and accompanied by coffee, for their breakfasts, their rice-cookers eased the process of preparing more varied and nutritious Japanese-style meals for dinner. Vacuum cleaners swept *tatami* floors and washing machines cleaned traditional futon covers. After-work groups of colleagues, in their uniform suits and ties or skirts and blouses, might sip whisky in bar surroundings that could be anywhere in the world, or they might take off their shoes and sit on cushions round a low table, consuming sake or beer with Japanese-style nibbles. For the broad mass of Japanese people, the world of material goods became rapidly richer, more complex and more varied, as the economy became more and more productive, but the result was a distinctive pattern of consumption that incorporated the new products of mass manufacturing into the historically created, once-elite, Japanese lifestyle that rising incomes now made a reality for the majority.

[48] Yoshimi 2006: 76.

Consuming and saving: the individual and society

Japanese people's avid acquisition and enjoyment of the new forms of food and drink, wardrobes of Western-style clothes and sets of household appliances that the economic miracle offered them contrasts with their reputation for Confucian frugality – their status as the world's number-one savers went long unchallenged – and for valuing a kind of group homogeneity – 'the nail that sticks out gets hit' – that might have been the despair of advertisers used to selling consumer goods on the basis that they make their purchasers stand out in a crowd. Post-Occupation governments appear to have given priority to heavy industrial growth and to the physical and financial infrastructure that promoted it, hitting on the tax cut of 1957 and the Income-Doubling Plan of 1960, both often held to demonstrate a positive attitude towards the improvement of living standards, almost by accident.[49] The traditions of pre-war savings campaigns were revived and the tax-breaks and other incentives to save, particularly through the convenient network of post offices, were firmly maintained. How then did Japanese people reconcile their role as consumers, and indeed as the drivers of the domestic-market growth that sustained most of the big names of Japanese manufacturing, with their prodigious saving activities and with the social values that continued to underlie their work and family lives?

In many ways, the post-war approach to saving continued the pre-war tradition of treating it not so much as the antithesis of consumption, but rather as a rational long-term strategy for achieving a better standard of life. Regular saving was promoted both as a means to building up the funds necessary to secure the relatively expensive consumer durables, and ultimately the house, that defined the good life and – following a model that would have proved grist to the mill of proponents of the life-cycle theory of saving – as necessary for a family planning to achieve a desired pattern of consumption over its lifetime. A well-known savings-association advertisement of the early 1970s plots a typical couple's potential saving and expenditure needs against the events of a 'calm and composed ['awatenai'] life plan': marriage; the birth of a son, then a daughter; their children's educational and then marriage expenses; their trip to Europe; and eventually their 'comfortable old age'.[50] Consumption and saving become visibly two sides of the same coin for those seeking, account-book in hand, the long-term security and comfort that had eluded most Japanese families in the past.

[49] Partner 1999: 186–8.   [50] Plath 1980: 89.

In this context, as in the past, consumption expenditure could always be justified if it was 'rational' and contributed to the long-term welfare, education and general 'modernity' of the consuming household. The short-term, evanescent enjoyment of expenditure on wedding festivities or village drinking parties might be frowned on as 'backward' and wasteful, but, as advertisers were well aware, the purchase of a fridge or washing machine could easily be justified as an investment yielding returns in the health and efficiency of the 'rational', 'modern' family living the bright life. Consuming more meat and dairy produce meant moving towards the apparently more nutritious Western diet, and processed foods could be given an aura of scientific healthiness and convenience. Attempts to portray the television as an educational device proved less convincing, though, and consumers were clearly not always unwilling to spend their hard-earned cash on modern goods that simply offered enjoyment and status.

At the same time, with incomes rising fast more or less across the board, taxes low and families small, it was not necessarily hard to increase both spending and saving simultaneously. Nonetheless, there were still plenty of families who could not easily manage this, amidst the many pressures to acquire the goods that marked respectable middle-class status, and consumer credit was in fact widely used. It typically took the form of instalment purchase, a practice pioneered by sewing-machine manufacturers in the pre-war period but widespread in the marketing of larger household appliances by the 1950s. Andrew Gordon quotes estimates that at least half of the televisions, fridges and washing machines entering Japanese homes by the early 1960s were being bought on instalment, while employers and department stores co-operated to devise systems enabling employees to buy goods 'on ticket', with repayments deducted from salaries.[51] Concern that such schemes encouraged overspending was expressed in Japan, as elsewhere, but credit organisations and business representatives justified them on the grounds that they enabled more households to obtain the large-scale modern goods without which the rational bright life was impossible, while incidentally helping to generate the home market that Japanese manufacturers needed. Continued ambivalence towards consumer credit was nonetheless reflected in heavy regulation, and borrowing not tied to specific purchases remained limited and shady.[52]

[51] Gordon 2006: 145–7.
[52] Apart from instalment credit to finance specific large-scale purchases, the only real sources of personal loan finance were the so-called *sarakin* (salaryman finance) companies who charged very high interest rates and were, as David Flath puts it, 'notorious for their aggressive collection efforts' (Flath 2000: 265).

While Japanese people thus, on the whole, found ways to feel happy about the growth in consumption that the miracle made possible, it was nonetheless clear that such growth did have implications for the nature of their society in the modern industrial era. The rapid and uniform spread of the same set of consumer durables and the same array of processed food and drink more or less throughout the country produced what was thought of as 'homogenisation'. This involved the disappearance of regional variations in lifestyles, but more significantly was also part of the process of creating the 'middle mass' that seemed to characterise miracle-period Japan. The growing perception of the majority of the population that they were 'middle-class' depended on their ability to purchase and utilise the goods that symbolised that status – an eclectic mix of key electrical appliances, quasi-Western food and drink products, a scattering of Western-style furniture or household knick-knacks and Western-style clothes, alongside high-quality rice, futon, Japanese-style restaurant eating, kimono for big occasions and a Japanese-style bath.[53] While subtle variation within this pattern was certainly possible, its basic structure was predetermined in the desire to become part of the 'middle mass' that lived the bright life.

The 'homogeneity' of the emerging mass market demonstrated itself most dramatically in the phenomena of fads and panics, to which Japanese consumers seemed to become particularly prone. The 'panda craze', for example, sparked by the arrival of Ran-Ran and Kan-Kan from China to mark the resumption of Sino-Japanese relations in 1972, generated enormous queues at Ueno Zoo and a vast amount of panda merchandise, as consumers joined in with each other in acquiring symbolic products.[54] The first oil crisis of 1973 triggered panic-buying of an assortment of goods, most notably toilet paper, stockpiling of which produced frantic queues and shortages. The community of consumers nationwide thus found expression not only in the purchase of the same sets of goods, but also in the enthusiasms and fears that the mass market could generate.

Nonetheless, beneath this surface homogenisation, Japanese consumers continued to find ways to differentiate themselves as members of a wider society. This differentiation might have been based more on gender and age than, as perhaps in the past, on class or family status, but long-standing approaches to the appropriateness of particular goods to particular social categories were carried through and adapted to the expanded range of products available. The art of judging the right gift

---

[53] See Ivy 1993: 249.
[54] For illustrations of the panda craze, see Nitta, Tanaka and Koyama 2003: 12–13.

appropriate to the status relation between giver and recipient needed
to be expanded to cover tinned fruit and imported whisky as well as
Japanese-style confectionery, tea and high-class sake. Japanese women
had to learn which hairstyle or skirt length was appropriate to their age
and marital status in relation to Western-style clothes, just as they had
done with kimono. Moreover, beneath the apparent homogeneity of the
sets of goods crammed into the mass-produced housing spaces that constituted urban homes, income differences could still be demonstrated.
In the world of newfangled electrical appliances, manufacturers' repu-
tations were often all there was to go on in assessing quality, so that
the brand-name on your television set did matter; a fridge arriving in a
department store's delivery van impressed neighbours in a way that the
local electrical shop's much cheaper model could not.[55] With Japanese-
style items too, as many more people came to be able to afford good-
quality produce, differentiation according to price and type began to
grow more important: rice, tea or sake from particular regions or with
special qualities – once appreciated only by elite gourmands – were now
being differentiated for the mass market.

Although 'homogenisation' was thus by no means complete, the
growth of 'middle-mass' consumption continued to be celebrated as
evidence of the equalisation and democratisation that enabled many
more people than in the past to enjoy a comfortable life surrounded by
both Japanese- and Western-style goods. The flip-side to this, though,
was that this new mass consumption was for the most part carried out
in the private or individualised context of *mai hōmu*. Western-style
goods might be 'rational', convenient and fun, but, in the hands of the
growing mass of nuclear families in their new suburban homes, they
could be seen as contributing to the breakdown of the wider family and
community relationships on which society had been based in the past.
The kimono and furniture that had once been handed down from generation to generation as the embodiment of the continuing family unit
were increasingly obsolete, and it was new fridges or washing machines
for their urban apartments that brides now wanted as their dowries. It
was the young daughter-in-law who knew, through her formal education and practical experience, how to operate in the world of electrical
goods and Western-style food, rendering unnecessary the deference to
her mother-in-law that had once been the condition for mastering the
skills of cooking or dressmaking. Communal activities, such as going
to the public bath-house or pooling cooking equipment in order to prepare a banquet, disappeared, as families came to possess their own

---

[55] Vogel 1963: 82.

private bathrooms and increasingly well-equipped kitchens. With their individual bedrooms, their lockable doors, their own washing, cooking and bathing facilities and the private entertainment offered by the TV and glass of beer from the fridge, homes lost the shared and public aspects that had been embodied in traditional architectural design and facilities for extended families and local communities. The new abundance of goods could be seen as bringing with it notions of individualism and privacy in the ownership and use of things that had not been part of earlier consumption practices.

However, while this may have given rise to a certain amount of nostalgia, it did not, through the miracle period, induce any overt rejection of Western-style goods and the values embodied in them. Instead, such goods were selectively 'domesticated', to use Joseph Tobin's word, and to some extent at least adapted to the requirements of social life in industrial Japan.[56] The Western-style food that Japanese people came to enjoy was eaten within a culinary and social context often very different from that of its countries of origin; beer came to be drunk in the manner of sake, from small glasses never filled by the drinker himself; prestigious foreign goods were widely utilised as gifts, even if subsequently stored away and never consumed. Thus products originating in the West became embedded in the nonetheless distinctive lifestyle that Japanese consumers of the miracle period created, as they came to utilise, socially as well as privately, the new variety and quantity of goods available to them.

In due course, the 'domestication' of initially imported goods and the technologies of their production succeeded to the extent that the Japanese-made versions came to be seen as embodying distinctively Japanese qualities. For the domestic market in the 1960s, these qualities already included superior technology, but this was combined with 'uniquely Japanese' aesthetic features. Colour televisions were advertised as employing technology that, unlike inferior foreign products, could display the warmth and subtlety of 'Japanese colour'; ranges of fridges, washing machines and televisions were developed with finishes mimicking the most admired Japanese woods and with names plucked from Japanese ancient history (Fig. 6.6). As Shunya Yoshimi points out, by this stage even intrinsically modern, Western-style products had become enmeshed in the process of defining 'Japaneseness' against the Western 'Other'.[57]

[56] See Joseph Tobin 1992a.
[57] Yoshimi 2006: 80–2.

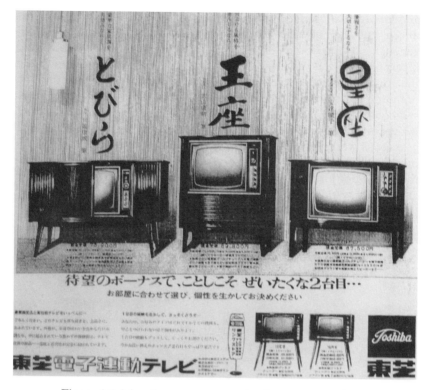

Figure 6.6 Advertisement encouraging buyers to spend their bonuses on televisions with historical names. Nitta, Tanaka and Koyama 2003: 143.

By the end of the high-growth period in the 1970s, the Japanese people who, thirty years earlier, had been struggling to survive on whatever they could scrape together, while gazing in awe on the wealth of goods that their American occupiers took for granted, were enjoying, in relative abundance and with pride, their own versions of those goods. In many ways, lifestyles had been transformed, as the swelling ranks of the 'middle masses' spent their rising incomes from steady urban industrial and white-collar employment on the household appliances, meat and dairy products and Western-style clothes that embodied the 'bright life' of the nuclear family glimpsed in American films. But their version of the bright life was lived out in a context very different from the idealised American suburbia of the films – in the small spaces of Japanese flats and houses, against a background of work practices, gender roles and family relationships by no means identical to those which had pro-duced the original American model and on the basis of a long indi-genous (though not always isolated) consumption history. It therefore incorporated both the 'domestication' of originally foreign goods and the 'modernisation', via new materials and production techniques, branding and marketing, of the Japanese-style goods that had come to symbolise a civilised Japanese way of life. This process had not been without its costs and anxieties, which were to come to the fore in the years of slower growth that followed the end of the miracle. But equally, by the 1980s, Japanese consumers were confidently sending out into the world not just the products they had both made and desired, but also the sophisticated, eclectic and distinctive tastes they had developed through the miracle years of consumption growth.

7 New tribes and nostalgia: consumption in the late twentieth century and beyond

There is more than one way of being a consumer society. Some of these are highly destructive of the human spirit; but others, especially those – like Japan – where the social bonds are already tight, may provide a way out: a zone of liberation, play and the imagination where other expressions of these are circumscribed. And furthermore, these can be exercised not apart from society ... not as spectacular acts of revolt, but entirely within the practice of everyday life.[1]

At a time when material prosperity has grown, Japanese consumers are asking for more ... The term 'breaking away from things' appears frequently in analyses of consumer trends in Japan. I interpret this to mean a transcendence of material values, and I believe the retail industry must provide the means to achieve this transcendence.[2]

Following the 'Nixon shock' of 1971, when the hitherto stable dollar was sharply devalued against the yen and other currencies, and the 'oil shock' of 1973, when the international price of the imported oil on which Japan's miracle growth had depended was dramatically forced up, the Japanese economy entered a period of instability, adjustment and much slower growth. By the end of the decade, however, stability had been restored and growth resumed at a respectable rate, though never again at the speed achieved in the 1960s. By this stage, Japanese manufacturers of cars, electrical goods and electronic parts were producing a continuous stream of innovative, high-quality products, and exports boomed, as Americans continued to consume beyond their means. Japanese holiday-makers and company men spent the resulting abundant foreign exchange on sightseeing and souvenirs all over the world, while Japanese businesses and financial institutions took advantage of the still prodigious saving capacity of their compatriots to invest in creating supply networks throughout Asia as well as manufacturing and marketing facilities in Europe and the United States. The

[1] Clammer 2000: 260.
[2] Tsutsumi Seiji, chairman of the Seibu Saison Group, in 1982; quoted in Creighton 1998a: 128.

era of 'internationalisation' (*kokusaika*) had begun and, as the 1980s progressed, Japanese people came to see themselves in a new light as regards the rest of the world and the goods that furnished it.

Japan's newfound international affluence encouraged those who could afford to do so to spend with more abandon than had been possible in earlier decades. The attempt to deal with the problem of Japan's trade surplus and the corresponding US deficit by pushing up the exchange value of the yen presented Japanese overseas investors and shoppers with further enhanced international spending power, and their buying sprees in the luxury markets of the world became legendary. Meanwhile, at home, businesses and individuals sought to buy assets, in particular land and housing as well as stocks and shares, pushing up prices to unsustainable levels in speculative markets. While asset prices were rising, those feeling rich continued to splash out on the best that money could buy, but at the end of the decade, with the Bank of Japan desperately trying to rein in the speculative spending, the 'bubble' burst, leaving businesses, banks and individuals unable to repay debts secured on assets whose prices had collapsed. The bursting of the bubble ushered in the 'lost decade' of the 1990s, when minimal growth, deflation and 're-structuring' threatened the jobs and careers of many who had grown used to security and affluence.

The Japanese consumers who shopped the world in the bubble years became renowned not just for their wads of dollars, but also for their sophisticated knowledge, their willingness to pay for the best quality or the most fashionable brand and in general the seriousness with which they approached the business of acquiring the right goods. But such dedicated consumers did not spring fully formed on to the world stage of the 1980s. They were the product of a consumption history that dated back to the Tokugawa period; our story will thus conclude by considering how that history came to culminate in the famed Japanese consumer of the bubble period.

Shopping in the city, late twentieth-century style

By the 1970s, the vast majority of Japanese people were settled in the cities and their suburbs and earning incomes that enabled them to consume in quantity and quality as never before. The urban environment within which they lived, conditioned as it was by scarcity of space and high population density, imposed constraints on household formation and the nature and cost of housing, hence on the forms that consumption might take, but also provided a more and more diverse and sophisticated range of opportunities for shopping and leisure expenditure.

Within this environment, consumers and advertisers between them created the world of fashion and product differentiation that reached its apotheosis in the bubble years of the 1980s.

House prices, traffic and parasitic children: urban
life in the late twentieth century

By the 1970s, the era of large-scale movement to urban areas was over, and by the 1980s the first generations to be born and brought up within the prosperity and security of the post-war cities were emerging into the economic world. Many of the younger generation born in rural areas had migrated, so that, although some larger-scale farm operations run by business-like younger people did begin to appear and great efforts were put into encouraging the use of the country-side for leisure and tourism, many villages remained home only to an ageing population of part-time farming couples, whose children and grandchildren now lived permanently in the city. For marketing and other purposes the urban population could now be broken down into the 'baby boom' generation, born in the late 1940s and 1950s, who consolidated the suburban lifestyle, and the 'new tribes' (*shinjinrui*), born into the age of television and electronic goods that began in the 1960s.[3]

These city-born generations were by now secure in their careers and settled enough to begin to demand more from their urban living environment than they had done during the frantic rush for material prosperity of the miracle years. The 1970s saw growing concern over the human and environmental costs that the previous decade's high-speed growth had inflicted. A number of serious cases of industrial pollution, resulting in significant illness and deaths, came to light, and anxiety over air quality in the cities mounted, as growing numbers of cars and lorries jammed into congested city centres. The neglect, in the rush to create housing and industrial facilities, of public open space and social amenities in general became more keenly felt, as families began to consider their and their children's future in the city. The well-known description of the Japanese, attributed to a European diplomat, as 'workaholics living in rabbit hutches' hit home precisely because many Japanese themselves were now coming to ask for more in terms of their quality of life than merely the – now undoubtedly abundant and high-quality – food, clothing and household goods that the economic miracle had made available to them.

---

[3] For a more detailed breakdown, see Ueno 1998: 204.

A major concern in this was certainly housing. Many families wanted to translate their now reliable income and prospects into home-ownership and/or more space in which to bring up their children. This was, however, problematic within the densely populated urban areas of the coastal strip and necessitated building on every possible scrap of urban land, as well as expanding the suburbs still further out into the countryside. This put pressure on land and house prices, culminating in the phenomenal and unsustainable prices paid for urban real estate during the bubble years. Despite their valiant saving efforts and all possible help from their parents, couples wanting to own their own homes had to take out often huge mortgages, and rising housing costs ate into the disposable income available for consumption.

Nonetheless, growing numbers succeeded in escaping the cramped and poorly built apartments of the miracle years into larger flats or small 'dream homes' in the suburbs. This might mean a long commute for father, or even renting him a pied-à-terre in the city, but it made individual bedrooms and a larger living area, as well as parking space and maybe a tiny garden, a possibility. New and refurbished houses and flats tended to be largely Western-style, with typically only one room remaining *tatami*-floored; they therefore offered increased scope for the purchase of the Western-style furniture with which many people were now most at home. In Tokyo, virtually all the traditional-style wooden housing that had survived earthquake and fire-bombing was pulled down, as owners found it much more convenient and comfortable, as well as profitable, to sell off part of the land for building and construct for themselves a modern concrete house equipped with a proper kitchen and bathroom, a sofa and air-conditioning. For younger people, in the cities at least, sitting on the floor and eating from low tables became something done only when being consciously Japanese.

Another way to make the most of available space was to keep the family small, and the birth rate stayed low, so that, although many couples continued to have to accommodate ageing parents at some point, households with more than two children became a rarity.[4] However, those children, as they grew up, were tending to postpone until later and later the point when they left home and set up their own independent households. After their years in education (often living at home), low starting salaries in new jobs rendered the cost of renting or buying a proper home prohibitive for many young people. For this reason and

---

[4] Average household size fell from 5.07 people in 1950 to 3.01 in 1990 (*Kokumin seikatsu hakusho* 2007: Table 1.2).

no doubt others, marriage was often delayed and the average age at first marriage steadily rose. As a result, through the 1980s and 1990s, growing numbers of young people continued to live with their parents as 'parasite singles', putting off the evil hour when they would have to devote some of their income to their own housing costs.[5] Their spending power hence remained conversely large so that, while their parents struggled to pay the mortgage, they sustained the market for fashions and mobile phones.

The spread of housing further and further out from the urban centres where most people still worked was facilitated by continued development of the communications network. New bullet train lines were built out to the north and east of Tokyo, making commuting from towns well away in the mountains or up the coast possible, if expensive. Urban train and underground networks continued to expand; new airports were developed so that, for longer-distance travel round the country, flying became an option. Even the road system was improved, with motorways constructed along the main coastal routes and expressways cutting through urban neighbourhoods. Nonetheless, much of Japan remained unsuited to the car: residential neighbourhoods had grown up as patchworks of narrow streets and paths difficult to navigate at any speed in a vehicle; given the premium on land, parking space was very limited and expensive; away from the cities, most major roads remained two-lane and highly congested, so that traffic speeds were very low. Despite greatly expanded car ownership (see pp. 202–3) and use of vehicular freight, public transport or the bicycle was still often the most practical option.

By the 1980s, a newfound national confidence, as well as unprecedented access to funds, was being expressed in the hiring of celebrity international architects to design, in Tokyo and other cities, some of the most exciting new buildings in the world, while grand projects created smart new resort areas on land reclaimed at enormous cost from the sea. While such developments sometimes involved fabulously expensive housing complexes, they typically centred on office blocks, glamorous retail sites or public buildings, such as the monumental municipal government building in central Tokyo, and with the re-development that surrounds them, they have helped to create the elegant and sophisticated business and shopping areas of the great cities.

---

[5] The average age at first marriage rose from 25.9 for men and 23.0 for women in 1950 to 28.4 for men and 25.9 for women in 1990. By 2000, it had reached 28.8 and 27.0 respectively and was still rising (*Kokumin seikatsu hakusho* 2007: Table 1.3). By the late 1990s, it was estimated that, in the age group 25–34, 19 per cent of men and 14 per cent of women continued to live with their parents (Rebick and Takenaka 2006: 9).

Away from these glossy centres, however, the living environment of most of those who lived and worked in the urban Japan of the 1980s and 1990s was still that of the densely packed residential and commercial neighbourhoods that had characterised towns and cities up and down the country ever since economic growth began. For many, housing space and quality had certainly improved since the 1960s, with private bathrooms, air-conditioning and Western-style furnishings now standard. Concrete walls, steel windows and vinyl flooring had replaced any remaining damp and draughty wood; solid partitions and lockable doors ensured new levels of privacy; balconies and tiny gardens provided oases of greenery. But still the relative space and solidity of urban housing in European or American cities remained unattainable in crowded, earthquake-prone Japan, while the streets and shopping arcades, thronged with bicycles, buses and taxis and lined with small shops, remained in some ways recognisably those of much earlier times (Fig. 7.1). Open spaces, speeding traffic and slumbering suburbia were no more part of the Japanese urban landscape than they had ever been.

Shopping, fashion and advertising

By the 1970s, and even more so in the 1980s, Japanese people were faced with an array of consumption choices far greater than anything they had experienced before. The infrastructure within which they made their choices and bought their goods adjusted to this situation in a number of ways, but not by any means straightforwardly along the lines laid down in the Anglo-American mass-marketing world. Japanese consumers developed their taste for fashion, branding and product differentiation in a retail environment that could encompass both the extremes of niche marketing and the overwhelming, must-have fad. With their substantial disposable incomes to spend, they exercised the skills of discrimination and judgement – of fitting the product to the situation – that they had built up across the range of Western- and Japanese-style goods now available to them within a retail and advertising world adapted to the practices that had developed out of the long history of consumption in Japan.

With the multiplication of everyday goods to be sold and with intensifying external pressure on the government, in the light of Japan's trade surplus, to level the playing field for large-scale retailers, life for the small shop became harder. The 'welfare' role of the small shop became less relevant as the public pension and welfare system improved and as younger generations took over retail establishments. In most late

Figure 7.1 A bus negotiates a shopping street in Kichijōji, a largely residential area of Tokyo.

twentieth-century urban localities, the streets of small shops and stalls selling fresh food, confectionery, hardware, medicines and cosmetics, books and magazines, and everyday goods in general were still to be found (Fig. 7.2), and rice merchants and liquor stores still offered personal service, although the tofu stalls and *tatami*-makers were gradually fading away. By the early 1990s, half of all food shops, for instance, still employed only one or two people, although the number of such small shops had declined sharply since the early 1970s.[6] Market liberalisation hit specialist rice-dealers and liquor stores particularly hard, but in

[6] Food and Agriculture Policy Research Center 1997: 77.

Figure 7.2 A Tokyo hardware shop, typical of the small-scale retailers still to be found in most urban residential areas.

general the tide of the supermarket became increasingly difficult to hold back, so that branches of chains such as Daiei and Itoyōkadō, selling the full range of food and drink, as well as clothes and household goods, were eventually to be found on the station plazas of most urban neigh-bourhoods.[7] Convenience stores, belonging to chains such as 7-Eleven, continued their march along the routes to and from the station, offering anonymous service from an army of students doing part-time jobs. By the time of the post-bubble recession, there were even discount stores and '100-yen shops', selling all manner of bargains. Although the out-of-town hypermarket, and any kind of retail outlet that depended on customers using cars, remained rare, everyday shopping, in urban areas at least, was gradually becoming less of a social activity.

Meanwhile, although housewives might buy many of their everyday groceries from a local supermarket, if not small local shops, and single students bought their pot noodles and cans of Coca-Cola in a 7-Eleven, much of the large array of less basic goods was now to be found in spe-cialised shops, typically located in the shopping centres that had come into existence in particular areas, often around key stations, in the cities.

[7] Advances in packaging eventually overcame the resistance to buying fresh food from supermarkets and all now sell pre-packed fresh fish, meat, etc. (Kikkawa 1998: 117).

Department stores – themselves often now constructed as collections of small retail outlets under one roof – remained the focus of these centres, but around them clustered arcades and underground shopping malls lined with smaller shops. These might sell particular specialised items or fashion goods in individual styles or brands, some, such as Parco and Loft, offering lifestyles consciously younger and trendier than those embodied in the goods sold in the old, respectable department stores.[8] Some, such as Muji or the amazing do-it-yourself and hobby store Tokyū Hands, were successful enough to expand and develop branch chains; others succeeded or failed as niche outlets according to their ability to keep up with trends. In centres such as Ikebukuro, Shibuya and later Omotesandō in Tokyo, Motomachi in Yokohama, Dōtonbori in Osaka and many, many more in a shifting hierarchy of fashionableness, crowds strolled through shopping malls and department stores, enjoying the atmosphere and abundance of goods, as once their Tokugawa forebears (though in much smaller numbers) might have done (Fig. 7.3).

Advertising was, of course, central to the process of product differentiation and fashion creation that made shopping a serious leisure activity, and the advertising industry, already big by the 1970s, continued to grow, largely under the control of Japan's one big advertising agency, Dentsū.[9] By this stage, television was becoming the major medium for advertising, with many new commercial channels being established, but the whole gamut of advertising possibilities – print media, billboards, sports sponsorship – continued to be employed as appropriate (Fig. 7.4). Although the healthy-looking housewife and her happy family still appeared regularly in advertisements for food and household products, much more sophisticated imagery was increasingly employed in many fields. The use – or misuse – of English (or occasionally other European languages) in brand names and advertising copy was much remarked by foreign visitors and analysts, but represented just one of many ways of suggesting international style and sophistication. By contrast, for some products, it was a nostalgic image of true 'Japaneseness' that advertising sought to convey, by means of rice fields, Japanese-style interiors and women in kimono.

[8] Joseph Tobin 1992a: 15. 'Fashion buildings', such as Parco, Lumine and 109, are 'segmented to create buildings with very defined consumer targets. In Shibuya, the main 109 building caters for late teen girls and young women, whilst 109-2 focuses on younger teenage children' (Larke and Causton 2005: 230).
[9] By the mid-1980s, Japan's advertising industry was the second-largest in the world in expenditure terms, though still way behind the United States in both total and per capita expenditure (Bowring and Kornicki 1993: 267).

Figure 7.3 A shop specialising in imported tea in Motomachi, the smart shopping area of Yokohama that originated as the location of shops catering to foreign residents after the opening of the ports in the middle of the nineteenth century.

Figure 7.4 Billboard advertisements for attractions in Asakusa, the amusement area for Tokyo dwellers since Tokugawa times.

Top-down advertising was not, however, the only way in which consumers were influenced to buy particular products. The continued propensity for fads and panics meant that certain products or brands mysteriously (to the foreign eye at least) emerged as must-have symbols of belonging to a particular group or category. The phenomenal success of the 'Hello Kitty' image, now also widely popular in other parts of East Asia, was a classic 1980s example, with the stylised cat eventually to be found on almost anything a schoolgirl might buy.[10] The overwhelming popularity of things and images considered 'cute' ('kawaii') – Hello Kitty of course, but also many other cuddly animals (like the pandas beloved of an earlier generation) and numerous manga characters and their merchandise – seemed to reflect the desires and demands of an increasingly significant market of girls and young women whose purchases appear to have been driven more by word-of-mouth communication and copying within social groups than any advertising campaign.

Japanese consumers thus set out on their 1980s buying spree amidst a huge array of retail establishments, ranging from the local supermarket or convenience store to the warrens of small, specialised and usually expensive shops in fashionable shopping centres. Like their counterparts all over the developed world, they were bombarded with information and images encouraging them to buy particular products. But they faced the unprecedented choice now available to them against the background of their historically determined pattern of consumption and their long-standing experience of selecting and using goods for enjoyment and meaning within their own economic and social contexts. The results are to be found in the consumption patterns observed in their everyday lives, and these are the subject of the next section.

Consumption in practice in the post-miracle years

By the 1980s, the much wider array of differentiated goods and services that the economic growth of the miracle period and after made available to shoppers, together with the efforts of advertisers to imbue these products with image and meaning, had made the choice of what to buy an increasingly complex one for Japanese consumers. At the same time, their growing experience of the rest of the world, through trade, tourism and the media, situated their consumer choices within a more internationalised context than had been the case previously. As

---

[10] Kitty was actually born in 1974, but her huge popularity stems from a 1980s revamp that made her more cute and cuddly. See *Nipponia* no. 40 (2007): 18.

consumers set about enjoying the possibilities that Japan's international economic strength opened up, they devised patterns of consumption, in their food and drink, their clothes, their household surroundings and their leisure activities, that enabled them to deploy fashion and style, from at home and abroad, in distinctive ways that reflected a widening range of individual and group identities. Nonetheless, these patterns were still conditioned in many ways by the structures and institutions – eating patterns, clothing styles, housing construction and the whole infrastructure of consumption – that remained as the legacy of earlier stages in Japanese consumption history.

Food and drink

By the 1970s, Japanese consumers were in a position to enjoy a much greater range of food and drink choices than had been available before the economic miracle, while needing to spend a declining proportion of their rising incomes on securing what they wanted to eat and drink. The share of food in total household expenditure (the Engel coefficient) declined from the 50 per cent level of the late 1940s to below 25 per cent by the early 1990s. The proportion of per capita calorie intake derived from rice, as the basic grain staple, fell from over 50 per cent in the 1950s to less than 25 per cent by the beginning of the 1990s, while the shares of livestock products (meat, eggs and dairy produce) on the one hand and oils and fats on the other rose sharply.[11] In these aggregate terms, therefore, Japanese people were coming to consume something closer to the more varied and in some respects more nutritious, though also more fattening, diet of the industrial West. Necessarily, given the diversification and, to some extent, 'Westernisation' of the diet, the proportion of food components that could be supplied by Japanese farmers and fishermen declined, and by the 1980s Japan was the world's largest food importer, significantly more dependent on foreign produce than most other developed countries.

Meanwhile, as in the West, a growing share of food expenditure was devoted to processed products, and Japanese people were able to enjoy the much greater range of foods, as well as the convenience, made possible by everything from commercially made sauces and seasonings, through tinned, dried and frozen foods, to pre-packed pizza. Processed foods – increasingly bought from supermarkets – helped housewives to

---

[11] Food and Agriculture Policy Research Center 1997: 14, 3. See also Appendix, Tables 4 and 6. The Engel coefficient nonetheless remained significantly higher than those of the US and major European countries (Rothacher: 1989: 95).

cope with the demands on their time, including, for many, more or less part-time work as well as the management of the household, care of elderly parents and the education of children, and with the complexities of catering for families who were less and less frequently able to assemble together at the same time for meals. Although the image of Japanese processed food typically involves the solitary student eating pot noodles in front of the television, it was in forms such as commercially made pickles, pre-packed *gyōza* dumplings, processed fish products or curry-sauce bases, heated up if necessary and served as elements in family meals, that its consumption really grew. Pre-packed *o-nigiri* rice balls, with fillings traditional (*umeboshi* pickled plums) and new (tuna mayonnaise), became the equivalent of sandwiches and a staple of the convenience store.[12]

In practice, therefore, the diversification of the diet continued, as before, around the basic 'rice plus side dishes' format, which remained the standard model for family meals at home. Surveys carried out in the early 1990s indicated a 50:50 split between rice and toast as the chosen breakfast, while noodles or bread served as a change from rice for lunch. Most evening meals, however, still involved rice, even if now eaten with a more predominant main dish within the range of accompaniments.[13] Rice, miso soup and green tea still headed the list of the most common dinner components, although beer followed closely behind. Supermarket shelves and chill-cabinets continued to display a range of pickled vegetables (to accompany plain rice) baffling to the foreign shopper, alongside processed cheese, pasta salads and sliced bread. At the same time, the demand for fresh food, especially fish, to be prepared at home did not disappear, and daily shopping trips, involving detailed inspection of the fish, fruit and vegetables on offer, to local shops or markets remained a fact of life for many housewives.

In the context of this continuing preference for Japanese-style food, the relative affluence that many households had achieved by the 1980s expressed itself in increasing product differentiation and quality-consciousness in relation to 'traditional' products. The (partial) freeing up of the rice distribution system in the 1980s led to competition to supply the particular varieties of rice considered most tasty, and branding (together with pricing) by variety and region of cultivation

---

[12] Here they compete with bread products, with the result that much of the bread consumed in Japan is sold flavoured and sweetened with some kind of topping, as the kind of ready-to-eat food in which convenience stores specialise (Larke and Causton 2005: 151–2).

[13] Food and Agriculture Policy Research Center 1997: 18–20.

Figure 7.5 Rice of different varieties on sale in Kyoto market.

became widespread (Fig. 7.5).[14] Preference for the best sashimi looked set to result in the extinction of the blue-fin tuna, while farmers throughout the world have laboured to supply the mass of Japanese consumers with types of fruit and vegetable once regarded as the height of luxury in Japanese cuisine (Fig. 7.6). The phenomenal prices paid in department stores for particularly large or beautiful specimens of fruit caught the headlines in the West, but more significant was the price differentiation, according to quality and image, increasingly observed in relation to products such as sake, soy sauce and tea. Sake connoisseurs savoured differentiated regional varieties and even *shōchū*, the spirit in which the poor had once drowned their sorrows, was sold in fancy bottles and became fashionable as a cocktail ingredient.[15]

This spreading demand for quality and differentiation in food and drink was also reflected in restaurant eating. Expenditure on eating out continued to grow rapidly during the 1970s and 1980s,[16] expanding and diversifying the practice of going to a restaurant as a leisure

---

[14] For details, see Francks 1998. The imported rice forced on Japan under multi-lateral trade agreements has never succeeded in overcoming the belief among consumers that home-grown rice tastes best.

[15] See S. Smith 1992.   [16] Cwiertka 2006: 165.

Figure 7.6 Fresh mushrooms, some from China and the United States, on sale in the Tsukiji indoor market in Tokyo.

activity that urban Japanese had been enjoying since the Tokugawa period. Establishments serving what had become accepted as Japanese cuisine, ranging from bars – some modelled on the *izakaya* of old – providing Japanese-style snacks with drinks, through sushi bars and restaurants offering speciality regional cuisine, to exclusive venues serving elaborate, seasonal, *kaiseki* menus, continued to predomin-ate in the entertainment quarters of towns and cities. However, it was also in the sphere of eating out that 'internationalisation' was most to be observed in relation to food and drink. 'Foreign' fast-food outlets became ubiquitous features of shopping malls, although the experience of a McDonald's in Japan was not the same in terms of either food or ambience as that to be had in the United States or indeed other parts of Asia.[17] Japanese diners became familiar with Italian, French, Indian and regional Chinese cuisine, elements of which began to find their

[17] See Watson 1997.

way into home-cooking too, and the popularity of Korean food was reflected in the huge demand that developed for *kimchi* pickled cabbage, which became a regular snack to have with beer and a standard addition to the range of pickles served with rice.

Meanwhile, as Japanese travellers and tourists took their food tastes abroad with them, Japanese food itself became increasingly part of the world of 'international cuisine'. Japanese restaurants in London and New York were originally established as a way of relieving homesick Japanese businessmen of some of their valuable yen, but were before long opening their doors to those of the local population who could afford to demonstrate an acquired taste for their exotic and beautifully presented meals. Eventually the international fashion for things Japanese produced more downmarket versions of Japanese or pseudo-Japanese food, supplied through chains of sushi and noodle bars, and London office workers were eventually buying, as packed lunches from Marks and Spencer, something approximating the sets of sushi that Edo tradesmen once snacked on. Just as Japanese consumers adapted 'foreign' food items to their own tastes and circumstances, so Japanese food abroad developed in its own way, eventually impacting back on what people in Japan ate and how they viewed it. New varieties of sushi designed in California or Hawaii were to be found on offer in Tokyo sushi bars; the fashionable took their sake with ice, while diluting their whisky with hot water and drinking it warm in the manner traditional with sake.[18]

Japanese food, for all its distinctiveness, had of course always been enmeshed in the international traffic in foodstuffs and ways of cooking and eating, but by the end of the twentieth century the web of influences was thus becoming ever more complex. Kōbe beef, the history of which goes back to the efforts to supply the foreigners who came to the port in the middle of the nineteenth century with the meat they craved, made the return trip as the ultimate beef-eating experience for wealthy Europeans and Americans. By the end of the twentieth century, Japanese consumers were not only fitting a much wider range of food and drink items into their historically determined meal patterns and changing forms of social activity, but were also viewing their cuisine as part of a globalised food culture.[19] This has involved not

---

[18] S. Smith 1992: 153. According to the *Guardian* newspaper (4 August 2008), for brewers of high-class sake in Japan, 'the best hope for a revival in the domestic market may rest on triggering a knock-on effect among ambivalent Japanese who decide to give sake another chance once they see how well it is going down among the style-conscious drinkers of London, New York and, increasingly, Moscow and Beijing'.

[19] For an indication of just how complex and post-modern this process can become, see Jeffrey Tobin 1992. The Japanese chef in his restaurant in Hawaii whom Tobin

only observing foreigners eating sushi with mayonnaise but even, just possibly, considering it themselves.

Clothing With their relatively abundant, post-miracle incomes, Japanese men and women of the 1970s and 1980s were able to accumulate wardrobes of Western-style clothes that served both the practical purposes of everyday life and the enjoyment of changing fashions. The continued prevalence of what amounted to uniforms associated with occupations – ranging from the obvious, such as white coats for doctors, through the particular forms of semi-traditional headgear, footwear and other accessories worn by tradespeople, to the much more subtly uniform male suits and female skirts and tops worn by company office workers – placed some restrictions on clothing choice but, when off duty, Japanese consumers were by now following global fashion with as much interest as their counterparts elsewhere in the developed world and at this stage with rather greater financial resources than many. The kimono was firmly relegated to strictly formal and/or very specifically Japanese occasions and shoppers spent their lunch-breaks and weekends trying on or window-shopping for branded fashion goods and designer accessories in the fashion boutiques and department stores that dominated shopping centres.

As a result, the fashion trends of the Western world continued to sweep through Japan too. Jeans and T-shirt, though of whatever was the correct brand of the moment, were standard leisurewear by the 1980s; hippie and punk styles, though without the political connotations they possessed in the West, each had their day.[20] Within this framework, however, fashions were increasingly defined and refined according to an agenda set by Japanese clothing consumers. Particular magazines became the fashion bibles of their times, prescribing the labels to be desired and the places where current style was to be seen. Motomachi in Yokohama gave way to Shibuya in Tokyo, only to be superseded in the 1990s by the smart areas of Nagoya and Kōbe where rich young ladies drove to big-brand shops in expensive cars.[21] Increasingly, however, individuals and groups developed their own takes on the trends of the day, stepping out, in the tradition of *o-share* that their forebears had established, in the varied and carefully constructed street fashions that

---

studies is creating 'a Japanese representation of a French chef's representation of Japanese cuisine' (161).

[20] For details and illustrations, see Jō 2007: 277–91.

[21] Jō 2007: 290–1.

impressed even Western celebrity designers. Dressing entirely in one designer brand or in a reconstructed version of school uniform, going to extremes with fake tan or white make-up, eventually even dressing up as a manga character ('cos-play') – all could be seen as forms of self-expression that made their own comment on the world of fashion and media that had given birth to them.[22]

The wherewithal to create such fashions was to be found in the vast array of clothes and accessory shops, large and small, that came and went in the shopping centres of the cities. Although international fashion chains, such as Benetton and Gap, and brands, such as Levi's, sold as well in Japan as anywhere else, and those who could afford it, in Japan or on their trips abroad, snapped up Armani suits and Gucci accessories, much of the clothing available in the Japanese market was designed and produced in Japan, even if it was given some kind of foreign-looking label. On this basis, Japanese designers did also begin to attempt to break into the world of international (though French-dominated) *haute couture*, in some cases with considerable success. Whether their Japanese backgrounds influenced their designs is perhaps open to doubt – the concept of 'Japanese fashion' is problematic for them, as for their Parisian competitors[23] – and the kimono has been an influential inspiration, from time to time, for non-Japanese fashion designers as well. However, the eventual incorporation of Japanese designers into the international fashion world was an indicator of the importance attached to the Japanese market by clothes producers and the attention paid to the intricacies of fashion, design and branding by Japanese consumers.

Those unable to afford the products of Paris and Milan, and perhaps more constrained by the demands of everyday life and work, also nonetheless found their own ways of employing and enjoying fashion in clothing. Even men, outside the office at least, followed trends in jeans and wore slightly more exciting ties. As had once been the case with the kimono, accessories continued to provide scope for adding a fashionable or high-class touch to an otherwise inexpensive outfit. By the bubble period, therefore, Japanese clothes-buyers had come to apply to their consumption of Western-style fashion something of the attention to detail and fashion nuance, as well as the ability to read the relation of quality and style in clothing to income, status and group membership, that they had once applied to kimono collars and *obi* colours.

---

[22] For an example of the serious cultural and gender-based analysis that such trends can produce, see Kinsella 2005.

[23] See Kondo 1992.

Mai hōmu *and* mai kā

As more and more people, through the 1970s and 1980s, moved into houses with more and more Western-style rooms and facilities, expenditure on the furniture and equipment required by different forms of cooking, eating and relaxing necessarily climbed. With fridges and washing machines now standard, microwave ovens and other more specialised electrical gadgets began to clutter up the still small space of the dining kitchen; ever larger and grander TVs stood alongside high-quality stereo systems; dining tables and chairs, sofas and armchairs filled up living areas; an air-conditioner was increasingly regarded as essential to comfortable living (see Appendix, Table 7). Continuing diversification in the elements making up meals necessitated a stock of Western-style plates and bowls, forks and spoons, mugs and glasses. Pictures and ornaments decorated the bookcases and coffee tables that no living room could now be without. Meanwhile, stocks of Japanese-style equipment – Japanese-style bowls and plates, chopsticks and drinking cups, ornamental vases, dolls and hangings and of course everything for the bath – still had to be maintained, if not improved in quality and variety.

Finding appropriate ways to furnish and decorate a house with such a mixture of elements had presented a challenge to homemakers ever since the middle classes had begun to move into suburban 'culture houses' and live 'modern lives' in the inter-war period. By the later decades of the twentieth century, the problems involved in choosing and adapting Western-style elements for the house faced the majority of housewives (usually), who now lived in housing equipped for more and more varied furnishings and had the resources to buy them. Whereas in the past the rules for furnishing in Japanese style had been reasonably clear, and in the post-war and miracle years the purchase of new goods – a large proportion of them electrical consumer durables – could be based on their functionality and 'rationality', by the 1980s Western-style furnishings had become more a matter of status and lifestyle choice. Home improvements involving Western-style furniture and decorations were advertised and promoted as the props to a more individualised and pleasurable way of life, unencumbered by the obligations to wider family and community implied by Japanese-style housing.[24] Home decoration magazines suggested ways in which even a small apartment might be re-decorated by the enterprising housewife in her own individual style to create a comfortable environment in which

---

[24] Rosenberger 1992.

she and her husband (and possibly children) could lead a relaxed life and entertain their freely chosen friends. Curtains and carpets could replace or conceal Japanese-style fixtures; Western-style lights, ornaments and mats could be used to suggest sophistication; Japanese-style clutter could be cleared away to create space in which to do one's own thing.

Meanwhile, many of the families who were in this way creating *mai hōmu* as a zone of privacy and individuality were by now able to extend that zone to include *mai kā*. The Japanese media dubbed 1966, the year when the number of cars in Japan came to exceed 10 million, 'the first year of the My-Car Era';[25] from then on the car became both affordable and necessary to the 'middle mass' family, with ownership rates exceeding 50 per cent of households in 1980 and 75 per cent in 1990.[26] There had been motor vehicles in Japan since the beginning of the twentieth century, and by the inter-war years taxis and buses were a familiar part of the urban scene, although private car ownership was limited to the very rich. The Occupation forces arrived equipped with a vast array of vehicles, and the American love affair with the car – as symbol of freedom, individuality and masculinity – began to permeate Japan. However, the Japanese-made cars that were all that was then available remained relatively expensive and not always very reliable, and it was the motorcycle – the Honda 50 especially – that mechanised and liberated personal transport in the crowded cities of the 1950s and early 1960s. Thereafter, however, as Japanese manufacturers mastered the art of producing small, reliable and relatively cheap family cars in a range of distinctive models (each with its own foreign-sounding name), the car became an essential household acquisition. The phenomenal export success of Japanese vehicle producers was based on the resulting rapidly growing home market of families establishing themselves, by the 1970s, in their own suburban homes and seeking to demonstrate and enjoy their newfound privacy and independence.

Nonetheless, Japan remained a far from ideal environment for car use: traffic congestion and the consequent air pollution became a massive problem in towns and cities; negotiating urban sidestreets was virtually impossible without local knowledge; and parking had to be pre-planned. Commuting by car was not an option in the cities and, if

---

[25] 'Mai kā gannen'. See Plath 1992: 230.

[26] Appendix, Table 7, based on the government survey of households of two or more people. The number of passenger cars in use per 1,000 people had risen to over 300 by the early 1990s, a figure still significantly below those for the United States and, though less so, France and Germany, but not far below that for the UK (Keizai Kōhō Center 1997: Table 10.9).

Figure 7.7 How to accommodate the car, the washing and the garden in contemporary Tokyo.

cars were used during the week, it was typically by wives and children. However, on Sundays, husbands took to the wheel and the outing by car to a scenic site or a family restaurant became a defining symbol of the nuclear family in its own little world. The 'Western parlor on wheels',[27] even if it rarely left the valuable parking space that it occupied, was decorated with ornaments, cleaned and tidied, and even blessed at a shrine, as an extension of the family's own private space and individual identity. The car, even if not greatly used as a means of transport, had embedded itself into the lifestyle of Japanese families as an extension of the private and partially Western-style homes that they were by now able to create for themselves (Fig. 7.7).

In this context, some of the features of the Japanese 'traditional' house and lifestyle, abandoned in the rush to acquire sofas, carpets and solid walls, began to take on new meaning. For those able to afford them, a Japanese-style garden, a tea-ceremony space, a *tatami* room fitted out with *tokonoma* and *shoji* screens, even a kettle (of the antique black type) hanging over a fake *irori* fire-pit became luxury elements in interior design (Fig. 7.8). This style was not, as Nancy Rosenberger

[27] Plath 1992: 236.

Figure 7.8 A contemporary version of the *irori* hearth and suspended kettle (compare Fig. 3.2), on sale in Tokyo in 2007.

points out, derived from the world of 'tattered tatami and torn shoji' inhabited by most people in the past, but reflected rather the samurai villas and castles preserved as stately homes and settings for TV 'samurai dramas'. In this re-created form, Japanese style had become, for the wealthy, 'one alternative among many, a commodity to be self-consciously chosen and consumed'.[28] In home furnishings, as in much

[28] Rosenberger 1992: 122.

else, the traditional items that had become consumer goods prior to or alongside the influx of products generated by industrialisation and internationalisation were re-created in the light of the new.

Leisure and travel

Japanese people had of course always enjoyed a variety of leisure pursuits and forms of travel. In the Tokugawa period, the urban population frequented amusement parks and the theatre, while villagers came together for festivals and to enjoy the performances of travelling storytellers and puppet-theatre groups. In rural and urban areas alike, the upper, and increasingly also the middle, classes engaged in poetry-writing, *nō* chanting, painting and calligraphy, and trips to pilgrimage sites or beauty spots were common. By the first half of the twentieth century, in urban areas at least, new possibilities were opening up: there were cinemas, concerts, funfairs and variety shows to go to, baseball matches to watch and trips to the seaside or mountain resorts to make. By the 1950s and 1960s, television was transforming the landscape of leisure activity, both by commercialising activities such as sport and by luring audiences with entertainment that could be enjoyed in the privacy and solitude of the home. But golf ranges, fishing pools and pachinko parlours, along with all the establishments offering drink, sex and fun in the *sakariba* areas of cities where men (mostly) went to relax, all continued to supply commercialised entertainment, while the providers of classes and equipment for flower-arranging, the tea ceremony and a whole range of traditional 'hobbies' grew to be big businesses. Through the miracle years, the commodification of leisure activities thus became virtually complete.

By the 1980s, therefore, deciding what to do with your leisure time had become much more significantly a matter of consumer choice. Persistently long (though nonetheless declining) work hours meant that Japanese people continued to have less free time and fewer holidays than their European counterparts at least, but rising incomes opened up many more options for the time that there was. The high value of the yen in the 1980s made foreign travel a mass possibility in a way that it had not been before, and no European historic site, from the Tower of London to the Acropolis, was complete without its camera-wielding Japanese coach party. Over time, fashions in foreign travel widened and shifted: the honeymoon in Hawaii and the whistle-stop tour of European capitals gave way to the golf trip to the Philippines and the beach holiday in Australia. But, wherever they went, Japanese travellers consistently took their consumption habits with them.

As a result, it was shopping, according to Japanese principles and customs, that often provided the focus of the holiday.[29] In part this reflected the opportunity to buy (cheaply) status-symbol items – Prada handbags, Burberry coats, Scotch whisky, Wedgwood china – that were expensive or hard to find at home. But mainly it was a matter of souvenir gifts (*omiyage*), as it had been for Japanese travellers, at home and abroad, ever since Tokugawa times – at home, a regional variety of sake was a standard gift to take back from a trip; abroad, it was Johnny Walker or Chivas Regal.[30] *Omiyage* would include the kinds of typical local product that everyone buys as souvenirs, but also, and more significantly, international branded goods – perfume, whisky, designer accessories, branded sportswear and so on – to take back as customary and necessary gifts to family, friends, colleagues and superiors. In major Japanese tourist destinations, such as Waikiki in Hawaii, specialist Japanese shopping centres came to cater to the honeymoon couples and parties of office-ladies who arrived clutching their shopping guides and checklists of gift-recipients. Shopping abroad in the 1980s had become an extension of shopping at home.

For those without the time or resources to take holidays abroad, something of the experience could be gained from visiting Tokyo Disneyland, which opened in 1984, or the various 'foreign villages' that were set up as tourist attractions around the country. However, just as the experience of 'real' foreign countries was to some extent 'Japanised' by the facilities and practices that surrounded foreign travel, so the theme parks, while 'keeping the exotic exotic', adapted it into a form that was comfortable and accessible to their Japanese visitors. As Waikiki filled up with Japanese shopping malls, so Tokyo Disneyland was constructed to provide more space for shopping than its American original, selling more expensive, higher-quality goods to meet the need for *omiyage*.[31]

Meanwhile, there were more strictly Japanese leisure activities to consume at home. Some of these – such as skiing or mountain climbing (both necessitating extremely expensive clothing and equipment) – could be classed as relatively new, but many involved traditional facilities or pursuits adapted to the needs of the modern mass-market consumer. Company groups enjoyed bonding sessions at hot-spring resorts; groups of friends or colleagues picnicked under the cherry blossom in

---

[29] Japanese tourists to Hawaii in the 1980s, for instance, spent nearly three times as much per person per day as their North American and European counterparts; 30 per cent of this was on gifts and souvenirs, compared with only 9 per cent for US tourists (Nitta 1992: 205).
[30] Nitta 1992: 207.   [31] Brannen 1992.

famous parks; coach parties went to view the autumn colours in Kyoto. Japanese-style inns (*ryokan*) continued to offer the 'authentic' experience of 'traditional' food, furnishings and customs to those for whom they had become almost as exotic as the foreign 'Other'. Although the real countryside (as opposed to mountains for climbing and forests to hike in) has never had much appeal to the urban Japanese, villages struggling to survive in the face of agricultural decline re-branded themselves as tourist locations where visitors could experience, or feel nostalgia for, 'traditional' rural ways of life.

On a day-to-day level too, new forms of leisure activity – from watching TV to participating in Western sports, playing classical music or attending a rock concert – were pursued alongside 'traditional Japanese' ones that adapted to the needs and aspirations of late twentieth-century consumers. Many traditional arts and crafts – martial arts, flower-arranging, traditional music and dance, poetry-writing – attracted large numbers of practitioners as hobbies or routes to personal accomplishment. For the mothers of marriageable daughters, the tea-ceremony courses, like the English-language classes, to which they dispatched their offspring offered a useful qualification in the marriage market. Television turned sumo into a huge commercial spectacle, and *go* and mah-jong acquired their slots in the schedules too. Here, though, they competed with baseball, golf, soccer and tennis, as well as the massively popular gambling sports of horse-racing and speed-boat racing, themselves subtly adapted to the ways of life of their Japanese participants and audiences. The leisure activities of the post-miracle years had become commodified consumer choices, but, whether Western-derived or 'traditional', nonetheless offered sources of personal satisfaction and social interaction that fitted into the internationalised but still distinctive everyday lives of Japanese consumers.

The ambivalent consumer[32]

During the bubble years of the 1980s, Japan could be portrayed as home to millions of the world's most archetypal consumers. Huge sums were spent on designer goods, impossibly expensive meals and entertainment, luxury cars and exotic foreign travel. Japanese people appeared to have become thoroughly immersed in the business of defining themselves by means of the goods they acquired and the 1980 novel *Nantonaku kurisutaru* (Somehow, Crystal), which described the lives of affluent

---

[32] The term devised as the title of a major collection of papers on saving and consumption in twentieth-century Asia (Garon and Maclachan 2006).

young people almost entirely in terms of the goods they bought and the places they went (complete with notes on the goods and where to buy them), became a best-seller and symbol of the times.[33] For Joseph Tobin, Japanese consumers of the 1980s were proving themselves less 'ambivalent' about the joys of consumption than their Anglo-American counterparts, demonstrating an almost childlike enjoyment of the things they were now able to buy.[34] Nonetheless, savings rates remained high, and by the 1990s the prolonged stagnation that followed the collapse of the bubble was being blamed on the reluctance of Japanese consumers to go out and spend for the nation. It seemed that perhaps, after all, the ultimate Japanese consumer had not really overcome an ambivalence towards consumption spending born of a century of exhortation to save and consume only 'rationally', not to mention an even older Confucian tradition of frugality.

By the end of the twentieth century, Japanese people clearly still regarded saving as a valuable and necessary part of their lives, especially when their economic circumstances were insecure, as in the 1990s, and, given the ways in which they had come to relate to goods in society, they were not always prepared to spend more for their own immediate gratification, even when urged to do so by the state. Like their counterparts elsewhere, they were also not by now without their doubts and questions over aspects of the world of consumption in which they lived. But two centuries of consumption history had produced not just consumers able to enjoy goods and to express their identity through them in what they saw as appropriate forms, but also a society in many respects held together by the particular ways in which goods had permeated social life. The anxieties and problems that late twentieth-century consumerism raised for Japanese people could therefore only be confronted by means of consumerist activity itself.

Goods in society

In Japan, as much as if not more than elsewhere in the developed world, goods had been associated with status from very early on and, as the market economy spread and incomes rose, growing numbers had become able to participate in a world in which differences between people were reflected in differences in what they ate and wore and the furnishings and fixtures of their everyday lives. New goods, many originating in the West but some from other parts of Asia, were incorporated

---

[33] For an analysis of *Nantonaku kurisutaru*, see Field 1989.
[34] Joseph Tobin 1992a: 21.

into structures of consumption as they adjusted to the economic, social and cultural changes wrought by economic growth and industrialisation. The emergence of the 'middle mass' as a result of the economic miracle appeared to blur this structure of differentiation – after all, everyone ended up with the same sets of electrical goods, the family saloon, the office uniform and the dining kitchen – and homogeneity and equality were important values that helped to define Japanese identity and justify Japan's economic success. But beneath this lay continuation of a whole set of practices whereby goods were differentiated, used and enjoyed within the context of economic change and the shifting structures of social groups and hierarchies. As John Clammer puts it, the art was 'to consume and to be known to consume, while simultaneously maintaining an ideology of equality'.[35]

The post-miracle culmination of the long history of Japanese consumption growth therefore in fact involved the conjunction of a complex pattern of product differentiation on the supply side with the segmentation of the market into what became known as 'micro masses' on the demand side. Japanese manufacturing systems and technology, epitomised by the so-called just-in-time system perfected in the motor industry during the 1960s, had long been designed to make possible the production of a range of subtly different versions of each model, each of which would slot into its particular niche in the market. Manufacturers were ranked by consumers according to the quality and price, hence status, of their products, and the naming and branding of goods was crucial to their success. Acquiring the right product, with all that it said about you – whether designer handbag, family car or fluffy toy to hang on your key-ring – from within a subtly differentiated range was central to the consumer's skill, and shoppers devoted much time and energy to researching within the mass of information available to help them. As *Nantonaku kurisutaru* had demonstrated, products with foreign names indicated all sorts of things about their purchasers that needed knowledge to decipher. Equally, though, just as in Tokugawa times, cachet was still attached to having the skill and knowledge, as well as the income, to buy the first autumn mushrooms of the season.

However, the 'rightness' of a product was not just a matter of the personal enjoyment of it, but was also bound up with its associations with the particular group or category to which the consumer belonged or aspired to belong. Goods such as clothes acted as markers of age, social or marital status and group identity, enabling producers to segment the market. Just as the colours and styles of kimono reflected the season,

---

[35] Clammer 1997: 4.

level of formality and social status to which the wearer aspired, so particular brands of T-shirt or jeans identified young people as belonging to particular groups or categories. Manufacturers and advertisers became adept at breaking down the 'middle mass' into 'micro masses,' subtly graded and differentiated within the vast middle class to which most people claimed to belong. Of course Japan is by no means unique in this respect, but the particular ways in which the growing quantity and variety of goods had been incorporated into consumers' everyday social lives over the course of their by-now long consumption history made product differentiation and segmentation, and the art of reading them, central to consumption practice, even in the era of mass production and mass marketing. Goods mattered because they helped to define the shifting groups and hierarchies of which Japanese society was made up.

This function of goods was instantiated and symbolised in the practice of gift-giving, which remained an important driver of consumption expenditure and a key mechanism whereby a changing variety of goods was used not just for personal enjoyment or for defining group identity, but also for cementing and symbolising social relationships.[36] While increased travel at home and abroad continued to expand the scope for *omiyage* purchases, traditional gift-giving at New Year and mid-summer, and at weddings, continued to operate, demanding ever greater knowledge on the part of the gift-giver as the range of appropriate items changed and social situations shifted. Meanwhile, new gift-giving occasions, such as Christmas and Valentine's Day, became increasingly entrenched, with their own customs and practices – female office workers must give their male superiors boxes of chocolates as Valentine's presents, for instance. The goods involved in such processes are rarely desired in themselves – in fact, a good deal of recycling of gifts goes on and the 'good' housewife keeps a stock-cupboard of past gifts that might come in handy in future. They remain symbols, carefully judged for appropriateness, in price, quality and nature, to the social relationship between giver and recipient rather than to what the recipient might like or enjoy. In the world of gifts, therefore, goods retain a social value distinct from the satisfaction of private, individualistic desires that other forms of consumption seek to satisfy.

---

[36] According to Larke and Causton, 12–15 per cent of department stores' annual sales take place during the traditional July and December gift-giving periods. 'Buying gifts at the right department store demonstrated that you had gone the extra mile, you hadn't skimped on cost, and you had made the effort to impress the recipient of the gift' (Larke and Causton 2005: 84, 88).

Consumption had thus become embedded as a necessary part of the system whereby Japanese society functioned and maintained itself, as well as playing a role as the largest element of aggregate demand in the economy. Goods had, in fact, been incorporated into everyday life not just as the means to satisfy personal desires but also as the oil that lubricated society. Even an object as humble and 'traditional' as the *bentō* packed-lunch box, symbolising traditional customs and family relationships but adapted to the demands of modern life, had become something that could 'allow Japanese to display individualism without losing their membership in a group... the opportunity of asserting their own identity, while stressing bonds with others'.[37] Japanese consumers did not therefore always just spend more for the sake of it, but rather as and when it could be justified by social practice as well as individual satisfaction. The guilt and doubt that might have attached to conspicuous consumption to achieve individual gratification – the 'frivolous' spending of *Nantonaku kurisutaru,* apparently abandoned in favour of saving when conditions were no longer appropriate – did not apply to the expenditure that had become part of what held society – its families, groups and hierarchies – together.

Questioning consumption through consumption

This social validation of consumption did not however mean that aspects of consumerism were never questioned, and the active and concerned consumer had become, by the 1980s, a significant element within civil society in Japan, as in Europe and the United States. What it did mean, though, was that consumers expressed and dealt with their anxieties not through the rejection of consumerism as such, but rather through its use in new ways. During the miracle years, the assumption seemed to have been that producers and consumers shared an overriding common interest in the achievement of economic growth and rising household incomes. By the 1980s, however, with the production and marketing of goods increasingly dominated by global big business, it could no longer be assumed that the success of corporate strategies necessarily coincided with the health and welfare of Japanese consumers and their environment. Like their counterparts elsewhere, Japanese consumers responded to this situation by organising themselves to campaign at the national political level, but they also, perhaps more successfully, devised new ways at the local and community level of acquiring goods in which they could feel confident. At the same time,

[37] Rodriguez del Alisal 2000: 41.

with the help of producers and retailers, it has to be said, they found the means to express their anxieties about their late twentieth-century consumerist world through the very products that they bought, as they sought 'transcendence of consumerism through consumerism'.[38] As a result, in the broader political, social and moral context, consumption in Japan continued to be practised and justified not solely as a matter of satisfying individual wants, but also as an activity with ramifications for the community and nation as a whole.

Given the ways in which goods had come to be used within Japanese society, their quality and safety were central to their value – serving anything less than the freshest fish or giving an imperfect present were not to be contemplated. A key part of the role of the housewife, as it had emerged since the inter-war years, was to develop the skills necessary to protect the family from impure products and ensure its social standing through the buying and giving of appropriately perfect goods. As long as most food was bought fresh from family-run shops and stalls, and durable goods from small-scale local suppliers or prestigious department stores, the housewife could rely on her personal relationships and local knowledge to carry out her role. By the 1980s, forces such as the growth in imports of consumer goods, the increased role of processed-food products and the growing share of impersonal supermarkets and convenience stores in the retail market put the knowledge required to ensure the quality and safety of goods beyond the reach of the individual housewife and appeared to place the consumer increasingly at the mercy of the producer.

Japanese consumers reacted to these trends by organising for their own protection. As elsewhere, a consumer movement was emerging by the 1970s, led by bodies such as the Housewives' Federation (Shufuren) in which women played significant roles. Although this movement was not unconcerned with issues that affected prices and consumer access to goods, such as anti-competitive business practices, much of its attention focused on developing the political and legislative means to ensure product quality and safety and to give consumers the information, via for example product labelling, that they now needed to make judgements about what they bought for their families. In general, though not absolute, terms, consumers and their emerging representative organisations seemed prepared to accept high prices and to ally with domestic producers in ways that might appear almost treacherous to an Anglo-American consumer activist, if that was what it took to guarantee that what was consumed was safe and wholesome.

[38] Creighton 1998a: 128.

In this environment, food products were bound to become the main focus of attention for consumers and their representatives. In 1983, consumer groups organised their most significant nationwide campaign to date in opposition to government moves, partly in response to foreign pressures, to relax the regulatory restrictions on the use of artificial food additives widely believed to be potentially harmful.[39] The eventual failure of the campaign was a considerable setback to the national consumer movement, but its scale and intensity did demonstrate the widespread concern among consumers about food safety. Subsequently, food scares, involving both imported and domestic products, continued to provoke panic and immediate import bans. When the domestic rice harvest failed in 1993, consumers panic-bought whatever supplies of trustworthy Japanese rice they could lay their hands on, while the stocks of foreign rice brought in by the government to stop the gap lay unsold, condemned in the media as dirty and contaminated, as well as less tasty than home-grown rice.[40] In this, as in other areas, consumers' representatives allied with farmers and other small businesses to support and protect, at whatever price, the goods that they associated with a safe and healthy Japanese lifestyle.

Meanwhile, consumers were also organising themselves at the local and grass-roots level to try to ensure that the goods they bought were safe and pure and that their provenance was known. The market for organic food began to grow and schemes which directly linked neighbourhood consumer groups with individual farmers also became popular. The consumer co-operative (*seikyō*) movement has a long history in Japan and has come to constitute 'a real alternative system' and 'a genuine social movement'.[41] *Seikyō* membership grew rapidly through the 1970s and 1980s, and by the early 2000s the membership of retail co-operatives had reached 16 million, nearly all of them women.[42] While many consumer co-operative organisations have come to operate effectively as shops, others developed as networks of communal buying groups with considerable influence. As a result, manufacturers and retailers often found co-operation with consumer groups to be in their interests, since those who did not match the co-operatives' standards in the quality and reliability of their products risked losing market share to them.[43]

[39] See Maclachlan 2002: ch. 7.   [40] Francks 1998: 11–12.   [41] Clammer 1997: 42.
[42] Japan Consumer Co-operative Union, Facts and Figures 2006 at jccu.coop/eng/public/pdf/ff_2006.pdf. However, although the Japanese consumer co-operative movement is among the largest in the world in terms of membership, it only accounts for around 2.5 per cent of total retail sales and 5–6 per cent of food sales.
[43] Maclachlan 2006: 252.

For many members, consumer co-operatives no doubt represented simply a convenient and sociable way of buying goods in which they could feel confident. The wider movement, however, was based on the principle that consumer goods, especially food, should be treated as 'life resources', rather than as branded and advertised commercial goods from which producers and retailers profit. The large-scale membership of *seikyō* and the influence in general of housewives' groups and consumer representatives, while in some ways a reflection of the abiding attraction of ideas of 'rationalisation' in daily life and the professionalisation of the housewife's role which go back to the inter-war years, clearly also arises from deep-seated concerns about the nature of commercial consumer goods and their welfare and environmental implications. The argument that agriculture is not a commercial activity producing consumer goods was being made by agricultural officials and farmers' representatives as far back as the turn of the century. However, in the era of globalised trade and food scares in which Japanese consumers found themselves by the 1980s and 1990s, growing numbers showed themselves willing to organise to acquire consumer goods in new ways and to adopt the role of 'consumer-as-citizen' that Patricia Maclachlan argues has become increasingly important in mobilising grass-roots consumer activism.[44]

Concerns about the implications of a consumerist economy for the safety and quality of products, especially food, could thus be addressed through practical steps to organise 'non-consumerist' ways of acquiring goods. Ultimately, however, given that the mass of Japanese consumers had indeed, over the generations, come to see goods as integrally involved in their social lives as Japanese citizens, vaguer anxieties about the world of consumption in which they lived could really only be expressed by means of consumer goods themselves. The affluence which large numbers of Japanese people had been able to achieve by the 1980s produced not just debate over the human and environmental costs incurred in the successful pursuit of economic growth, but also the luxury of nostalgia for what might have been lost in the process. Japan had entered the age of 'things other than things' (*mono igai no mono*), when department stores discovered that an image as a promoter of culture – staging art exhibitions and cultural events – and even philosophy – providing the means to a 'meaningful human life' – was by no means detrimental to sales.[45]

Central to the 'things other than things' which were felt to have been lost was 'traditional rural life', which meant in this context not

---

[44] Maclachlan 2002: esp. 251–3.   [45] Creighton 1998b.

relentless agricultural toil, but rather the local products and tourist experiences that embodied the urban consumer's idea of the natural countryside and the close rural community. *Furusato* – literally 'old village' but implying rural roots and home cooking – became a key marketing term and department stores gave over whole floors to the '*furusato* products' – food and craft goods beautifully packaged and tied to rural localities – that commodified nostalgia and embodied a sense of belonging to a small community which was otherwise hard to realise in the modern city.[46]

Nostalgia could be applied to urban areas as well, though. During the 'Edo boom' of the 1980s and 1990s, the old city became the urban equivalent of the *furusato*, embodying the lost 'Other' world of Japanese tradition and community against which the globalised modernity of contemporary Japan had to be viewed.[47] Interest in the history of urban everyday life was embodied in the Edo-Tokyo Museum, eventually opened in 1993 in a monumental new building in the city, but also found expression in the search for those few 'traditional' urban neighbourhoods that had survived both bombing and re-development.[48] The 'nostalgia boom' encompassed anything from the tenement row-houses in which pre-war urban workers had once lived to the *rāmen* noodle restaurants that had blossomed in the cities in the 1950s.[49] As Jordan Sand points out, such nostalgia was directed at whatever embodied 'rootedness and community ... low-tech, small and intimate spaces ... territory outside the dominance of the state, capitalism or global culture centered in the West'. As such, it could be seen as 'an expression of ambivalence about modern life – and therefore potentially a reaction against consumerism'.[50] Yet, in the context of late twentieth-century Japan, that expression could only take the form of consumption activities, such as buying retro and 'anachro-modern' goods through which one could 'feel the gap' between the past and the present, or eating at cheap old-fashioned restaurants selected from the *B-grade Gourmet* guide.[51] So profoundly had the world of goods become incorporated into Japanese society that ambivalence about consumption could only be expressed through the supremely consumerist – though in fact very long-standing – medium of the restaurant guide.

[46] See Creighton 1998a.   [47] See Gluck 1998.
[48] For an analysis of the Edo-Tokyo Museum and its meaning, see Sand 2001.
[49] The *Rāmen* Museum in Yokohama centres on a wonderful, nostalgia-inducing mock-up of a 1950s urban neighbourhood within which are located replicas of *rāmen* restaurants serving various local varieties of the noodle and soup dish. The museum shop sells pre-packed gourmet versions, devised by named chefs, to take away and prepare at home.
[50] Sand 2006: 86, 84.   [51] Sand 2006: 97–8.

Although Japanese people remained more willing than some of their Western counterparts to defer consumption through saving and exhibited a concern with the quality, safety and authenticity of what they bought that gave consumers' representatives considerable influence, there could be no reversing of the long history that had embedded goods in particular ways within the changing structure of Japanese economic and social life. Indeed, in the heady times of the bubble, consumers demonstrated none of the puritanical guilt that the possession of luxuries sometimes evokes elsewhere, but rather an ability to enjoy and play with differentiated goods that led some to portray Japan as the archetype of the post-modern society in which brands, images and advertising constitute whatever reality there is.[52] Over the longer term too, it had come to be through goods that many aspects of social relationships were expressed, validating their acquisition, enjoyment and display not as the satisfaction of desires or the expression of individuality, but as what held society together. The ambivalence that Japanese people appeared to feel towards consumption in fact reflected just how seriously they took the goods that it involved and the practices that surrounded it.

Of course by no means all Japanese goods have been consumed within the framework of social relationships – the pot noodle and the Walkman are after all Japanese inventions. By the 1990s, with the spread of the mobile phone, the development of ever more sophisticated computer games and the massive popularity of manga and anime, Japanese consumers, especially the younger ones, seemed to be turning to forms of consumption that were a good deal more solitary and/or less socially conditioned than those practised up to then. At the extreme, the phenomenon of young people, often labelled *otaku*, who withdrew from society into a solitary world of manga and computer-game reality, emerged as a much talked-about social and cultural issue, along with other forms of anti-social behaviour among the young. For the most part, such problems were blamed on social and institutional structures such as those of the education system rather than on the goods that made a solitary or anti-social life possible. Moreover, *otaku* do share their world with other *otaku*, even if only via electronic or other media, and are 'active consumers', selecting from and playing with the array of virtual products available to them. It has even been argued that they in fact represent the post-modern reincarnation of the Edo connoisseur/flâneur (the *tsū*), refining their appreciation of both craftsmanship and style not in relation to the textiles, cuisine and cool chic cultivated by

---

[52] See Miyoshi and Harootunian 1989.

their Edo forebears, but rather through absorption in manga, anime and video games in all their various forms.[53] It is not therefore a foregone conclusion that those who, by means of consumer goods, have become able to retreat so effectively into their own worlds will necessarily lose the long-honed capacity of Japanese people to use goods in the socially conditioned ways that have, up to now, validated their acquisition.

[53] Steinberg 2004.

8 The Japanese consumer past and present

This book has attempted to tell a long story: from the stylish kimono accessories that young women paraded through the streets of eighteenth-century Edo to the street fashions created by their descendants in 1990s Tokyo; from the sushi and noodles with which the working people of pre-modern Edo and Osaka filled themselves up to the menus of elegant late twentieth-century restaurants in Tokyo and New York; from the clocks and bicycles and sewing machines that began to clutter Japanese homes in the early twentieth century to the electronic gadgets without which Japanese people, like their counterparts elsewhere in the modern world, are nowadays lost. The argument has been that the Japanese consumer, whose tastes and habits many in the world have now come to share, has a history – one which goes back a long way and incorporates both 'indigenous' consumer goods and selected elements of the foreign lifestyles confronting Japanese people over the years – that has to be recognised in any explanation of the growth and development of the Japanese economy.

The starting point of this story, in Japan as in the Europe of the 'consumer revolution', hence lies in changes in attitudes to goods and their uses in society that had begun well before anything resembling modern industrial production existed and in advance of the arrival of those who brought with them the goods and lifestyles of the industrial West. The association between goods and political and social status, which sumptuary regulations vainly tried to maintain, began to break down in the cities almost as soon as the conditions for the expansion of the commercial economy, and the production and distribution systems that went with it, became established under the 'Pax Tokugawa'. While those growing richer on the profits of commercial growth enjoyed the 'floating world' of transient pleasures – as pictured in prints that were also advertisements – in the restaurants, tea-houses and shops of the great cities, those who worked for them snacked on street food, smoked and drank in open-air bars, and bought quack medicines, hair ornaments and children's toys at fairs and festivals.

218

By the nineteenth century, the commercial elite in the countryside were also coming to use and enjoy goods in new ways, picking up the tastes of their urban counterparts and developing them to suit their own circumstances, as they sought to establish their economic and social position in their world. Carrying out home improvements, providing a daughter with a fashionable trousseau, eating white rice with the kinds of fresh and processed accompaniments that city people dined on, exchanging books, poems, calligraphy and tea-ceremony experiences with neighbouring country gentlemen: all combined consumption for personal enjoyment with the expression of status-enhancing style and cultivation. For more ordinary farmers and rural workers, the sophisticated food and drink, clothes and cultural pursuits of the cities remained out of reach, but nonetheless some white rice to mix with other grains, preserved fish bought from a door-to-door fish-merchant, the occasional treat of shop-bought confectionery, a comb or a bright new kimono collar persuasively sold by a passing peddler all became increasingly possible when and where the commercial economy raised incomes and opened up market connections with the wider world.

This growing consumption of goods was inextricably linked with the expansion of the 'traditional' economy now recognised as taking place through to the end of the nineteenth century and beyond. Output growth in commercial agriculture and manufacturing generated the money incomes that fuelled growing demand for consumer goods, as more and more households and small businesses, in the countryside as much as in the towns and cities, engaged in the production of processed food products, textiles and household goods. As in Europe, the growing demand for cheaper yet more fashionable clothes, for populuxe clothing accessories and household equipment, for tea, tobacco and sugar, fuelled pre-industrial growth and created consumer markets that preceded the introduction of the factory system and mass production, whether home-grown or imported. In fact, in the Japanese case, the small-scale producers who generated the wide and differentiated range of consumer goods that was being formed in the Tokugawa period continued, with the help of their own borrowings from amongst the technological and marketing possibilities opened up by exposure to the industrial West, to meet a large part of consumer demand through to the post-Second World War period. The pre-industrial consumer and the industries that met his/her demand were to prove not so much a precursor or 'necessary analogue' to Japan's industrial revolution as a continuous, though modernising, presence within it.

As a result, by the middle of the nineteenth century, when Japanese people were able to observe – in the flesh or via the media – the influx of Europeans and Americans, with their strange costumes, their devotion to meat-eating and their predilection for beer, Japanese cities were clearly already well endowed with specialist shops, restaurants of many different kinds and leaders of fashion and style fully conversant with the ways in which goods could be deployed in the pursuit of taste and distinction. Thereafter, the skills of the pre-industrial consumer were to be applied to finding out about, accommodating and enjoying some of the new goods that contact with the West presented, but pre-existing tastes and practices – the 'rice plus side dishes' meal pattern; the social functions of goods as gifts and of eating out and drinking with colleagues and neighbours; the structure and fixtures of Japanese-style housing; even, for a long while, the kimono and all its accessories – were by no means forgotten. New, Western-style goods were acquired – though largely only by the better-off and urban middle classes – where they served a purpose, whether as symbols of style (Western-style hats and umbrellas), as elements in a more convenient and 'rational' lifestyle (matches and aspirin, electric heaters and kitchen tables) or simply as sources of fun (ice cream, cinema, beer and baseball). More significant, however, for the everyday lives of the majority of people, as they adapted to urban industrial growth and its impact on social and family life, was the 'modernisation' of the 'traditional' goods that continued to meet most of their consumption needs. Sake and soy sauce became branded products, advertised in the new national media, while machine-made kimono material brought fashion within the reach of the ordinary girl.

The 'domestication' of Western-style goods within a consumption pattern largely framed by the pioneering consumers of Tokugawa-period cities, combined with the fact that, before long, Japanese manufacturers proved able to meet much of the demand for such goods, meant that the creative absorption of Western industrial modernity invoked less anxiety and resistance than was to be experienced in, for example, China, then and since. As Kenneth Pomeranz has shown, prior to the 'Great Divergence' in the eighteenth century, levels of consumption of key goods such as textiles and sugar were higher in significant parts of China than in European countries on the brink of the industrial revolution, so that the pre-industrial consumer, both of 'everyday luxuries' and of fashionable elite durable goods, appears to have been as prevalent as in England or, for that matter, Japan.[1] Subsequently, however, the association of Western-style goods with Western, and eventually Japanese, imperialism – and with a lifestyle that many appeared not to find desirable – precluded both the easy absorption of new goods into

[1] Pomeranz 2000: ch. 3.

pre-existing consumption patterns and the 'modernisation' of trad-itional products, as well as generating agonised debate over national identity.[2] In Japan, on the other hand, in reality much more secure against the predations of the West, state and society were able to utilise new goods, and the technology that produced them, first to demon-strate 'civilisation and enlightenment' to the world and then to carve out a modern Japanese identity ultimately as threatening to China as that of the West. Although strands of nostalgia for 'traditional Japan', and the goods and moral values in which it was seen to be embodied, were already appearing in the inter-war years and the war-time state did try, for its own reasons, to redirect Japanese consumers towards their pre-industrial selves, the clock could no longer be turned back. Hence, while the post-war Chinese state, like many of its contemporary Third World counterparts, continued to try to defy the lure of Western products, Japanese producers and consumers were eagerly turning tel-evisions and stereos into expressions of a 'unique' Japanese identity.

As a result, and despite the Japanese reputation for frugality, con-sumption was to remain a key element in the growth of the economy, both as a major component of demand and as a basis for the innovation and product development that enabled Japanese producers to expand their output and ultimately to sell their products to the rest of the world. Through the pre-Second World War decades, growth in domestic con-sumption demand proved more significant, for much of the time, as a source of overall economic growth than did investment or exports. In the post-war years, Japanese consumers' efforts to re-build their lives, and their embrace of first processed food, Western-style clothes, and tables and chairs for their new homes, then washing machines, televisions and cars, provided the markets for older businesses, large and small, turning swords into ploughshares after the war, and in due course for Honda, Nissan, Sony and all the other Japanese producers which are now household names across the world.

Many of the goods that have emerged out of this process are by now perfectly familiar to us and indeed symbolic of global modernity or post-modernity. However, in their home environment in Japan, they are used and enjoyed within a consumption context by no means identical to those within which their exported versions find a place. That context is embodied in the physical infrastructure of homes and public places, in the patterns of Japanese people's everyday social and family lives and in the whole array of complementary consumer goods now available. It is the product of a consumption history that goes back to the eighteenth

---

[2] See Gerth 2003.

century and has since come to reflect both the impact of Western industrialisation and modernisation and the indigenous developments that have given rise, on the one hand, to war and disaster and, on the other, to unprecedented economic growth and prosperity.

In its concern for product differentiation and quality and its emphasis on both fashion and the appropriateness of goods to status and situation; in its continued inclusion of distinctively Japanese goods, even though now produced and marketed in the most modern of ways; in its serious approach to goods and their social functions – in these and many more ways the world of Japanese consumption that has emerged from its long history remains distinctive, despite the fact that so many of the products that fit into it have come to appeal to consumers elsewhere. Perhaps what the Japanese case illustrates above all is that every nation has a consumption history of its own that cannot be ignored, either as part of its own emerging economic story or as a piece in the global jigsaw that makes up the world of consumption in which we now all live.

Statistical appendix

The tables in this appendix bring together available statistical data on the macro-economic role of consumption within the Japanese economy and the growth and structure of consumption expenditure by individuals and households. Pre-war figures are drawn from the results of the massive, long-term project to produce and publish series of historical statistics on all aspects of the Japanese economy, which was carried out at the Institute of Economic Research at Hitotsubashi University. In particular, volume VI (Shinohara 1967) of the resulting multi-volume collection provides series on the consumption of a wide range of products, calculated on the basis of available data on production and the other elements making up supply in the domestic market. Representative goods particularly relevant to the content of this book have been selected where appropriate, and various conversions – from Japanese to metric units; from money to real terms; from total to per capita values – have been carried out as necessary. Meanwhile, Ohkawa and Shinohara 1979 conveniently brings together and analyses data from the other volumes in the series.

For the post-war period, by contrast, 'purpose-built' statistical sources on consumption exist in the form of surveys of household income and expenditure carried out by government statisticians. These are available in government publications – e.g. the annual white paper on 'national life' (*Kokumin seikatsu hakusho*) produced by the Cabinet Office – but many have now been conveniently assembled by the Statistics Bureau of the Ministry of Internal Affairs and Communications as *Historical Statistics of Japan* at www.stat.go.jp/english/data/chouki/index.htm. Descriptions of the methods used in the collection of the data are also given on this site.

Pre-war and post-war statistics are not therefore straightforwardly comparable; in particular, pre-war data are calculated where appropriate on a per capita basis and using 1934–6 prices, whereas post-war data are available on a per household basis, using 1990 prices. For reference, average household size remained at around 5 people from 1920 until 1950, thereafter declining steadily to reach 3 by 1990.

Table 1. Share of consumption in gross national expenditure (GNE), 1885–1995

	GNE ¥m	Personal consumption expenditure ¥m	Share of consumption in GNE %		GNE ¥bn	Personal consumption expenditure ¥bn	Share of consumption in GNE %
1885	806	652	80.9	1955	8,399.1	5,501.9	65.5
1890	1056	869	82.3	1960	15,998.0	9,395.4	58.7
1895	1552	1160	74.7	1965	32,772.8	19,239.2	58.7
1900	2414	1914	79.3	1970	73,188.4	38,332.5	52.4
1905	3084	2278	73.9	1975	148,169.9	84,762.7	57.2
1910	3925	2967	75.6	1980	240,098.5	141,324.3	58.9
1915	4991	3616	72.5	1985	321,555.9	188,759.5	58.7
1920	15896	11326	71.3	1990	432,971.9	249,288.5	57.6
1925	16265	12740	78.3	1995	487,211.6	290,523.6	59.6
1930	14671	10850	74.0				
1935	18298	12668	69.2				
1940	36851	20290	55.1				

Note: 1 billion = 1,000,000,000.
Sources: Pre-war: Ohkawa and Shinohara 1979: Table A1. Post-war: *Historical Statistics of Japan* Table 3.1.

Table 2. *Consumption in the overall growth of the economy over long-swing phases, 1887–1969 (average annual rates; 1934–6 prices)*

	Growth rate of real personal consumption expenditure %	Relative contribution of growth in individual components to overall growth in expenditure %				
		Personal consumption	Investment	Government expenditure	Exports	Imports
1887–97	3.15	82.1	17.9	12.3	8.0	–20.4
1897–1904	1.02	45.0	8.5	57.1	25.9	–36.5
1904–19	2.99	68.7	30.7	–0.3	21.7	–20.6
1919–30	2.60	93.9	9.6	23.7	26.3	–53.5
1930–38	2.23	33.1	41.5	16.3	35.6	–26.3
1953–69	7.90	49.8	46.4	5.0	13.2	–14.6

Note: Rounding means that components do not necessarily add up to 100.
Source: Ohkawa and Shinohara 1979: Table 1.7.w

Table 3. *Growth and structure of private consumption expenditure, 1874–1940 (ten-year averages)*

	Real per capita consumption expenditure, ¥, 1934–6 prices	Composition of consumption expenditure, current prices, %							
		Food	Clothing	Housing	Heating and lighting	Health and hygiene	Transport and communications	Social entertainment and leisure	Education and leisure
1874–83	80.1	65.7	7.8	7.2	5.5	3.8	0.3	5.8	3.9
1882–91	98.3	63.8	7.9	8.8	4.2	4.7	0.5	6.0	4.1
1892–1901	119.4	63.0	9.5	8.0	3.0	4.2	1.2	7.1	4.0
1902–11	122.4	63.2	8.2	8.8	3.3	3.0	2.0	7.2	4.3
1912–21	144.1	60.4	13.3	7.5	3.9	3.3	2.6	3.9	5.1
1922–31	179.2	56.0	10.9	11.4	4.2	4.2	3.6	3.4	6.3
1931–40	189.3	49.5	12.9	12.4	4.4	5.7	4.2	2.9	8.0

Source: Calculated from Shinohara 1967: Tables 1.9 and 1.2.

Table 4. *Growth and structure of private consumption expenditure, 1955–1995*

| | Real annual per capita consumption expenditure, ¥, 1990 prices | Composition of consumption expenditure, current prices, % | | | | | | | | | |
		Food	Housing	Heating and lighting	House-hold goods	Clothing	Health and hygiene	Transport and communi-cation	Education	Leisure and culture	Other
1955	340,782										
1960	490,258										
1965	705,213	38.1	4.4	5.0	5.0	10.1	2.5	3.5	3.9	7.1	20.4
1970	1,044,156	34.1	4.9	4.4	5.0	9.5	2.7	5.2	2.7	9.0	22.6
1975	1,273,945	32.0	4.9	4.5	5.0	9.2	2.5	6.1	2.8	8.4	24.8
1980	1,477,263	29.0	4.6	5.7	4.3	7.9	2.5	8.0	3.6	8.5	25.8
1985	1,657,524	27.0	4.6	6.5	4.3	7.2	2.5	9.1	4.0	8.9	26.0
1990	2,0155,08	25.4	4.8	5.5	4.0	7.4	2.8	9.5	4.7	9.7	26.3
1995	2,184,984	23.7	6.5	6.1	3.8	6.1	3.0	10.0	4.7	9.6	26.6

Note: Rounding means that components do not necessarily add up to 100.
Sources: Calculated from *Historical Statistics of Japan* Table 3.1; *Kokumin seikatsu hakusho 2007:* Statistical Appendix, Table 2-1-1.

Table 5. *Per capita consumption of selected goods, 1875–1940 (quantities as given; expenditure in ¥ in real terms, 1934–6 prices)*

	Rice* (kg)	Meat* (kg)	Soy sauce* (kg)	Sake (litres)	Beer (litres)	Confectionery (¥)	Tobacco (¥)	Clothing (¥)	Furniture and utensils (¥)
1875	96.1	0.23	12.4	17.0	0.01				
1880	105.1	0.27	17.9	17.0	0.02				
1885	99.0	0.53	12.7	13.5	0.03	2.7	0.6	6.1	1.0
1890	103.2	0.48	13.0	16.0	0.08	4.0	0.7	7.5	0.9
1895	117.0	0.77	15.0	19.8	0.10	4.2	1.1	12.7	1.4
1900	106.3	0.89	15.6	19.0	0.43	6.4	1.6	12.4	1.4
1905	153.0	0.88	11.5	13.8	0.40	5.6	2.5	9.2	1.2
1910	132.9	1.03	14.5	17.2	0.45	5.6	3.5	12.3	1.6
1915	139.0	1.11	12.5	15.5	0.69	5.2	3.1	12.3	2.2
1920	131.5	1.42	14.7	19.8	1.59	7.1	3.3	19.7	3.1
1925	136.8	1.82	15.0	19.1	2.31	10.4	3.7	18.1	3.4
1930	134.9	1.70	14.9	14.7	2.09	11.7	5.0	17.2	3.5
1935	127.1	1.83	13.3	12.2	2.32	11.6	4.8	24.0	4.3
1940	140.7	1.96	13.0	6.9	3.37	11.7	5.4	20.9	9.0

* Based on net food supply, after allowance for waste and other uses; otherwise on total supply of the product on the domestic market.
Source: Calculated from Shinohara 1967: Tables 9, 11, 39, 40, 51, 53, 54, 55, 58, 59, 62, 63, 75, 76, 78, 79, 86; population from Andō 1979: 4–5; consumer price index 1934–6 = 100, Ohkawa and Shinohara 1979: Table A50.

Table 6. *Average annual quantities purchased by households, selected consumer items, 1965–1995*

	Rice (kg)	White bread (kg)	Fresh fish (kg)	Fresh meat (kg)	Cheese (grams)	Oils and fats (kg)	Soy sauce (litres)	Miso (kg)	Mayon-naise and other dressings (grams)	Sake (litres)	Beer (litres)	Women's kimono	Women's skirts	Visits to *sentō* public bath
1965	339	17	62	26	516	7	30	18	1750	19	21	0.4	0.6	116
1970	251	20	55	33	1057	9	23	16	2902	22	30	0.5	0.7	90
1975	199	25	55	40	1376	12	19	14	3337	23	41	0.3	1.6	54
1980	172	26	50	47	1455	14	17	13	4190	18	47	0.2	1.9	28
1985	155	21	47	46	1484	13	14	11	4424	15	42	0.1	1.7	15
1990	124	18	42	44	1705	12	12	10	4324	13	55	0.1	1.8	7
1995	105	20	42	44	2105	11	11	9	4559	13	59	0.1	1.2	5

Source: Historical Statistics of Japan: Table 20.3.

Table 7. *Percentages of households possessing selected consumer durables, 1964–1995*

	Dining set	Refrig- erator	Washing machine	Vacuum cleaner	Sewing machine	Elec- tric fan	Room air- conditioner	Electric *kotatsu* heater	B&W TV	Colour TV	Stereo	Passen- ger car	Bicycle
1964	38.2	61.4	26.8	76.2	49.9	1.7	50.7	87.8		9.0	6.0	72.9
1965	13.6*	51.4	68.5	32.2	77.4	59.6	2.0	57.8	90.0		13.5	9.2	73.1
1970	27.4	89.1	91.4	68.3	84.5	83.2	5.9	81.4	90.2	26.3	31.2	22.1	67.1
1975	43.9	96.7	97.6	91.2	84.7	94.3	17.2	91.3	48.7	90.3	52.1	41.2	77.0
1980	60.9	99.1	98.8	95.8	83.8	95.4	39.2	93.2	22.8	98.2	57.1	57.2	78.4
1985	64.5	98.4	98.1	97.4	81.2		52.3	91.9		99.1	59.9	67.4	80.1
1990	69.4	98.2	99.5	98.8	80.9		63.7			99.4	59.3	77.3	81.3
1995		97.8	99.0	98.3	79.1		77.2			98.9	57.7	80.0	79.4

Note: Based on surveys of households of two persons or more.

* 1966.

Source: Historical Statistics of Japan: Table 20.7; *Kokumin seikatsu hakusho* 2007: Statistical Appendix, Table 2-1-6

References

Akaishi, Takatsugu and Steinmo, Sven 2006. 'Consumption taxes and the welfare state in Sweden and Japan', in Garon and Maclachlan (eds.), pp. 213–35.

Altman, Albert 1986. 'The press', in Jansen and Rozman (eds.), pp. 231–47.

Andō Yoshio 1979. *Kindai nihon keizai shi yōran* (An outline of modern Japanese economic history), 2nd edn. Tokyo: Tōkyō Daigaku Shuppan Kai.

Asahi Shinbun (ed.) 1933. *Changing Japan Seen through the Camera*. Tokyo: Asahi Shinbun.

Bauer, Arnold 2001. *Goods, Power, History: Latin America's Material Culture*. Cambridge: Cambridge University Press.

Beasley, William 1973. *The Meiji Restoration*. Oxford: Oxford University Press.

Berg, Maxine 2005. *Luxury and Pleasure in Eighteenth-Century Britain*. Oxford: Oxford University Press.

Bernstein, Gail Lee 2005. *Isami's House: Three Centuries of a Japanese Family*. Berkeley: University of California Press.

Bestor, Theodore 2004. *Tsukiji: The Fish Market at the Center of the World*. Berkeley: University of California Press.

Bowring, Richard and Kornicki, Peter (eds.) 1993. *The Cambridge Encyclopedia of Japan*. Cambridge: Cambridge University Press.

Brannen, Mary Yoko 1992. '"Bwana Mickey": constructing cultural consumption at Tokyo Disneyland' in Tobin, Joseph (ed.), pp. 216–34.

Brook, Timothy 1998. *The Confusions of Pleasure: Commerce and Culture in Ming China*. Berkeley: University of California Press.

Brown, Kendall and Minichiello, Sharon 2001. *Taishō Chic: Japanese Modernity, Nostalgia and Deco*. Honolulu: Honolulu Academy of Arts.

Chūbachi, Masayoshi and Taira, Koji 1976. 'Poverty in modern Japan: perceptions and realities', in Patrick, Hugh (ed.), *Japanese Industrialization and Its Social Consequences*. Berkeley: University of California Press, pp. 391–438.

Clammer, John 1997. *Contemporary Urban Japan: A Sociology of Consumption*. Oxford: Blackwell.

    2000. 'The global and the local: gender, class and the internationalisation of consumption in a Tokyo neighbourhood', in Ashkenazi, Michael and Clammer, John (eds.), *Consumption and Material Culture in Contemporary Japan*. London: Kegan Paul, pp. 244–83.

Creighton, Millie 1998a. 'Pre-industrial dreaming in post-industrial Japan: department stores and the commoditization of community values', *Japan Forum* 10: 127–49

1998b. 'Something more: Japanese department stores' marketing of a "meaningful human life"', in MacPherson (ed.), pp. 206–30.

Cwiertka, Katarzyna 2006. *Modern Japanese Cuisine*. London: Reaktion Books.

de Grazia, Victoria 1998. 'Changing consumption regimes in Europe, 1930–1970', in Strasser, Susan, McGovern, Charles and Judt, Matthias (eds.), *Getting and Spending: European and American Consumer Societies in the Twentieth Century*. Cambridge: Cambridge University Press, pp. 59–83.

Dore, Ronald 1978. *Shinohata: A Portrait of a Japanese Village*. London: Allen Lane.

Dower, John 2000. *Embracing Defeat: Japan in the Aftermath of World War II*. London: Penguin.

Dubro, Alec and Kaplan, David 1987. *Yakuza*. London: Futura.

Dunn, Charles 1969. *Everyday Life in Traditional Japan*. London: Batsford.

Embree, John 1964. *Suye Mura*, revised edn. Chicago: University of Chicago Press.

Ericson, Steven 1996. *The Sound of the Whistle: Railroads and the State in Meiji Japan*. Cambridge, MA: Harvard University Press.

Fairchilds, Cissie 1994. 'The production and marketing of populuxe goods in eighteenth-century Paris', in Brewer, John and Porter, Roy (eds.), *Consumption and the World of Goods*. London: Routledge, pp. 228–48.

Field, Norma 1989. '*Somehow*: the postmodern as atmosphere', in Miyoshi and Harootunian (eds.), pp. 169–88.

Fine, Ben and Leopold, Ellen 1990. 'Consumerism and the industrial revolution', *Social History* 15: 165–73.

Flath, David 2000. *The Japanese Economy*. Oxford: Oxford University Press.

Food and Agriculture Policy Research Center 1997. *Structural Changes in Japan's Food System*. Tokyo: Food and Agriculture Policy Research Center.

Francks, Penelope 1998. 'Agriculture and the state in industrial East Asia: the rise and fall of the Food Control System in Japan', *Japan Forum* 10: 1–16.

2007. 'Consuming rice: food, "traditional" products and the history of consumption in Japan', *Japan Forum* 19: 147–68.

2009. 'Inconspicuous consumption: sake, beer and the birth of the consumer in Japan', *Journal of Asian Studies* 68(1):135–64.

Fruin, Mark 1983. *Kikkoman*. Cambridge, MA: Harvard University Press.

Furukawa Hiroshi (ed.) 1979. *Saga: Meiji, Taishō, Shōwa shashin shū* (Saga: Meiji, Taishō, Shōwa photograph collection). Tokyo: Kokusho Kankō Kai.

Garon, Sheldon 1998. 'Fashioning a culture of diligence and thrift: savings and frugality campaigns in Japan, 1900–1931', in Minichiello (ed.), pp. 312–34.

2000. 'Luxury is the enemy: mobilizing savings and popularizing thrift in wartime Japan', *Journal of Japanese Studies* 26: 41–78.

Garon, Sheldon and Maclachlan, Patricia (eds.) 2006. *The Ambivalent Consumer*. Ithaca: Cornell University Press.

Gerth, Karl 2003. *China Made: Consumer Culture and the Creation of the Nation*. Cambridge, MA: Harvard University Press.

Glennie, Paul 1995. 'Consumption within historical studies', in Miller, Daniel (ed.), *Acknowledging Consumption*. London: Routledge, pp. 164–203.

Gluck, Carol 1998. 'The invention of Edo', in Vlastos, Stephen (ed.), *Mirror of Modernity*. Berkeley: University of California Press, pp. 262–84.

Gordon, Andrew 2006 'From Singer to *shinpan*: consumer credit in modern Japan', in Garon and Maclachlan (eds.), pp. 137–62.

    2007. 'Consumption, leisure and the middle class in transwar Japan', *Social Science Japan Journal* 10: 1–21.

Hanes, Jeffrey 1998. 'Media culture in Taishō Osaka', in Minichiello (ed.), pp. 267–87.

Hanley, Susan 1997. *Everyday Things in Premodern Japan*. Berkeley: University of California Press.

Hanley, Susan and Yamamura, Kozo 1977. *Economic and Demographic Change in Preindustrial Japan, 1600–1868*. Princeton: Princeton University Press.

Hareven, Tamara 2002. *The Silk Weavers of Kyoto*. Berkeley: University of California Press.

Havens, Thomas 1978. *Valley of Darkness: The Japanese People and World War II*. New York: Norton.

Hayashi, Reiko 1994. 'Provisioning Edo in the early eighteenth century', in McClain, Merriman and Udagawa (eds.), pp. 211–33.

Hazama, Hiroshi 1976. 'Historical changes in the life style of industrial workers', in Patrick, Hugh (ed.), *Japanese Industrialization and Its Social Consequences*. Berkeley: University of California Press, pp. 21–52.

Historical Statistics of Japan. Ministry of Internal Affairs and Communications, Statistics Bureau: www.stat.go.jp/english/data/chouki/index.htm.

Hitotsubashi Daigaku Keizai Kenkyū-jo (ed.) 1961. *Nihon keizai tōkei*, (Economic statistics of Japan). Tokyo: Iwanami Shoten.

Horioka, Charles 1993. 'Consuming and saving', in Gordon, Andrew (ed.), *Postwar Japan as History*. Berkeley: University of California Press, pp. 259–92.

Hunter, Janet 2003. *Women and the Labour Market in Japan's Industrialising Economy*. London: RoutledgeCurzon.

Ihara Saikaku 1688/1959. *The Japanese Family Storehouse*, trans. by G. W. Sargent. Cambridge: Cambridge University Press.

Ioku Shigehiko 1999. 'Kindai ni okeru chihō shōyū jōzōgyō no hatten to shijō' (The development of the regional soy-sauce brewing industry and the market in the early modern period), in Hayashi Reiko and Amano Masatoshi (eds.), *Higashi to nishi no shōyū shi* (The history of soy sauce, east and west). Tokyo: Yoshikawa Kōbunkan, pp. 231–55.

Ishige, Naomichi 2001. *The History and Culture of Japanese Food*. London: Kegan Paul.

Ivy, Marilyn 1993. 'Formations of mass culture', in Gordon, Andrew (ed.), *Postwar Japan as History*. Berkeley: University of California Press, pp. 239–58.

Jansen, Marius 1989. 'Japan in the early nineteenth century', in Jansen, Marius (ed.), *The Cambridge History of Japan V: The Nineteenth Century*. Cambridge: Cambridge University Press, pp. 50–115.

Jansen, Marius and Rozman, Gilbert (eds.) 1986. *Japan in Transition*. Princeton: Princeton University Press.

Jardine, Lisa 1996. *Worldly Goods*. London: Macmillan.

Jō Kazuo 2007. *Nihon no fuasshion* (Japanese fashion). Kyoto: Seigensha.

Johnson, Chalmers 1982. *MITI and the Japanese Miracle: The Growth of Industrial Policy, 1925–1975*. Stanford: Stanford University Press.

Jones, Colin and Spang, Rebecca 1999. 'Sans-culottes, *sans café*, *sans tabac*: shifting realms of necessity and luxury in eighteenth-century France', in Berg, Maxine and Clifford, Helen (eds.), *Consumers and Luxury: Consumer Culture in Europe 1650–1850*. Manchester: Manchester University Press, pp. 63–87.

Kanzaki Noritake 2000. 'Ryōriya no sake, izakaya no sake' (Sake in restaurants and *izakaya*), in Umesao Tadao and Yoshida Shūji (eds.), *Sake to Nihon bunmei* (Sake and Japanese culture). Tokyo: Kōbundō, pp. 145–60.

Katz, Richard 1998. *Japan: The System that Soured*. New York: M.E. Sharpe.

Kayō Nobufumi 1958. *Nihon nōgyō kiso tōkei* (Basic statistics of Japanese agriculture). Tokyo: Nōrinsuisangyō Seisansei Kōjō Kaigi.

Keizai Kōhō Center 1997. *Japan: An International Comparison*. Tokyo: Keizai Kōhō Center.

Kikkawa Takeo 1998. 'Shōhi kakumei to ryūtsū kakumei' (The consumption revolution and the distribution revolution), in Tōkyō Daigaku Shakai Kagaku Kenkyū-jo (ed.), *20-seiki shisutemu 3: keizai seichō II* (The twentieth-century system 3: economic growth II). Tokyo: Tōkyō Daigaku Shuppan Kai, pp. 99–137.

Kinsella, Sharon 2005. 'Blackfaces, witches and racism against girls', in Miller, Laura and Bardsley, Jan (eds.), *Bad Girls of Japan*, Basingstoke: Palgrave Macmillan, pp. 142–57.

Kirin Bīru (ed.) 1984. *Bīru to Nihonjin* (The Japanese and beer). Tokyo: Sanseidō.

Kitō Hiroshi 1998. 'Edo jidai no beishoku' (Rice consumption in the Edo period), in Haga Noboru and Ishikawa Hiroko (eds.), *Zenshū Nihon no shoku bunka III: kome, mugi, zakkoku, mame* (Japanese food culture III: rice, other grains, beans). Tokyo: Yūzankaku, pp. 47–58.

Kōdō Seichō Ki o Kangaeru Kai (ed.) 2005. *Kōdō seichō to Nihonjin II: kazoku no seikatsu* (The Japanese and the economic miracle II: family life). Tokyo: Nihon Edeitā Sukūru Shuppan-bu.

Koizumi Kazuko 1994. 'Kurashi no dōgu' (Household utensils), in Iwanami Kōza (ed.), *Nihon tsūshi XIII* (Japanese history series XIII). Tokyo: Iwanami Shoten, pp. 339–61.

Kokumin seikatsu hakusho (White paper on Japanese life) 2007, Tokyo: Naikaku fu.

Kondo, Dorinne 1992. 'The aesthetics and politics of Japanese identity in the fashion industry', in Tobin, Joseph (ed.), pp. 176–203.

Kosuge Keiko 1991. *Nihon daidokoro bunka shi* (A history of Japanese kitchen culture). Tokyo: Yūzankaku Shuppan.

Kubo Masataka (ed.) 1991. *Kaden seihin ni miru kurashi no sengo shi* (The postwar history of everyday life seen through household goods). Tokyo: Mirion Shobo.

Kuroda Masahiro 1993. 'Price and goods control in the Japanese postwar inflationary period', in Teranishi, Juro and Kosai, Yutaka (eds.), *The Japanese Experience of Economic Reforms*. Basingstoke, UK: Macmillan, pp. 31–60.

Larke, Roy and Causton, Michael 2005. *Japan: A Modern Retail Superpower*. Basingstoke, UK: Palgrave Macmillan.

Latham, A.J.H. 1999. 'Rice is a luxury, not a necessity', in Flynn, Dennis, Frost, Lionel and Latham, A.J.H. (eds.), *Pacific Centuries: Pacific and Pacific Rim History since the Sixteenth Century*. London: Routledge, pp. 110–24.

Leupp, Gary 1992. *Servants, Shophands and Laborers in the Cities of Tokugawa Japan*. Princeton: Princeton University Press.

Lewis, Michael 1990. *Rioters and Citizens: Mass Protest in Imperial Japan*. Berkeley: University of California Press.

Lockwood, William 1968. *The Economic Development of Japan*, 2nd edn. Princeton: Princeton University Press.

Maclachlan, Patricia 2002. *Consumer Politics in Postwar Japan: The Institutional Boundaries of Citizen Action*. New York: Columbia University Press.
   2006. 'Global trends vs. local conditions: genetically modified foods and contemporary consumerism in the United States, Japan and Britain', in Garon and Maclachlan (eds.), pp. 236–59.

Macpherson, Kerrie (ed.) 1998. *Asian Department Stores*. Richmond, UK: Curzon.

Maruyama Yasunari 1999. 'Kinsei ni okeru daimyō minshū no shoku seikatsu' (Food of the *daimyō* and people in the Tokugawa period), in Ishikawa Haruko and Haga Noboru (eds.), *Shoku seikatsu to tabemono shi zenshū: Nihon no shoku bunka II*. (Diet and food history series: Japanese food culture II). Tokyo: Yūzankaku Shuppan, pp. 173–98.

McClain, James 1994. 'Edobashi: power, space and popular culture in Edo' in McClain, Merriman and Udagawa (eds.), pp. 105–31.
   1999. 'Space, power, wealth and status in seventeenth-century Osaka', in McClain, James and Wakita, Osamu (eds.), *Osaka: The Merchants' Capital of Early Modern Japan*. Ithaca: Cornell University Press, pp. 44–79.

McClain, James and Merriman, John 1994. 'Edo and Paris: cities and power' in McClain, Merriman and Udagawa (eds.), pp. 3–38.

McClain, James, Merriman, John and Udagawa, Kaoru (eds.) 1994. *Edo and Paris*. Ithaca and London: Cornell University Press.

McKendrick, Neil 1982. 'The consumer revolution of eighteenth-century England', in McKendrick, Neil, Brewer, John and Plumb, J.H. (eds.), *The Birth of a Consumer Society*. London: Europa Publications, pp. 9–33.

Metzler, Mark 2006. *Lever of Empire: The International Gold Standard and the Crisis of Liberalism in Prewar Japan*. Berkeley: University of California Press.

Mills, Edwin and Ohta, Katsutoshi 1976. 'Urbanization and urban problems', in Patrick, Hugh and Rosovsky, Henry (eds.), *Asia's New Giant*. Washington, DC: Brookings Institution Press, pp. 673–752.

Minichiello, Sharon (ed.) 1998. *Japan's Competing Modernities*. Honolulu: University of Hawai'i Press.

Mintz, Sidney 1985. *Sweetness and Power: The Place of Sugar in Modern History*. New York: Penguin.

Miyamoto Mataji and Hirano Takashi 1996. 'Shōgyō' (Commerce), in Nishikawa Shunsaku, Odaka Kōnosuke and Saitō Osamu (eds.), *Nihon keizai no 200-nen* (200 years of the Japanese economy). Tokyo: Nihon Hyōronsha, pp. 339–70.

Miyoshi, Masao and Harootunian, Harry (eds.) 1989. *Postmodernism and Japan*. Durham, NC: Duke University Press.

Mochida Keizō 1990. *Nihon no kome* (Japanese rice). Tokyo: Chikuma Shobō.

Moeran, Brian 1998. 'The birth of the Japanese department store', in MacPherson (ed.), pp. 141–76.

Morris-Suzuki, Tessa 1994. *The Technological Transformation of Japan*. Cambridge: Cambridge University Press.

Najita, Tetsuo and Harootunian, Harry 1988. 'Japanese revolt against the West: political and cultural criticism in the twentieth century', in Duus, Peter (ed.), *The Cambridge History of Japan VI: The Twentieth Century*. Cambridge: Cambridge University Press, pp. 711–74.

Nakae Katsumi 2007. *Edo no kurashi* (Life in Edo). Tokyo: Seishun Shuppansha.

Nakagawa, Keiichi and Rosovsky, Henry 1963. 'The case of the dying kimono: the influence of changing fashions on the Japanese woollen industry', *Business History Review* 37: 59–80.

Nakai, Nobuhiko and McClain, James 1991. 'Commercial change and urban growth in early modern Japan', in Hall, John (ed.), *The Cambridge History of Japan IV: Early Modern Japan*. Cambridge: Cambridge University Press, pp. 519–95.

Nakamura Keiko 2005. *Shōwa modan kimono* (Modern kimono of the Shōwa period). Tokyo: Kawade Shobō Shinsha.

Nakanishi Satoru 2000. 'Bunmei kaika to minshū seikatsu' (*Bunmei kaika* and ordinary life), in Ishii Kanji, Hara Akira and Takeda Haruhito (eds.), *Nihon keizai shi I: bakumatsu ishin ki* (Japanese economic history I: the late Tokugawa and Restoration period). Tokyo: Tōkyō Daigaku Shuppankai, pp. 217–823.

Nakano, Makiko 1995. *Makiko's Diary: A Merchant Wife in 1910 Kyoto*, trans. by Kazuko Smith. Stanford: Stanford University Press.

Narimatsu Saeko 1989. 'Kinsei goki no nikki ni miru shōya kazoku no seikatsu' (The lives of village elite families seen through late Tokugawa diaries), in Hayami Akira, Saitō Osamu and Sugiyama Shinya (eds.), *Tokugawa shakai kara no tenbō* (The view from Tokugawa society). Tokyo: Dōbunkan, pp. 161–90.

Narita, Ryūichi 1998. 'Women in the motherland: Oku Mumeo through wartime and postwar', in Yamanouchi, Yasushi, Koschmann, J. Victor and Narita, Ryūichi (eds.), *Total War and Mobilization*. Ithaca: Cornell University East Asia Program, pp. 137–58.

Nishikawa, Shunsaku 1986. 'Grain consumption: the case of Chōshū', in Jansen and Rozman (eds.), pp. 421–46.

Nishiyama, Matsunosuke 1997. *Edo Culture: Daily Life and Diversions in Urban Japan, 1600–1868*, trans. by Gerald Groemer. Honolulu: University of Hawai'i Press.

Nitta, Fumiteru 1992. 'Shopping for souvenirs in Hawai'i', in Tobin, Joseph (ed.), pp. 204–15.

Nitta Tarō, Tanaka Yūji and Koyama Shūko 2003. *Tōkyō ryūkō seikatsu* (Fashionable life in Tokyo). Tokyo: Kawade Shobō.

Noma Seiroku 1974. *Japanese Costume and Textile Arts*. New York: Weatherhill.

Ogi Shinzō 1970. *Shōwa shomin bunka shi I* (History of Shōwa popular culture I). Tokyo: Nihon Hōsō Shuppan Kyōkai.

   1999. 'Tōkyō shomin no shoku seikatsu' (The diets of ordinary Tokyo people), in Ishikawa Haruko and Haga Noboru (eds.), *Shoku seikatsu to tabemono shi zenshū: Nihon no shoku bunka II* (Diet and food history series: Japanese food culture II). Tokyo: Yūzankaku Shuppan, pp. 225–67.

Ohkawa, Kazushi and Shinohara, Miyohei (eds.) 1979. *Patterns of Japanese Economic Development*, New Haven and London: Yale University Press.

Ohnuki-Tierney, Emiko 1993. *Rice as Self*. Princeton: Princeton University Press.

Overton, Mark, Whittle, Jane, Dean, Darron and Hann, Andrew 2004. *Production and Consumption in English Households, 1600–1750*. London: Routledge.

Partner, Simon 1999. *Assembled in Japan: Electrical Goods and the Making of the Japanese Consumer*. Berkeley: University of California Press.

   2001. 'Taming the wilderness: the lifestyle improvement movement in rural Japan', *Monumenta Nipponica* 56: 487–520.

   2004. *Toshié: A Story of Village Life in Twentieth-Century Japan*. Berkeley: University of California Press.

Plath, David 1980. *Long Engagements: Maturity in Modern Japan*. Stanford: Stanford University Press.

   1992. 'My-car-ism: motorizing the Showa self', in Gluck, Carol and Graubard, Stephen (eds.), *Showa: The Japan of Hirohito*. New York: Norton, pp. 229–44.

Platt, Brian 2000. 'Elegance, prosperity, crisis: three generations of Tokugawa village elites', *Monumenta Nipponica* 55: 45–81.

Pomeranz, Kenneth 2000. *The Great Divergence: China, Europe and the Making of the Modern World Economy*. Princeton: Princeton University Press.

Pratt, Edward 1999. *Japan's Rural Elite: The Economic Foundations of the Gōnō*. Cambridge, MA: Harvard University Asia Center.

Ravina, Mark 1999. *Land and Lordship in Early Modern Japan*. Stanford: Stanford University Press.

Rebick, Marcus and Takenaka, Ayumi 2006. 'The changing Japanese family', in Rebick, Marcus and Takenaka, Ayumi (eds.), *The Changing Japanese Family*. London: Routledge, pp. 3–16.

Roberts, John 1973. *Mitsui: Three Centuries of Japanese Business*. New York: Weatherhill.

Roberts, Luke 1998. *Mercantilism in a Japanese Domain*. Cambridge: Cambridge University Press.

   2002. 'Mori Yoshiki', in Walthall, Anne (ed.), *The Human Tradition in Modern Japan*. Wilmington, DE: Scholarly Resources, pp. 25–42.

Rodriguez del Alisal, Maria-Dolores 2000. 'Japanese lunch boxes: from convenience snack to the convenience store', in Ashkenazi, Michael and

Clammer, John (eds.), *Consumption and Material Culture in Contemporary Japan*, London: Kegan Paul, pp. 40–80.

Rosenberger, Nancy 1992. 'Images of the West: home style in Japanese magazines', in Tobin, Joseph (ed.), pp. 106–25.

Rothacher, Albrecht 1989. *Japan's Agro-Food Sector*. New York: St Martin's Press.

Rozman, Gilbert 1974. 'Edo's importance in changing Tokugawa society', *Journal of Japanese Studies* 1: 91–112.

Rubinger, Richard 2007. *Popular Literacy in Early Modern Japan*. Honolulu: University of Hawai'i Press.

Saitō Osamu and Ozeki Manabu 2004. 'Daiichi sekai daisen mae no Yamanashi nōson ni okeru shōhi no kōzō' (The structure of consumption in pre-First World War Yamanashi villages), in Ariizumi Sadao (ed.), *Yamanashi kindai shi henshū* (Modern history of Yamanashi collection). Tokyo: Iwata Shoin, pp. 153–81.

Saitō, Osamu and Tanimoto, Masayuki 2004. 'The transformation of traditional industries', in Hayami, Akira, Saitō, Osamu and Toby, Ronald (eds.), *Emergence of Economic Society in Japan 1600–1859*. Oxford: Oxford University Press, pp. 268–300.

Sand, Jordan 2000. 'The cultured life as contested space: dwelling and discourse in the 1920s', in Tipton and Clark (eds.), pp. 99–118.

   2001. 'Monumentalizing the everyday: the Edo–Tokyo Museum', *Critical Asian Studies* 33: 351–78.

   2003. *House and Home in Modern Japan*. Cambridge, MA: Harvard University Press.

   2006. 'The ambivalence of the new breed: nostalgic consumerism in 1980s and 1990s Japan', in Garon and Maclachlan (eds.), pp. 85–108.

Sarti, Raffaella 2002. *Europe at Home: Family and Material Culture 1500–1800*. New Haven and London: Yale University Press.

Sasama Yoshifumi 1979. *Nihon shokuhin kōgyō shi* (History of the Japanese processed-food industry). Tokyo: Tōyō Keizai Shinposha.

Sato, Barbara Hamill 2000. 'An alternate informant: middle-class women and mass magazines in 1920s Japan', in Tipton and Clark (eds.), pp. 137–53.

Scherer, Anke 1999. 'Drawbacks to control on food distribution: food shortages, the black market and economic crime', in Pauer, Erich (ed.), *Japan's War Economy*. London: Routledge, pp. 106–23.

Seidensticker, Edward 1983. *Low City, High City*. London: Allen Lane.

Shammas, Carole 1990. *The Pre-Industrial Consumer in England and America*. Oxford: Clarendon Press.

Shimazaki, Tōson 1987. *Before the Dawn*, trans. by William Naff. Honolulu: University of Hawai'i Press.

Shimbo Hiroshi and Hasegawa Akira 1988. 'Shōhin seisan, ryūtsū no dainamikkusu' (The dynamics of commodity production and trade), in Miyamoto Mataji and Hayami Akira (eds.), *Nihon keizai shi I: keizai shakai no seiritsu* (Japanese economic history I: the establishment of economic society). Tokyo: Iwanami Shoten, pp. 217–70.

   2004. 'The dynamics of market economy and production', in Akira, Hayami, Saitō, Osamu and Toby, Ronald (eds.), *Emergence of Economic Society in Japan 1600–1859*. Oxford: Oxford University Press, pp. 157–91.

Shimbo Hiroshi and Saitō Osamu 1989. 'Gaisetsu' (Outline), in Shimbo Hiroshi and Saitō Osamu (eds.), *Nihon keizai shi II: Kindai seichō no taidō* (Japanese economic history II: the beginnings of modern growth). Tokyo: Iwanami Shoten, pp. 1–65.

Shinohara Miyohei 1967. *Chōki keizai tōkei VI: kojin shōhi shishutsu* (Long-term economic statistics VI: personal consumption expenditure). Tokyo: Tōyō Keizai Shinpo Sha.

Shively, Donald 1964. 'Sumptuary regulation and status in early Tokugawa Japan', *Harvard Journal of Asiatic Studies* 25: 123–64.

  1991. 'Popular culture', in Hall, John (ed.), *The Cambridge History of Japan IV: Early Modern Japan*. Cambridge: Cambridge University Press, pp. 706–70.

Silverberg, Miriam 1992. 'Constructing the Japanese ethnography of modernity', *Journal of Asian Studies* 51: 30–54.

Smethurst, Richard 2007. *From Foot Soldier to Finance Minister: Takahashi Korekiyo, Japan's Keynes*. Cambridge, MA: Harvard University Press.

Smith, Kerry 2001. *A Time of Crisis*. Cambridge, MA: Harvard University Press.

Smith, Stephen 1992. 'Drinking etiquette in a changing beverage market', in Tobin, Joseph (ed.), pp. 143–58.

Steinberg, Marc 2004. 'Otaku consumption, superflat art and the return to Edo', *Japan Forum* 16: 449–71.

Styles, John and Vickery, Amanda 2006. 'Introduction', in Styles, John and Vickery, Amanda (eds.), *Gender, Taste and Material Culture in Britain and North America, 1700–1830*. New Haven: Yale University Press, pp. 1–34.

Taeuber, Irene 1958. *The Population of Japan*. Princeton: Princeton University Press.

Takemura Tamio 2004. *Taishō bunka* (Taishō culture). Tokyo: Sangensha.

Takenaka Makoto 2003. *Edo shumin no ishokujū* (Clothing, food and housing of ordinary people in Edo). Tokyo: Gakken

Takeuchi, Johzen 1991. *The Role of Labour-Intensive Sectors in Japanese Industrialization*. Tokyo: United Nations University Press.

Tamura Hitoshi 2004. *Fuasshon no shakai keizai shi* (The socio-economic history of fashion). Tokyo: Nihon Keizai Hyōronsha.

Tanimoto, Masayuki 1992. 'The evolution of indigenous cotton textile manufacturing before and after the opening of the ports', *Japanese Yearbook on Business History* 9: 29–56.

  (ed.) 2006a. *The Role of Tradition in Japan's Industrialization*. Oxford: Oxford University Press.

  2006b 'The role of tradition in Japan's industrialization: another path to industrialization', in Tanimoto (ed.), pp. 3–44.

Thompson, Lee 1998. 'The invention of the *yokozuna* and the championship system, or, Futahaguro's revenge', in Vlastos, Stephen (ed.), *Mirror of Modernity: Invented Traditions of Modern Japan*. Berkeley: University of California Press, pp. 174–90.

Tipton, Elise 2000. 'The café: contested space of modernity in interwar Japan', in Tipton and Clark (eds.), pp. 119–36.

Tipton, Elise and Clark, John (eds.), 2002. *Being Modern in Japan: Culture and Society from the 1910s to the 1930s*, Honolulu: University of Hawai'i Press.

Tobin, Jeffrey 1992. 'A Japanese-French restaurant in Hawai'i' in Tobin, Joseph (ed.) 1992b, pp. 159–75.

Tobin, Joseph 1992a. 'Introduction: domesticating the West', in Tobin, Joseph (ed.), pp. 1–41.

(ed.) 1992b. *Re-Made in Japan: Everyday Life and Consumer Taste in a Changing Society*. New Haven: Yale University Press.

Trentmann, Frank 2004. 'Beyond consumerism: new historical perspectives on consumption', *Journal of Contemporary History* 39: 373–401.

Uchida Seizō 2002. *Kieta modan Tōkyō* (Disappearing modern Tokyo). Tokyo: Kawade Shobō.

Ueno, Chizuko 1998. 'Seibu Department Store and image marketing: Japanese consumerism in the post-war period', in MacPherson (ed.), pp. 177–205.

Umemura Mataji, Takamatsu Nobukiyo and Itō Shigeru 1983. *Chōki keizai tōkei XIII: chiiki keizai tōkei* (Long-term economic statistics XIII: regional economic statistics). Tokyo: Tōyō Keizai Shinposha.

Uno, Kathleen 1993. 'One day at a time: work and domestic activities of urban lower-class women in early twentieth-century Japan', in Hunter, Janet (ed.), *Japanese Women Working*. London: Routledge, pp. 37–68.

Van Assche, Annie (ed.) 2005. *Fashioning Kimono: Dress and Modernity in Early Twentieth-Century Japan*. Milan: Five Continents Editions.

Vaporis, Constantine 1997. 'To Edo and back: alternate attendance and Japanese culture in the early modern period', *Journal of Japanese Studies* 23: 25–68.

Vogel, Ezra 1963. *Japan's New Middle Class* 2nd edn. Berkeley: University of California Press.

Walsh, Claire 2006. 'Shops, shopping, and the art of decision-making in eighteenth-century England', in Styles, John and Vickery, Amanda, (eds.), *Gender, Taste and Material Culture*. New Haven: Yale University Press, pp. 151–78.

Walthall, Anne 2002. 'Nishiyama Hide', in Walthall, Anne (ed.), *The Human Tradition in Modern Japan*. Wilmington, DE: Scholarly Resources, pp. 45–60.

Waswo, Ann 2001. *Housing in Postwar Japan: A Social History*. Richmond, UK: Curzon.

Watanabe Minoru 1964. *Nihon shoku seikatsu shi* (History of the Japanese diet). Tokyo: Yoshikawa Kōbunkan.

Watson, James (ed.) 1997. *Golden Arches East: McDonald's in East Asia*. Stanford: Stanford University Press.

Weatherill, Lorna 1996. *Consumer Behaviour and Material Culture in Britain, 1660–1760*, 2nd edn. London: Routledge.

Weisenfeld, Gennifer 2000. 'Japanese modernism and consumerism', in Tipton and Clark (eds.), pp. 75–98.

Welch, Evelyn 2005. *Shopping in the Renaissance: Consumer Cultures in Italy, 1400–1600*. New Haven: Yale University Press.

Wigen, Karen 1995. *The Making of a Japanese Periphery*. Berkeley: University of California Press.

Wray, William 1986. 'Shipping: from sail to steam', in Jansen and Rozman (eds.), pp. 248–72.

Yamada, Takehisa 2006. 'The export-oriented industrialization of Japanese pottery: the adoption and adaptation of overseas technology and market information', in Tanimoto (ed.), pp. 217–40.

Yamaguchi Kazuo 1963. *Meiji zenki keizai no bunseki* (A study of the early Meiji economy). Tokyo: Tokyo Daigaku Shuppansha.

Yamakawa, Kikue 2001. *Women of the Mito Domain: Recollections of Samurai Family Life*, trans. by Kate Wildman Nakai. Stanford: Stanford University Press.

Yamashita, Samuel Hideo 2005. *Leaves from an Autumn of Emergencies: Selections from the Wartime Diaries of Ordinary Japanese*. Honolulu: University of Hawai'i Press.

Yano, Christine 1998. 'Defining the modern nation in Japanese popular song, 1914–1932', in Minichiello (ed.), pp. 247–66.

Yoshikawa Hiroshi 1997. *Kōdō seichō* (High-speed growth). Tokyo: Yomiuri Shinbunsha.

Yoshimi, Shunya 2006. 'Consuming America, producing Japan', in Garon and Maclachlan (eds.), pp. 63–84.

Young, Louise 1999. 'Marketing the modern: department stores, consumer culture, and the new middle class in interwar Japan', *International Labor and Working-Class History* 55: 52–70.

Index

accessories 32, 34, 98–9
  1920s men's 128
  Western-style 130–1
account books 138, 142
advertising 123, 191n9, **192**
  in 1970s/1980s 191
  by department stores 113
  in economic-miracle period 162–3
  in inter-war period 120
  in Meiji period 85–7, **86**
  of *meisen* kimono 130
  and newspapers 79
  in Tokugawa period 19
agricultural co-operatives 159–60
agriculture, as non-commercial activity
  214
aid, post-war 148, 150
  and Western-style food 164
Akihabara (district of Tokyo) 150,
  150n12, **150**
alcohol *see* beer, sake, *shōchū*, whisky
alternate attendance *see sankin kōtai*
'ambivalence' towards consumption 7,
  208, 215, 216
Americans, in post-war Tokyo 150–2
Ameyokochō (district of Tokyo) **24**, 150,
  151
amusement parks 117
amusement quarters (*sakariba*) 26, 157,
  205
animal products 56–7
anthropology 2, 5, 7
apartments 80, 155, **155**
  see also housing
appappa (shift dress) 131
apron 131, **132**, 142
architects 112, 135, 187
Asakusa (amusement area of Tokyo) **192**

'baby boom' generation 185
bars **24**, 58, 96, **96**
bartering, during war-time 149

baseball 117
bath-houses (*sentō*) 25, 64
bathrooms 64, 172
bazaars (*kankōba*) 83, 83n21, **84**
bedding 38, 63–4, 172, 173
bedrooms 142, 156
beef 57, 94
  Kōbe 198
beer
  advertising of 85–6, **86**
  domestic production of 103
  in economic-miracle period 166
  growth in consumption of 127
beer halls 83, 116, 121, 127
Before the Dawn (novel) 50n5, 51n9
bentō (picnic boxes) 25, 46n91,
  133, 211
beri-beri 29, 51, 124
bicycles 101–2, 133
black markets 148–50, 149n7
branding 85–7, 120, 162, 179, 209
  of sake 95
bread 56, 125, 150, 165, 195n12, 195
breweries (sake and soy-sauce) 57, 58, 70
'bright life' (*akarui seikatsu*) 162, 177
  and electrical goods 175
'bubble economy' 5, 9, 184, 186, 216
burger chains 166
  McDonald's 197

cafés 83, 116–17, 121, 126, 127n16
  waitresses in 117
cars, 133
  inter-war production of 120
  and the Occupation 202
  ownership rates of 202
  production of 202
  and urban environment 187, **203**
  use of 202–3
  see also mai kā
castle-towns 48, 67
ceramics 25, 37

242

production of 70, 104
charcoal 36
chefs 31, 94
children, as consumers 39
 see also toys
China 108, 137, 178
 'national products' in 103n67
 resistance to Western-style goods in
  220–1
 war in 9, 147
Chinese food, 95, 115, 125, 164
 see also restaurants, Chinese
chocolate 93, 126
cigarettes, advertising of 85
cinemas 81, 118, **119**, 121
cities
 generations in 185
 post-war rebuilding of 154
 role in Tokugawa economy 12
 as sites of consumption 11–12
 see also urbanisation
'civilisation and enlightenment' 83, 98,
  101, 137, 221
Clammer, John 209
clothing
 fashions in 1950s and 1960s 171
 home-made 59
 Japanese-style men's 128, 169
 retailers of 170
 Western-style 97–9, 129, 169–70
 see also accessories, kimono, suits,
  uniforms
coffee 126, 167
coffee shops (*kissaten*) 117, 166
commercial class *see* merchant class
commercial design 120
'Complete Guide to the Speciality
  Products of the Domains
  of Japan' 55
confectionery 30, 57, 93, 126
conscription 81–2
consumer co-operatives (*seikyō*) 160,
  213–14
consumer credit 114, 142, 177
consumer movement 212–13
'consumer revolution', in Europe 5, 218
consumerism 5, 7, 142
 in contemporary Japan 7
 outside the West 7
 questioning of 211–12
consumption expenditure
 contribution to economic growth 139,
  158, 221
 post-war growth in 158
 as 'rational' 177

consumption history, of Europe and
  North America 5–7
consumption tax 148n6
convenience stores 159, 190
cookery books 27
'cos-play' 200
cosmetics 131
cotton textiles 60
 and 'cotton revolution' 60
 imports of 99
 production of 16, 70
'culture houses' 135, 141, 171, 201
'culture life' (*bunka seikatsu*) 134, 163
curry-rice 125, **126**
cute ('kawaii') 193

daimyō (feudal lords) 12
 abolition of 77
 diets of 50
 domain incomes of 49
 Edo residences of 14
 role in Tokugawa system 13
 and status-based consumption 40–1
 and urban decline 47
danchi (housing estates) 154, **155**
'dark valley' 146, 152
Dentsū (advertising agency) 120, 191
department stores 84, 113–14, 121, 122,
  129, 191, 214
 during economic miracle 160
 and *meisen* kimono 130
 restaurants in 115, 166
Depression (1930s) 144
dining-kitchen (DK) 172, 201
distribution system
 complexity of 161
 post-war 150
 Tokugawa period 15–16, 66–7
 see also retail system
doburoku (home-brewed sake) 58, 59, 95
Dodge Line (1949) 147
'domestication' of foreign goods 180, 220
Dōtonbori (Osaka shopping area) 113,
  191
'double life' 136
Dower, John 151
drinking practices 25, 58, 95–7, 166–7
'drug foods' 127

economic growth 4
 'economic miracle' 145–6
 in late nineteenth century 102–3
 slow-down in 183
 in Tokugawa countryside 66
 in Tokugawa period 8

Edo (pre-1868 Tokyo)
  consuming in 1
  expansion of 13
  food of 30
  and local products 72
  location of 12
  population of 11
  restaurants in 22
  and *sankin kōtai* 13, 14
  spread of fashion in 43
'Edo boom' 215
Edo-Tokyo Museum 215
electrical goods 2, 133, 171, 173–5, **174**,
    201
  and the 'bright life' 162–3
  and 'classes' 174
  diffusion of 173
  marketing of 173
  retailing of 159, 161
electricity, *see* public utilities
Embree, John 124
empire, Japanese 75
  and domestic market 4
  as source of tropical produce 124
emulation 6
Engel coefficient 194
environmental problems 156, 185
exhibitions 83
exports 75, 146, 175, 183
  of cars 202

fads 178, 193
fashion
  in 1980s/1990s clothing 199
  and cities 11
  diffusion in clothing 100
  in inter-war clothing 128
  and inter-war Japanese-style clothes
    129–31
  miracle-period trends in 170–1
  in Tokugawa cities 19
  in Tokugawa-period clothing 33–5, 61
  and Western-style clothing 169
fashion designers 200
female education 121
festivals/fairs 26, 118
feudal lords *see daimyō*
fish 57, 90, 124, 195
flats, *see* apartments
food additives 213
Food Control System 147–8, 153, 165
food scares 213
food stalls 23, **23**
  see also yatai
footwear 32, 98
foreign travel 205–6

'foreign villages' 206
formality, in clothing 33
furniture/furnishings 35, 38, 101, 134–5,
    172–3, 201
  'traditional' style 203–5, **204**
furusato (village home) 215
furoshiki (wrapping cloth) 100
futon, *see* bedding

gambling 26
Garon, Sheldon 140
geisha 34, 85, **86**, 99
genkan (hall) 101, 112
gift-giving 157, 178, 210
  and department stores 160
  see also omiyage
Ginza (district of Tokyo) 81, 83, 83n22,
    83n23, 113, 171
glass 133
globalisation, and Japanese goods 1–2
gold standard 139, 140
'good wife, wise mother' 142
Gordon, Andrew 177
government, attitude to consumption
    176
  history of 137–8
grain (non-rice) 56, 89, 89n33, 123–4
'Great Divergence' 220
gyōza (Chinese-style dumplings) 164

hair-styles 32, 98, 131
  perms (*pāmanento*) 131n45
hairdressers 55, 131n45
hakama (Japanese-style trousers) 32, 98
haneri (kimono collar) 131
Hanes, Jeffrey 118
Hankyū railway company/department
    store 113, 115
haori (jacket) 32, 100
Harajuku (area of Tokyo) 152, 171
hats 99, 131
  see also accessories
Hawaii 205, 206, 206n29
heating 101
  see also kotatsu
'Hello Kitty' 193
hobbies 207
holidays 117, 205–6
home-ownership 186
'homogenisation' 178
  differentiation within 178–9
hot-spring resorts 117, 206
Housewife's Friend (Shufu no tomo) 121
housewives 121, **122**, **132**, 134, 194
  and home furnishings 201
  and modernity 142

in post-war advertising 162
in post-war households 157
and product safety 212
and 'rational' consumption 138
Housewives' League/Federation
    (Shufuren) 152, 212
housing, 35, 38
    in 1970s and 1980s 186, 188
    changes with urbanisation 101
    cost of 186
    and eating practices 94
    in inter-war cities 111, 112
    in suburbs 111–12
    post-war construction of 154–6
    of rural elite 52
    rural improvement in 62–3
    of samurai 62–3
    in tenements 80
    see also apartments, danchi,
        row-houses
housing ladder 156

ice cream 93, 95
iki (cool/chic style) 45
imports 103
    of food 194
    and 'nationality' of consumer goods
        103n67
    of textiles 62, 99
indigo 72n56
individualism 179–80, 201
'industrial policy' 148
industrial revolution
    and consumption 6, 7
    and mass production/modernity 7
    and nineteenth-century Japan 8
Inoue Junnosuke 139
instalment credit, see consumer credit
'internationalisation' (kokusaika) 184
    and eating-out 197–8
irori (fire-pit) 36, 63, 65, 88, 203, 204
Ishibashi Tanzan 140
Ishida Baigan 43
izakaya (bar/restaurant) 23, 197

Japanese/Chinese cooking
    (chūka ryōri) 125, 166

kaiseki (set menu) meal pattern 22, 28,
    115, 197
    and cooking 35
    and dining equipment 36
kamado (cooking stove) 36, 37, 63, 101,
    166
Kansai region 13
    brewing in 24

Keiō railway company/department store
    113
kemari (football) 52n11
Keynes, John Maynard 140
Kikkoman 30, 93
kimchi (Korean picked cabbage) 198
kimono 98, 106, 129
    construction of 32
    decline of 169–70
    inter-war fashions in 129–30
    in Tokugawa period 31–4
kitchen equipment 36, 38, 53n13, 63,
    101, 172
kitchens 64, 88, 101, 106, 135, 172
    in Edo-period cities 36, 38
    rural improvements in 63, 144
knives 36
Kon Wajirō 128
Korean food 198
kosode (kimono outer garment), see
    kimono
kotatsu (heater) 38, 101, 173
Kyoto 13
    and clothes 27
    craft producers in 16
    as imperial capital 13
    population of 12

lacquer-ware 37
land reform 153
land-tax reform 77
leisure activity 158
    in 1950s/1960s 205
    in 1980s 205
    commodification of 205, 207
    company-based 157, 158
    early twentieth-century 117–18, 205
    in Tokugawa period 205
'life-cycle' saving 176
lighting 55, 81
literacy 79
living standards 4, 152
local products 72–3, 215
    see also meibutsu
London 12
    shopping and the 'season' in 11
'lost decade' 184
'luxury' 43, 61, 90, 138, 140

Maclachlan, Patricia 214
Maeda Masana 140n73
mai hōmu (my home) 146, 172, 179,
    201
mai kā (my car) 202–3
mail order 128
manga 200, 216

manufacturing output, in Tokugawa
    period 69
market towns 67
marketing 162
markets, in Edo and Osaka 17
mass consumption 159
mass market 7, 144, 178
mass production 7, 109, 118
    limitations of in Japan 119
McKendrick, Neil 5–6
meat 94, 124, 125, 165
    see also beef
meibutsu (souvenir products) 72
Meiji reforms 81
Meiji Restoration (1868) 8, 75
meisen silk 129–30, 130n44, **130**, 170n36
merchant class
    and clothing fashion 34
    and urban consumption 41
    in urban population 14
Metzler, Mark 139
'micro masses' 209, 210
middle classes 110, 111, 128
    and beer 127
    and home decoration 134
    ideal homes of 136
    inter-war lifestyle of 144
    miracle-period consumption pattern
        of 178
    and miracle-period meal patterns 168
    and Western-style goods in Meiji
        period 102
'middle masses' 123, 146, 178, 209, 210
'middling sort' 135
    and consumption in Europe 6
migrants, to cities 80, 156
milk 125
'milk halls' 95
mingei (folk art) 143
miso (bean paste) 26, 28, 29, 94
    commercialisation of 91
    uses of 91
Mitsui (Echigoya) textile store 17, **18**,
    19, 34
Mitsukoshi department store 113, **114**
mochi (pounded rice) 30
'modern boys/girls' 9, 118, 142
'modern goods' 7
'modern life' 109
    and gender roles 141
'modernisation' 123, 220
    of clothing 128
    of eating patterns 124
monpe (traditional trousers) 132, 132n53
Motomachi (district of Yokohama) 191,
    192, 199

motorcycles 202

Nakano Makiko 82, 91, 94, 96
Nantonaku kurisutaru (novel) 5, 207, 209,
    211
'narrowness' of Japanese domestic market
    4, 5
'new tribes' (*shinjinrui*) 185
newspapers 79, 120, 121
'Nixon shock' (1971) 183
noodles (*soba, udon*) 24, 30, 56, 92
    see also rāmen
nostalgia 214–15
nuclear family 157
    and the car 203
    and decline of wider family group 179
    gender roles within 157

o-nigiri (rice balls) 195
o-share (dressing up) 130n44, 199
obi (kimono sash) 32
    Nishijin 106
Occupation, of Japan (1945–52) 9, 145,
    147
    and the car 202
Oda Nobunaga 27
Ohnuki-Tierney, Emiko 87n27
'oil shock' 183
omiyage (souvenir gifts) 206, 210
    spending on 206n29
opening of ports/to the West 67, 74–5
Osaka 29, 67
    as distribution hub 16, 66
    and food 27
    population of 12
    as port 13
otaku (computer nerds) 216–17
outcaste (*eta*) community in Osaka 16
'overcoming modernity' 143

pack-horse transport 78
paintings 134
palanquins 39
pan-pan girls 151
'panda craze' 178
panic-buying 178, 213
'parasite singles' 9, 187
Paris 11, 12
patriarch, from northeast 53, 78, 121
peddlers 17, 67–8, 68n52, **68**
    see also travelling salespeople
Perry, Commodore Matthew 74–5
pickles 26
Pomeranz, Kenneth 220
population
    growth of 87

rural 81
Tokugawa urban 13–15
trends in the 1970s/1980s 185
'populuxe' goods 6, 11
Post Office savings 138, 176
'pre-industrial consumer' 7, 219, 220
prints (woodblock) 15, 19, 31, 39, 44, 218
processed-food products 91, 92, 93, 165, 194
production techniques in 104
product differentiation 104, 106, 179, 195–6, 209
and local industry in Tokugawa period 71–3
in soy sauce 57
prostitution 26
public utilities 111, 135, 156

railways 78–9, 123
developments in 1970s/1980s 187
and leisure travel 117
passenger travel on 78, 78n10
post-war suburban 154
and shopping centres 113
rāmen (Chinese-style noodles) 125, **167**
instant 165
museum of 215n49
and nostalgia 215
'rationalisation' 135, 214
of consumption 138, 162
rationing 140, 147, 164
refrigerators 166, 172
regulation, of consumption 148
restaurant guides 27, **43**, **44**, 215
restaurants **167**
in 1970s/1980s 196
Chinese 115, 125
in economic-miracle period 166, 168
in Edo 22, 43
Japanese, abroad 198
in Meiji period 94–5
origins of 22n26
Western-style 94, 115, 125
retail system
in 1980s 188–91
in post-war period 159–61
small shops in 105
and trade friction 161
in Tokugawa cities 17
in Tokugawa countryside 66–9
see also shops, shopping
rice
branding of 195, **196**
in contemporary diet 195
and Food Control System 147, 153
imports of 89, 90

in *kaiseki* meal pattern 29
and late twentieth-century consumerism 9
marketing in Tokugawa period 29
in mixed-grain combinations 56, 88, 124
and nutritional deficiencies 124
panic-buying of 213
per capita consumption of 89, 89n32, 165
polishing 29
post-war diversification away from 165
price of 90
in rural diet 55–6
share in calorie intake 194
share in grain consumption 89
supply of 89
in Western-style meals 125
white, as 'civilised' 88
rice-cookers 166, 173
rice merchants 29
'rice plus side dishes' meal structure 87, 88, 106, 123–4, 164, 165, 168, 195
see also kaiseki meal pattern
Rice Riots (1918) 90, 124
roads 156, 187
Roppongi (area of Tokyo) 152
Rosenberger, Nancy 203
row-houses 15, 35, 111, 215
as shops 19
rural depopulation 185
rural elite, 219
consumption patterns of 51–3
cultural pursuits of 52–3
in early Meiji period 81
economic and political role of 51
emulation by 52
travel by 53
rural households
market involvement of 54–5
post-war consumption by 153–4
rural/urban inequality 110
ryokan (Japanese-style inns) 207

safety, of products 212–13
Saikaku (Ihara Saikaku) 11n1, 42n80, 43, 47n1
sakariba, see amusement quarters
sake **96**, 198n18
changing patterns of consumption of 95–7
consumption in Edo 24–5
decline in consumption of 166
differentiation of 196

sake (*cont.*)
  home-brewed/unrefined, *see doburoku*
  rural consumption 58–9
salarymen 111
samurai
  attitudes to consumption 41
  consumption patterns of 49–51
  elite status of 48
  incomes of 14
  and urban construction 13
  as urban residents 14
'samurai dramas' 204
Sand, Jordan 134, 136, 215
sankin kōtai (alternate attendance) 13, 14,
    41, 48, 72
  consumption during 50–1
sarakin (salaryman loans) 177n53
Satsuma domain 16
saving, Japanese 2, 3, 7, 140, 176, 208
  government encouragement of 138, 148
  rate of 139
  war-time 140
seasonality, in clothing 33
'seclusion' policy 8, 13, 74
second-hand trade 33, 61
Seibu railway company 117
Seidensticker, Edward 136
seikatsu (life) 134
Seikō watch shop 83, 83n23
seikyō, *see* consumer co-operatives
self-sufficiency 55, 56–7
  in clothing 59
servants
  and clothing fashion 34–5, 61
  domestic 80, 135
  and *sankin kōtai* 50–1
  in Tokugawa cities 14–15
sewing machines 131, 133, 139, 169, 170
  and instalment credit 114
Shibuya (area of Tokyo) 113, 191n8, 199
Shimazaki Tōson, *see Before the Dawn*
Shinjuku (station/area of Tokyo) 113
Shirokiya store 17
shōchū (spirit alcohol) 58, 95n46, 196
shogun 8, 12, 41
shops **20, 85, 190, 192**
  and fashion 200
  in Meiji period 84–5
  in rural areas 69
  selling Western-style products 85
  small 105, 114n8, 115, 159, 188–90
  in Tokugawa cities 17–19
  for Western-style clothes 170
  see also convenience stores, department
    stores, retail system, supermarkets

shopping
  in 1970s/1980s 190
  and cities 11–12
  in early Meiji period 83
  in economic-miracle period 160–1
  in European history 6
  on holiday 206
  in rural areas 57
  and *sankin kōtai* 50
  in Tokugawa cities 17–21
side dishes 28, 124
  see also 'rice plus side dishes' meal
    structure
silk textiles 31, 60–1
  product development in 99
  see also meisen silk
small businesses, and consumer goods
    production 104–5, 120, 219
Smethurst, Richard 140n73
Smith, Adam 2
smoking 25, 57
  see also cigarettes
snacks 126
soft drinks 167
souvenirs *see omiyage*
soy sauce 29–30, 57–8, 92
  commercialisation of 91
soya beans 56, 90
'special procurements' 153
sport, commercialisation of 117
stations 79, 113
status, and goods 35, 209
  among feudal lords 40–1
storage chests 39
street fashion 130n44, 171, 199
street vendors 23
suburbs 109, 186
  housing in 111–12
  post-war expansion of 154
sugar 30, 93
suits (men's) 97, 99, 128, 169
sukiya (tea-house)-style houses 62–3
Sumiya restaurant 22n29, **37**
sumo wrestling 26, 117, 207
sumptuary laws 31, 35, 42–3, 218
supermarkets 159, 190
'supply-side' economic history 2–3, 5
  and post-war Japan 145
sushi 24, 30, 198
Suye Mura 124

tables 134, **135**, 172
'Taishō chic' 131
Taiwan, sugar from 93
Takahashi Korekiyo 140

Tamura Hitoshi 33
tatami matting 35, 101, 112
taxation 138
  see also consumption tax
tea 57, 92–3, 167
tea ceremony 28, 53, 205, 207
tea-houses 22, 25
television 118, 180, **181**
  and advertising 191
  post-war diffusion of 174, 174n48
textile production 33, 62, 70, 103–4,
  129
  see also cotton textiles, silk textiles,
    woollen textiles
theatre 81, 118
  kabuki 25
  rakugo (storytelling) 26
  Takarazuka 113, 118
theme parks 206
'three big Western foods' 125, **126**
toasters 165, 166
tobacco, *see* smoking
Tobin, Joseph 180, 208
tofu 27
tokonoma alcoves 35, 52, 112, 173
Tokugawa Ieyasu 12, 13
Tokugawa (Edo) period (1600–1868)
  economic growth during 8
Tokyo
  1980s building in 187
  housing in 186
  as scene of contemporary consumption
    1, 5
  station development in 113
  see also Edo
Tokyo Disneyland 206
tonya (wholesaler/dealer) 67
tourism
  in Tokugawa cities 15
  by Tokugawa rural elite 53
  and 'traditional' villages 207
  see also foreign travel
toys 39, 101
trade friction 105, 161
trade surplus 4, 184
'traditional goods' 220
  and economic growth 4, 219
  and modern life 9
transport
  in cities 81

traditional forms 78
  see also cars, railways, roads
travelling salespeople 19, **21**, 57, 82
  see also peddlers
trousseaux 33, 39, 60–1, 100
tsū (connoisseur) 45, 216

Ueno (district of Tokyo) 83, 150
umbrellas 99
uniforms 97–8, 129, 170, 199
United States, as lifestyle model 119, 136,
  152, 162, 181
  inter-war criticism of 143
urbanisation 8–9, 11, 47, 80, 110, 154

Valentine's Day 210
vegetables 56, 124, **197**

washing machines 145, 169, 172
Western-style goods 97, 136, 220
  in China 220
  in clothing 97–9
  and department stores 113
whisky 167
white-collar workers 80, 111
  and beer 127
  see also salarymen
women
  changing role in 'modern life' 142
  post-war political organisation of
    152
  as 'unreasonable' consumers 139, 142
  see also housewives
women's magazines 121, 131
woollen textiles 34, 61, 99–100
Worcestershire sauce 95n44, 126
'workaholics living in rabbit hutches' 185
World War II, effect on Japanese
  people 9
  see also black market, rationing

yakuza (gangsters) 68n52, 149
yatai (mobile food and drink stalls) 23
yen
  exchange rate of 184
  high value 5
Yoshimi Shunya 180
yukata see kimono

zoku (tribes) 171